Why Angola Matters

Report of a Conference
Held at Pembroke College, Cambridge
March 21-22, 1994

Edited by Keith Hart and Joanna Lewis

African Studies Centre
University of Cambridge

in association with

James Currey
London

First published 1995

ISBN 978 0 85255 394 7

James Currey
www.jamescurrey.com
is an imprint of Boydell & Brewer Ltd
PO Box 9, Woodbridge, Suffolk IP12 3DF, UK
and of Boydell & Brewer Inc.
668 Mt Hope Avenue, Rochester, NY 14620, USA
www.boydellandbrewer.com

University of Cambridge, African Studies Centre
Free School Lane
Cambridge
CB2 3RQ

Transferred to digital printing

Acknowledgements

Thanks to:
The Calouste-Gulbenkian Foundation and the Smuts Memorial Fund, Cambridge University
Salah Bander and Paula Munro for helping to organise the conference
Sir Roger Tomkys and Pembroke College
Marco Ramazzotti
Note takers: Gabriel Gbadamosi, Rod Brett, Katie-Jo Luxton
Tape-recording monitors: Eric Wood, Mark Chingono
Microphone-operators: Ato Quayson, Tel Owuso
Conference Photographer: Rosanne Tempest-Holt
Computer trouble-shooters: Peggy Owens, Sarah Bander, Phil Armstrong
Secretarial back-up: Irene Hughes
Proof-reading: Ruth Van Velson
Zed Nelson for his superb photographs
Patrick Verdon for saving our bacon

Produced and designed by Patrick Verdon
Cover Photograph by Zed Nelson

Contents

Page

For Davidson Nicol (1924 - 1994)

Introduction

Why Angola Matters

Keith Hart
and
Joanna Lewis

The world is turning and in 1994 many of the great events which help us to grasp its movement took place in Africa. South Africa and Rwanda dominated the headlines for much of the year, providing extreme symbols of human hope and despair. Things are turning in Angola too, as one of the world's longest and most destructive wars drags on through attenuated peace talks. But the cruel suffering of a people caught between two war machines does not often penetrate the consciousness of global television audiences.

It does not seem likely that a small gathering in a Cambridge college library could make much difference to this state of affairs. Even so, we took up the challenge of how to make people stop and think about Angola, to show that its problems are not out there, remote from our own lives, but rooted in the discontents of a world that we all share. We met to discuss how each of us would seek to persuade others that our own specific interest in the Angolan conflict should be a matter of general concern. And from this we hoped to build a case for the world to take a more active interest in Angola.

The working principle of 'Why Angola Matters', a conference called by the Cambridge African Studies Centre in March 1994, was thus to seek unity in division, to appeal to common interest rather than to score points in a debate. The presence of the protagonists and the intense feelings provoked by the war, as well as the great diversity of the participants, made this a difficult goal to realise. Throughout the two days the construction of a fragile community was under threat of subversion by forces analogous to those prolonging the war. Yet consensus won through and we came away from the meeting inspired by a common resolve not to be defeated by the enormity of Angola's problems.

If one major theme of the meeting was the tension between conflict and consensus, another was the problem of scale, how to bring a vast human tragedy down to a level where it made sense for individuals to commit their energies and emotions. One answer is to believe that human actions on a small scale meaningfully reflect and sometimes inform the large collective processes with which they are ultimately engaged. In any case, big ideas come best in small human packages, as interactions between persons. The real consequence of the conference was the fellowship generated among the participants, the renewed sense of work to be done and of people to do it with.

One antidote to a disabling sense of detachment from yet another image of human suffering being played out in the dark shadows of a world that bears no relation to our own is to explore the connections that in fact exist between the two. The line of bloody stumps belonging to civilian victims of anti-personnel mines, languishing in hospitals that have no electricity and no drugs, leads directly back to governments which refuse to curb arms exports to the Third World and to electorates which do not insist that they do so.

What then does this report seek to achieve? It is an attempt to communicate what happened in a form which comes closer than most conference proceedings to the spirit of the events themselves. We would like to convey something of the drama, the energy, and the passion which marked this extraordinary gathering. Obviously the dissemination of knowledge and information matters too. Several panelists produced scholarly pieces of work which we have reproduced. But our main concern is to show that great historical processes, over which we can aspire to exercise little direct influence, are ultimately the responsibility of people acting out their social lives in settings such as that chosen for our conference. The lesson of this meeting is that whatever it took for us to contain our differences and make common cause will be at a premium if the larger conflict is to be resolved. We hope that by presenting the connections between Angola and the wider world, we will promote the idea that crippling divisions between 'us and them' should give way to the more inclusive identity 'all of us'.

Accordingly, we have as our narrative line the microcosm of the conference itself. We want readers to share something of what it felt like to be in Pembroke's Old Library for those two days in March 1994; so we have retained the chronological flow of the verbal exchanges with minimal editing. The bulk of our report then is a script of what transpired, lightly modified by the legitimate desire of some authors to provide a written version of what they said. In this way we hope to reflect the spontaneity of the occasion. For the drama of passionate interventions broke through the prepared scripts and stale conventions which so often mark conferences of this kind. Indeed, there is a timeless quality to much of what is presented here, reflecting the human tragedy of Africa at war and for once transcending the contrived "news" of diplomatic statements leading nowhere.

Readers will also get much of what participants were exposed to: the invitation to participate and the conference programme; a list of those attending; Keith Hart's introductory essay. Some of the documentary fallout of the conference is also included towards the end.

The volume as a whole is aimed at an audience which has widely varying levels of familiarity with the topic. Readers will learn much about Angola from what our speakers say; but this is not intended to be a systematic source of information about that troubled land. We have kept editorial commentary down to introductions to the sessions, short biographical notes on the speakers, elucidation of some specific references and occasional interpretive notes. We apologise for any errors that may have crept into our transcription of the taped proceedings. In an effort to animate the pages, we have included some of the photographs taken during the two days. Each session begins with a short editorial setting the scene. We have also added occasional commentary in brackets with italics added.

We feel it necessary also to place the events of March 21-22 in the context of their own prehistory, for the conference was not envisaged in its final form from the beginning, and this prehistory to an extent shaped the pattern of events to follow. Indeed major changes in the composition of panels and audience were taking place right up to the opening; and two thirds of the 120 or so people who attended only made their intentions known in the last few days. Fluidity was a quality desired by the organisers, if not quite in this measure. Undoubtedly this openness to change lent a degree of spontaneity to the whole affair.

As reported in Keith Hart's opening essay (pages 168-172 below), the origins of 'Why Angola Matters' lay in an encounter with an Italian engineer visiting Cambridge. It was January 1993 and, in a serious escalation of the war renewed by UNITA after the September 1992 elections, some prominent government supporters were killed in Huambo. Marco Ramazzotti came into Hart's office and said "They are killing my friends in Angola. What are you going to do about it?" Although the African Studies Centre had no previous engagement with Angola, we were committed to breaking down the indifference of western academic institutions to the human dimensions of Africa's suffering. The result was an agreement to commit the Centre to some as yet unspecified involvement.

Ramazzotti was a supporter of the governing MPLA, a Communist and one-time soldier. He had no doubt about his allegiances; and through him Hart was drawn into acquaintance with members of the Angolan embassy in London, as well as with the Angola Emergency Campaign, an affiliate of the Anti-Apartheid Movement, with links to South Africa's ANC and Communist Party, as well as to the Labour left in Britain. This was before the Clinton regime recognised the Angolan government. UNITA was scoring heavy military successes and still seemed to enjoy the covert support of western governments and the South Africans. The main aims of the pro-MPLA campaign were to seek the diplomatic isolation of UNITA and to gain military and economic support from the western powers for the Angola government.

It appeared that a conference sponsored by Cambridge University might most usefully involve an audience of British businessmen and officials in discussing the prospects for Angola's economic reconstruction after the war. Informal approaches to the British Foreign Office indicated that an economic emphasis would be suitable; but hopes for an early resolution of the conflict were not sanguine and seemed to depend on America's initiative.

In May 1993 a small workshop on Angola took place in the African Studies Centre, involving a few academics and some members of the Angolan embassy, as well as a United Nations political officer who had attended the recently failed talks at Abidjan (José Campino). Things seemed to be going badly at this time, with more people dying than in any previous period of the war. The United Nations Security Council singled out UNITA for adverse comment and the USA recognised the Angolan government. In this climate a letter was composed by Hart, with the help of David Birmingham and Patrick Chabal, expressing the sentiments of the workshop. The letter was signed by over 100 Africanists in British universities and published in the Independent on June 27th. (See page 10). Some academics refused to sign it because it was too one-sided. It clearly reflects a phase of righteous confrontation in which UNITA is demonised (thereby provoking a long letter of protest from Isaias Samakuva, UNITA's London representative).

In the following summer, Hart and Ramazzotti drew up plans for a major conference, having won some financial support from Cambridge University's Smuts Memorial Fund and the Calouste-Gulbenkian Foundation. The tension here was between emphasising economic reconstruction (Hart) and the political history of the war (Ramazzotti). These aims were reconciled under the rubric of "Democracy and Development in Angola". It was designed as a large-scale international conference with invited papers from a global list of luminaries. Such a conference needed a lot of money and the format would be fixed well in advance, culminating in a fat volume of proceedings. We explored leads to the European Community in Brussels and Strasbourg, mainly through left-wing politicians in Britain and Italy. In September these efforts came to nothing and Ramazzotti left Cambridge.

Shortly afterwards the Harambee Centre and a group of NGOs in Cambridge ran a one-day seminar called 'Africa Matters' to which Hart gave the opening address. The aim was to inform and, more important, touch the Cambridge public; to bridge the gap between ourselves and Africa. This was the concrete inspiration for the form that the conference eventually took. For in November, Joanna Lewis put her liminality (post-PhD, pre- full time job) to constructive use. As a newcomer to Angolan politics and ignorant of the British scene organised around it, she was able to approach potential speakers from all sides. In December, with no more money and time running out, Hart booked Pembroke College for a "workshop" on Angola in the following March. The name was a self-conscious attempt to minimise expectations, in case no-one came. This was a moment when the structures of society responsible for prolonging that interminable war seemed very alien; and the possibility of making an impact through a small academic initiative rather remote.

The striking feature of the next few months was the positive response evoked from so many people who saw the workshop as a way of expressing their own interest in Angola. The core staff of the Centre — Paula Munro, the secretary, and Salah Bander, the temporary communications officer — were engaged in a plethora of tasks needed to get the show on the road. Sir Roger Tomkys, Master of Pembroke College and a former Foreign Office mandarin, and Achol Deng, former Sudanese ambassador to the Netherlands, agreed to lend a hand when required. We often experienced severe disappointment; but even more often we were buoyed up by the sheer enthusiasm many talented people had for Angola. The early months of 1994 were something of a rollercoaster.

TUESDAY 29 JUNE 1993 — THE INDEPENDENT — 17

40 CITY ROAD, LONDON EC1Y 2DB Telephone 071-253-1222; general fax 071-956-1435

LETTERS TO THE EDITOR

International intervention in Angola

From Dr Keith Hart and others

Sir: The international community is faced with growing forces of fragmentation and division, which undermine prospects for peace and prosperity at the cost of great human suffering.

Angola deserves to be seen by everyone as an urgent test of our collective will to build a world fit to live in. An anti-colonial war there was brutally prolonged by the intervention of the superpowers and South Africa. After elections last September produced a legitimate majority government (at last recognised by the United States), the losing side, Unita, armed from South Africa and elsewhere, has reopened the war with devastating consequences. The United Nations Security Council blamed Unita unequivocally for the failure of the latest round of peace talks at Abidjan last month.

The humanitarian case for international intervention in Angola is overwhelming. An estimated 1,000 people are being killed daily, and the disruption of food supplies makes mass starvation likely. This war is a human disaster equalled in recent decades only by Afghanistan and Cambodia. Moreover, it involves most of Southern and Central Africa and threatens the future of the region as a whole. Yet the Western powers are largely content to stand aloof from the conflict.

We, the undersigned, and 90 other academic colleagues, are African specialists in British universities, and we call on the governments of Europe to stand up for democracy in Angola, by supporting the electoral process there and refusing to accept a *realpolitik* which will condemn much of Africa to another round of civil war and despotism.

This means that pressure must be brought to bear on Unita to accept the Abidjan protocol. The supply of arms and fuel to forces responsible for continuing the war must be stopped. It is time for our representatives to offer active support to a government that stands for integration, democracy and peace, against racial and ethnic division, dictatorship and war.

Europe's (and especially Britain's) long-term economic interest is deeply implicated in the Southern African region. Angola is yet another potentially rich country reduced to poverty and despair. We will never find a way out of global depression if we cannot see that our own future prosperity and theirs are bound together.

Yours faithfully,

Dr KEITH HART, director, Africa Studies Centre, Cambridge; Prof DAVID BIRMINGHAM, Kent; Dr PATRICK CHABAL, London; Dr GAVIN WILLIAMS, Oxford; Prof SHULA MARKS, London; Prof P. CAPLAN, London; Prof K. J. KING, Edinburgh; Prof LIONEL CLIFFE, Leeds; Dr GRAHAM FURNISS, London

African Studies Centre
University of Cambridge

The first task was to ensure that the principal Angolan parties were represented; and that meant persuading UNITA that the Centre was now committed to a more even-handed approach than in the previous June. UNITA's London office agreed to come; but its head, Isaias Samakuva, was involved in the Lusaka peace talks and the precise nature of their representation remained doubtful right to the last minute. The Angolan embassy was supportive throughout and promised substantial government representation. We hoped for the participation of Lopo do Nascimento, Party Secretary of the MPLA; but in the end we were very grateful for a high-level delegation, including the Vice-minister of Foreign Affairs, George Chikoti, and the Ambassador to Britain, Antonio da Costa Fernandes. It is of some interest that both these men were non-MPLA members of the government with a history of association with UNITA

The prospect of the two protagonists meeting in public for the first time since the renewal of the war was a strong selling-point for the workshop; but it could be wrecked by a no-show. At the last minute, UNITA suggested an academic replacement who refused to be listed as a UNITA supporter, only for Mr. Samakuva to make a dramatic appearance straight from Lusaka, flanked by UNITA's representative in

Washington DC, Malik Chaka. In all the excitement, we perhaps neglected other Angolan interests. Professor Antonio Neto, head of the small Angolan Democratic Party, offered to come, but we could not fund his trip (he came anyway). We leapt at the chance to include Fernando Pacheco, the head of a prominent Angolan NGO (ADRA), on the programme. In retrospect, it seems obvious that we should have done more to invite Angolans living in the U.K.: but, as the transcript makes clear below, they made a powerful impact by simply turning up as members of the audience.

We learned the hard way that famous politicians and journalists had priorities which made forward planning very difficult. Baroness Chalker, the Minister for Overseas Development, confirmed her attendance and then was forced to withdraw her confirmation at the last moment. Even so a strong Foreign Office team included the British Ambassador to Angola, Richard Thomas. The Angola Emergency Campaign was unhappy about UNITA's participation and planned a demonstration (eventually called off), while agreeing to speak. Some very prominent broadcasters made tentative agreements to participate which had to be withdrawn because of overseas assignments. Despite this extreme volatility, which meant that the list of speakers had to be revised almost on a daily basis during the last two weeks, it became clear that the "workshop" was going to be a conference of some distinction. A last-minute flood of bookings meant that the audience would be of a size and variety to match.

The conference was organised as six sessions of one-and-a-half hours each spread over two days. Each addressed 'Why Angola Matters' from a particular perspective, dividing time equally between a panel of (usually) three speakers and the audience. The first day opened in Pembroke College's majestic Old Library with a session on Angola's significance for the world order. This panel gave strong representation to Africans and to associates of the African Studies Centre, mainly academics. As can be seen from the relatively few questions, the session was rather top-heavy and unwieldy. A divided presentation on the United Nations by Achol Deng and Mark Weller was followed by Jean-Emmanuel Pondi's statesmanlike review of Africans' interest in Angola and George Wright's vigorous expose of American foreign policy there. The drama was left for the afternoon's two sessions devoted to Angola itself and Britain respectively.

Peace talks had been going on in Lusaka, Zambia for several months; and part of the suspense of preceding weeks lay in the prospect of a dramatic announcement, which some diplomatic sources then thought was imminent. Yet the war was still going on and there was much bitterness on both sides, less perhaps between the professional diplomats who represented the opposed parties here than between their supporters. A clear majority of the audience seemed hostile to UNITA, while many of the Angolans present embraced an attitude of "a plague on both your houses". The Angolan government made a considerable concession by agreeing to appear alongside UNITA, since they did not recognise diplomatic parity with the rebels. UNITA, on the other hand, had to endure more aggressive questioning and seemed at times ready to walk away from the encounter.

There was thus tension between the notion that the government and UNITA were combatants whose mutual agreement was necessary for peace and the idea that one side was a legitimate government, while the other had embraced illegality when rejecting the 1992 election results. To this was added the history of racist colonialism and the Cold War, in which UNITA had attracted the support of South African whites and right-wing western regimes, while the MPLA had the support of the Soviet bloc and African nationalists. The Americans had recently switched sides, following the accession of a Democrat to the White House; but until quite recently it was assumed that UNITA received the covert backing of several western powers, as revealed by their being allowed to maintain diplomatic missions in western capitals despite what their opponents took to be systematic infringements of international law. Within Angola, the MPLA's base was the multi-racial population of the coastal cities, while UNITA drew the bulk of its support from the interior, where it currently held two-thirds of the country's territory. Fighting for control of the cities of Huambo and Cuito had been particularly severe.

A lot hinged on rival versions of recent and not-so-recent history. The MPLA and its allies in government claimed that the 1992 elections were declared "free and fair" by the U.N. representative, Margaret Anstee (she had); that UNITA's leader, Jonas Savimbi, refused to accept these results because he had been assured that he would win and could not tolerate sharing, never mind losing power; that UNITA, having failed to disarm, launched a coup attempt on the capital, Luanda; that this provoked rioting in the city against ethnic groups presumed to be UNITA supporters, but this had soon been stopped by government forces; whereupon UNITA launched a full-scale war with the logistical support of its South African and other foreign allies. Not everyone subscribes to all details of this story; but it is roughly the pro-government line and one with substantial acceptance outside the country.

UNITA's version of the crucial period around September 1992 is different. The U.N. and other observers were hasty in reaching a "free and fair" verdict since there was substantial vote-rigging and intimidation by the MPLA; Savimbi is a democrat with a mission to protect his supporters; there was no coup attempt; but a government-organised pogrom in Luanda ("ethnic cleansing") convinced UNITA that they and their supporters were not safe under the elected regime; so they reluctantly took to arms. The divergent constructions of history go even further back; but this was the form of the simmering dispute at the time of the Cambridge conference. Now American support for the government and the likelihood of an ANC-dominated regime in South Africa after the April elections meant that UNITA had a stronger interest than before in negotiating peace.

The Angolan session, supervised from the Chair by Sir Roger Tomkys, did not provide the anticipated fireworks. George Chikoti and Isaias Samakuva sat next to each other, on the same side of Sir Roger, emitting benign body language. Fernando Pacheco was the calming lusophone voice of "civil society". The Ambassador, who had been invited to open the session, as the government's representative in Britain, declined the privilege. The speeches were brief and to the point, delivered to a hushed audience. The subsequent questions were also relatively restrained. It was as if everyone saw the symbolic importance of maintaining at least the show of unity. There was a formal dance around the order of replies to questions. Nothing got out of control, but the dramatic tension was certainly high.

It was the British, paradoxically in view of their outdated reputation for self-restraint, who provided an outlet for the tension in the third and last session of the first day. Richard Thomas read a straightforward account of the British government's position which made clear its endorsement of the MPLA-led government, a major clarification since a few months earlier, before U.S. recognition of Luanda. This speech and off-the-cuff remarks made during dinner were destined to became the target of passionate commentary the following day. Tony Hodges, of the Economist Intelligence Unit, whose paper on the Angolan economy had been precirculated, gave a rousing synthesis of humanitarian and economic arguments. But it was the first woman speaker of the day, Victoria Brittain of The Guardian, who won the greatest round of applause and the most violent criticism, for a polemical speech which focused precisely on the disputed history of the last two years. Councillor Peter Brayshaw of the Angola Emergency Campaign left the audience in no doubt about his organisation's anti-UNITA stance. The Chair, Sir Hugh Byatt, a former ambassador who negotiated British recognition of the MPLA, was scrupulous not to show his own leanings. But Angolans in the audience came close to generating uproar in the face of this wholesale demonstration of British support for the Angolan government. The excitement was contained, however, and the conference adjourned for a peaceful sherry party and dinner.

Tuesday morning was dull and wet, after the previous day's brilliant sunshine and high drama. The fourth session was concerned with Angola's significance for the Southern African region. It was hoped to link up with forthcoming elections in South Africa and Mozambique, as well as arguing for Angola's importance for the regional economy. José Campino gave a tour of the United Nations' interest in various countries, including Angola. But the other two speakers more or less rejected the premise of the session. David Birmingham's lucid and original essay on language politics in Zaire, South Africa and Angola demonstrated the need to bring a broadly-based historical imagination to questions of Angola's future; while Reginald Green's admirable and iconoclastic review of the economy refuted any glib recourse to regionalism. It is a pity that attempts to recruit an ANC representative as a speaker failed.

After this somewhat confusing beginning, the fifth session proved to be the most populist of the conference, bringing together academics and NGOs to discuss the prospects for rehabilitation and reconstruction in Angola. It was also the only panel to feature a majority of women speakers. This was the occasion when the humanitarian tragedy of Angola was confronted most directly. Catherine Schulte-Hillen of Médecins sans Frontières was drawn into the contradictions of providing aid under war conditions; while Sue Fleming drew on her extensive Angolan experience to review grass-roots development there. Rae MacGrath's powerful speech on the subject of mines eradication, including a batch of the offending articles tipped out of a Marks and Spencer plastic bag, was the most moving moment of an emotional conference. For he spelt out in unequivocal language how a peace agreement will not signal an end to the violence nor to the suffering of the Angolan people.

But yet more climactic, the highlight of the session was an extraordinary speech from Teresa Santana, an Angolan living in Britain, who was asked to join the panel to say a few words. Taking her point of departure from a remark made by the British ambassador the previous evening, she vented her frustration with a government which treats refugees as "economic migrants" through an alliterative refrain built around repetition of the phrase "normal lives". The session ended with a most unlikely outbreak of disorder which the Chair, Joanna Lewis, barely rescued from fiasco.

The last session of the conference led straight into a discussion of its possible outcome. It consisted of four journalists — from print, radio, television and photography

— who had agreed to address the question of Africa's representation in the western media through a focus on Angola. Keith Somerville's informed paper, which had been circulated beforehand, was directly to the point. Ahmed Rajab complained about the low news value accorded to African events and personalities. Alex Holmes's honest admission that one dead Englishman was worth more to a home television audience than any number of dead Africans seemed to shock some. Finally Zed Nelson's talk, illustrated with his own photographs of Angola (some of them reproduced in this book with his kind permission), hinged on the need to balance "disaster" shots with more positive images of African society. This session reinforced a view of the media as relying on stock stereotypes which do little to escape from oscillation between shock/horror in the short term and indifference in the long term.

The audience was not quick to take up the opportunity to discuss what might be done to publicise the findings of the conference. But, after a slow start, the floor burst into life and, in an impressive display of baton-passing, the idea of a communication to the Lusaka peace talks was launched and consensus reached. The single voice of dissent came from the Angola Emergency Campaign whose leader, Peter Brayshaw, still at this late stage found it undesirable to put out a joint communique which might mask the differences between the various parties represented in the audience. It is indeed remarkable that, when the Angolan government representatives strongly supported a message of peace and reconciliation, their British allies insisted on fighting the good fight to the end.

Angolan participants enjoying the unexpected spring sunshine on arrival

Nevertheless, the conference delegated Keith Hart, with the assistance of José Campino, to send a goodwill message to the peace talks, stressing the interests of the people at large, beyond the two protagonists. It was accepted by the United Nations representative there, Alioune Blondin Beye. The exchange of letters is reprinted below (pages 150-151). For a moment it truly did seem that this extraordinarily diverse gathering had captured the general will of the people of Angola and of their friends everywhere.

In retrospect it was undoubtedly the women in the audience who were able to articulate most convincingly the fundamental injustices of the war in Angola and the real barriers to peace. They made it abundantly clear that if women had more political clout, there would be less violence in the world. But they took their cue from Rae McGrath.

He began by questioning the organisers' very terms of reference. He preferred not to discuss 'Why Angola Matters' but 'Why Angolans Matter'. He then went on to list individual victims by name, age, village, occupation and so on. McGrath spoke from the heart in plain and simple English. His appeal to our emotions, the personalisation of what until then was an intangible cycle of violence, was all the more potent for being delivered by a bearded burly ex-soldier from the North of England.

On the same platform Teresa Santana ridiculed the British Ambassador's alleged comment that there were people living normal lives in Angola by repeatedly asking the audience whether it was normal to live in fear of speaking out, of chronic hunger, of stepping on a mine, of death. This evocative picture of life in Angola was given by someone who usually would not have access to such a platform; and it was explicitly seen by some of the 'men in suits' present as a departure from the high intellectual standards expected.

It was the final session, however, which produced some outstanding contributions from women participants. Alison Tierney asked why it was that humanitarian action was usually the job of NGOs and not governments. But the most striking speech came from Fatima Pimental, at that time a leading member of the Angolan Community in the UK. It is worth repeating part of her statement here.

"Nobody wakes up one morning and says oh, I'm a democrat. Democracy requires understanding, tolerance and an awful lot of patience, and I'm afraid these are qualities that most human beings are not born with. They have to learn them and develop them....I believe that the Angolan people through their suffering are ready for democracy if only the two main parties would stop locking horns. Naturally in a situation of civil war there is a lot of healing to be done and the healing process can only take place once democracy becomes a reality. And this begins with peace. So in my view, the sooner the healing process can start, the better".

Pimental's contribution was enthusiastically recieved. She had given a voice to the feelings of many present and, as a result, resistance to the platform's desire to send a message to the peace talks at Lusaka was overcome. We all had to practice patience, tolerance and understanding during those two days at Pembroke, as we were forced to listen to opinions we would usually have dismissed from people we would prefer not to sit with. So why not others? The call for peace and an end to the suffering of the Angolan people was a message aimed at the politicians and the arms dealers, the men in suits; and it was the minority of women participants who found the language best able to express it.

In the months that followed, the organisers took a breather after the exertions of a hectic two days. Various items came into our hands after the event, such as Alex Vines' piece on visiting Cuito (pages 156-159), and these have been added to the text where suitable. The miracle of Mandela's peaceful revolution was soon surpassed in the news by the disaster in Rwanda. The enormity of Africa's (and the world's) crisis seems only to grow. The war in Angola, having gone increasingly the government's way, appears at the time of writing to have been arrested in a peace agreement (see Patrick Smith's afterword on the remainder of 1994, below pages - 160-164). The agony of the Angolan people, however, goes on.

We have dedicated this volume to the memory of Davidson Nicol who died while we were preparing it. The two obituaries (pages 190-191) make it clear why we feel that his life epitomised what is forward-looking in the work of the African Studies Centre. Like him each of us has found Cambridge University a means of bridging the gap between our particular origins and a world which cries out for a cosmopolitan outlook. Our different trajectories have intersected in a mutual concern for Africa's place in that world. We have found personal satisfaction and common cause in a shared institutional setting. Keith Hart's comments, written for the journal of the Royal African Society, celebrate the public figure in a way which disguises their personal relevance, while Joanna Lewis's highly personal reminiscences are framed by her awareness of Davidson Nicol's centrality in the construction of her public career. This sameness-in-difference, the basis of our editorial partnership and of the Centre's strategy, finds its symbol in the extraordinary life of our dear colleague and friend. It is the pervasive theme of the Angola conference, the need to construct human unity out of, but not despite our infinite variety.

The politics of affection

Something happened in Pembroke College on March 21-22, 1994. It may not have been very effective, but it was certainly affective. We hope those who read this book will find it affective too, will be able to the see how, despite the huge scope for the expression of conflict and difference, human compassion and mutual respect won the day. Nelson Mandela and his contentious ally, Desmond Tutu, have shown the way forward in world politics, if only the rest of us can discover how to join in — towards non-racial co-operation and consensus, rather than separation, division, opposition. They advocate a new tolerance, what we choose to call the politics of affection, an agreement to seek out reasons for getting on with each other, instead of harping on what keeps us apart. 'Why Angola Matters' was, in its own way, an example of this general aspiration.

For the conference brought a wide range of people together to negotiate their differences in a small version of the larger world. Those who are traditionally unrepresented at such gatherings were given a voice (as when the organisers yieded to pressure for an Angolan to join the platform on the second day); and the politicians were called to account by a forum in which the war's victims and their sympathisers were prominent. The unusual association of academics with "practical" men and women also lent spice to the attempt to contrive consensus out of diversity. Above all, this meeting, in providing an immediate local context for individuals to engage directly with global issues, enabled people to make new connections and perhaps to work together in future. That is why its outcome, for many if not all participants, was a message of hope.

Keith Hart & Joanna Lewis

DIRECTOR: DR KEITH HART
Tel. (0223) 334396/9
Library: 334398

FREE SCHOOL LANE
CAMBRIDGE
CB2 3RQ

WORKSHOP
WHY ANGOLA MATTERS

Pembroke College, Cambridge March 21-22, 1994

The African Studies Centre, Cambridge University intends to hold a two-day workshop concerned with Angola's significance for the rest of the world. There will be six sessions of one and a half hours, each with a panel of three speakers addressing why Angola matters from their perspective. After an opening session in which Angola's significance for the emergent world order will be considered, representatives of the country's main parties will put their own points of view to the workshop. The first day will conclude with Britain's interest in the Angolan question as defined by government and non-government organisations.

The second day will begin with Angola's political and economic importance for the Southern African region as a whole, not least for the transition to democracy in South Africa. Non-governmental organisations will discuss Angola as a vital test case for the world-wide problem of post-war reconstruction which faces peoples who wish to rebuild their shattered communities. Finally, prominent British journalists will examine reporting of Africa in the media; and the workshop will ask how we might stimulate public awareness of Angola's relevance to the future of the world we all live in.

Angola may or may not be on the verge of ending its ruinous war, one of the longest and most destructive the world has seen. The main aim of the workshop is to bring out the universal significance of its troubles, to show that the democracy and development we all aspire to are at stake there. This is manifestly true of the Southern African region, where attention will be focused on the imminent South African elections. But the proliferation of local wars threatens world peace everywhere and the task of rebuilding society anew is a general one. Above all, an increasingly integrated world community cannot afford to be indifferent to the consequences when a potentially wealthy country slides into fratricidal division and economic disaster.

The history of the Angolan conflict is a sorry tale of anti-colonial struggle complicated by superpower rivalry and racial politics. This workshop will emphasise the need for international co-operation and understanding in the search for a viable future. The plight of the people of Angola affects the humanity of everyone.

Keith Hart

AFRICAN STUDIES CENTRE

WHY ANGOLA MATTERS

Day One

Monday 21st March

10.30-11.00 Morning coffee

11.00-12.45 THE WORLD ORDER
Chair: Keith Hart(Director, African Studies Centre)

Achol Deng (African Studies Centre) and Mark Weller (RCIL, Cambridge) | The UN and Post-Civil War Peace-building; UN-Monitored Elections
Jean-Emmanuel Pondi (Pembroke College) African Global Diplomacy
George Wright (California State University, Chico) USA and Angola: The Prospects

1.00-2.00 Lunch

2.00-3.30 ANGOLA
Chair: Sir Roger Tomkys (Master, Pembroke College)

Opening Remarks: Antonio da Costa Fernandes (Angolan Ambassador to U.K.)
George Chikoti (Vice-Minister for Foreign Affairs)
Isaias Samakuva (UNITA London Representative)
Fernando Pacheco (ADRA, an Angolan NGO)

3.30-4.00 Afternoon Tea

4.00-5.30 BRITAIN
Chair: Sir Hugh Byatt (Former U.K. Ambassador to Angola)

Richard Thomas (U.K. Ambassador to Angola)
Victoria Brittain (The Guardian)
Tony Hodges (Economist Intelligence Unit)
Peter Brayshaw (Angola Emergency Campaign)

7.30- Dinner

Day Two

Tuesday 22nd March

9.15-10-45 THE SOUTHERN AFRICAN REGION
Chair: Patrick Chabal (Reader in Lusophone Studies, U. of London)

Jose Campino (United Nations) A UN Perspective on the Region
David Birmingham (U. of Kent) Regional Politics
Reginald Green (IDS, Sussex) Peace, Reconstruction, Rehabilitation, Regionalism

10.45-11.15 Morning Coffee

11.15-12.45 REBUILDING COMMUNITY AT WAR: A TEST CASE
Chair: Joanna Lewis (African Studies Centre)

Catrin Schulten-Hille (Medecins Sans Frontieres) Emergency Relief and Beyond
Rae McGrath (Mines Advisory Group) Land Mines Eradication
Sue Fleming (U. of Manchester) Grassroots Development

1.00-2.00 Lunch

2.00-3.30 AFRICA IN THE MEDIA
Chair: Keith Hart (African Studies Centre)

Keith Somerville (BBC World Service)
Ahmed Rajab (Africa Analysis)
Alex Holmes (ITV, World in Action)
Zed Nelson (Freelance Photo-journalist)

3.30-4.30 General Discussion,
Publicising the Results of the Workshop

4.30- Afternoon Tea

The African Studies Centre wishes to thank the Calouste-Gulbenkian Foundation and the Smuts Memorial Fund, Cambridge University for their generous support.

If you have any enquiries, please contact one of the workshop organisers:
Keith Hart
Joanna Lewis
Paula Munro
Salah Bander

List of Participants

Abrahams, Dr R Chairman – African Studies Centre
Aeschliman, Mr Alain – International Committee of the Red Cross
Attaran, Amir – Student, Wadham College, Oxford
Alexandre, Adao – Student, College of Ascension, Binningham
Amaral de Silva, Mr Dembo – Press Attache, Angolan Embassy
Antonio, Dr J M B – Head Dept. for Analysis & Econ Studies, Min Foreign Affairs, Angola
Arouni, Mr Hassan – BBC
Bander, Dr Salah – Research Associate, African Studies Centre, Cambridge
Barnardo, Mr M – Student, Oxford University
Bernardo, Mr K – Student, Hendon College
Birmingham, Prof. David – Eliot College, University of Kent
Bray, Mr Ian – OXFAM
Brayshaw, Councillor Peter – Angola Emergency Campaign
Brett, Mr Rod – Dept. of Social Anthropology, University of Cambridge
Brittain, Ms Victoria – The Guardian
Burgess, Ms Jan – Review of African Political Economy
Byatt, Sir Hugh – former Ambassador to Angola
Byatt, Lady
Calolita, Mr Ambrosio – Friends of Angola
Campino, Mr José – Political Affairs Officer, United Nations
Carvalho, Dr José – Economist, Angolan Embassy
Castelbranco, Mr Silvestre – Head, European Dept., Min Foreign Affairs, Angola
Chabal, Dr Patrick – King's College, University of London
Chaka, Mr Malike – UNITA USA representative
Chikoti, Dr George – Vice-Minister for Foreign Affairs of Angola
Chingono, Mr Mark – King's College, University of Cambridge
Clarke, Ms Francesca – ACTION AID
Cotton, Ms Anne – CAMFED
Cumandala, Pastor Mario – Friends of Angola
Da Costa Fernandes, Mr Antonio – Angolan Ambassador
Da Silva, Mrs Alice – Vice-Minister's Private secretary, Angolan Embassy
Davis, Ms Lois – Independent Film maker
Deng, Dr Achol – African Studies Centre, University of Cambridge
Dowden, Mr Richard – The Independent
Drummond, Mr Jim – Head Central & Southern Africa Dept., ODA
Edwards, Ms Ruth – Cambridge resident
Eldridge, Mr Chris – Save the Children Fund
Elghady, Mrs Penny – International Aid Dept., British Red Cross Society
Feldman, Ms Anna – Student, SOAS, University of London
Fleming, Dr Sue – International Development Centre, University of Manchester
Gbadamosi, Mr Gabriel – Author
Gibson, Ms Sam – Graduate student, Social & Pol. Sciences, Cambridge
Goncalves, Dr Adriano – Angolan Community in the UK
Green, Prof. Reginald – Institute of Development Studies, University of Sussex
Hardy, Ms Fiona – Student, Social Anthropology, University of Cambridge
Hart, Dr Keith – Director, African Studies Centre, University of Cambridge
Hawley, Ms Sara – BBC
Hawthorn, Dr Geoffrey – Social & Pol. Sciences, University of Cambridge
Hecht, Mr Toby – Student, Social Anthropology, University of Cambridge
Herle, Ms Anita – Arch & Anth, University of Cambridge
Hodges, Mr Tony – Economist Intelligence Unit
Holmes, Mr Alex – "World In Action"
Huby, Ms Anne-Marie – Médecins sans Frontières
Jarrah, Mr Raja – ACORD
Joaquim, Mr J M – Angolan Community in the UK
Kirkman, Mr Bill – Wolfson College, University of Cambridge
Kramer, Mr Chris – Africa Rights/SOASLamont, Mr Andrew – De Beers
Lehmann, Dr David – Social & Pol. Sciences, University of Cambridge

Lewis, Dr Joanna – Research Associate, African Studies Centre, Cambridge
Lonsdale, Dr J M – Trinity College, Cambridge
Luxton, Ms Katy-Jo – Student, Girton College
Mangueira, Mr Rui – Student, SOAS
Matthews, Mr John – Former UN Election Observer
McGrath, Mr Rae – The Mines Advisory Group
Meyer, Mr Guus – International Alert
Michael, Ms Cheryl-Ann – Jesus College, Cambridge
Miller, Ms Diana – Cambridge resident
Morrison, Mr Alastair – Defence Systems Ltd
Moss, Mr Todd – Student, SOAS, University of London
Munro, Ms Paula – African Studies Centre, University of Cambridge
Mubarak, Dr Khalid, African Studies Centre, University of Cambridge
Mupamhanga, Mr J H – Zimbabwe High Commission
Ncwana, Mr Sisa – African National Congress
Nelson, Mr Zed – Freelance Photo-journalist
Neto, Mr Antonio – Partido Democratico Angolano (PDA)
Noah, Mr Frank – Student, Centre International Studies, Cambridge
Nustad, Mr Knut – Wolfson College, Cambridge
O'Gorman, Ms Eleanor – Student, SPS, University of Cambridge
O'Neill, Ms Kathryn – Christian Aid (Southern Africa desk)
Pacheco, Mr Fernando – ADRA, (Angolan NGO)
Parreira, M M – Student, SOAS, University of London
Pawson, Ms Lara – SOAS, London
Peclard, Mr Didier – Student, SOAS
Pfister, Mr Roger – Student, Centre West African Studies, Birmingham
Phillipson, Dr David, Curator, Museum of Arch & Anth, University of Cambridge
Pimentel, Ms Fatima – Angolan Community in the UK
Pondi, Dr Jean-Emmanuel – Visiting Fellow, Pembroke College
Powis, Ms Jill – Amnesty International
Powles, Ms Julia – Student, University of Oxford
Pycroft, Dr Christopher – LIPAM, University of Liverpool
Quayson, Mr Ato – Pembroke College, Cambridge
Rajab, Mr Ahmed – Africa Analysis
Ramazzotti, Dr Marco – Consultant
Santana, Ms T – Middlesex University
Santana, Ms W – Student, Hendon College
Satangua, Mr Daniel – Angolan Community in the UK
Samakuva, Mr Isaias – UNITA
Schulte-Hillen, Ms Catrin – Médecins sans Frontières
Smith, Mr Patrick – Africa Confidential
Somerville, Mr Keith – BBC World Service
Synge, Mr Richard – Africa Analysis
Teka, Mr Tegegne – Churchill College, Cambridge
Thomas, Mr & Mrs Richard – UK Ambassador to Angola
Thomas, Ms Susie – Cambridge University Press Officer
Tierney, Ms Alison – London School of Economics
Tomkys, Sir Roger – Master, Pembroke College, Cambridge
Vines, Mr Alex – Human Rights Watch
Walsh, Mr Maurice – BBC, "The World Tonight"
Watson, Dr Helen – St John's College, Cambridge
Weller, Mr Mark – Research Centre International Law, Cambridge
Wells, Dr Robin – Africa Evangelical Fellowship
Whiteway, Mr Paul – Africa Department (Southern), Foreign & Commonwealth Office
Wong, Dr Lillian – Research & Analysis Dept., Foreign & Commonwealth Office
Wright, Prof. George – California State University

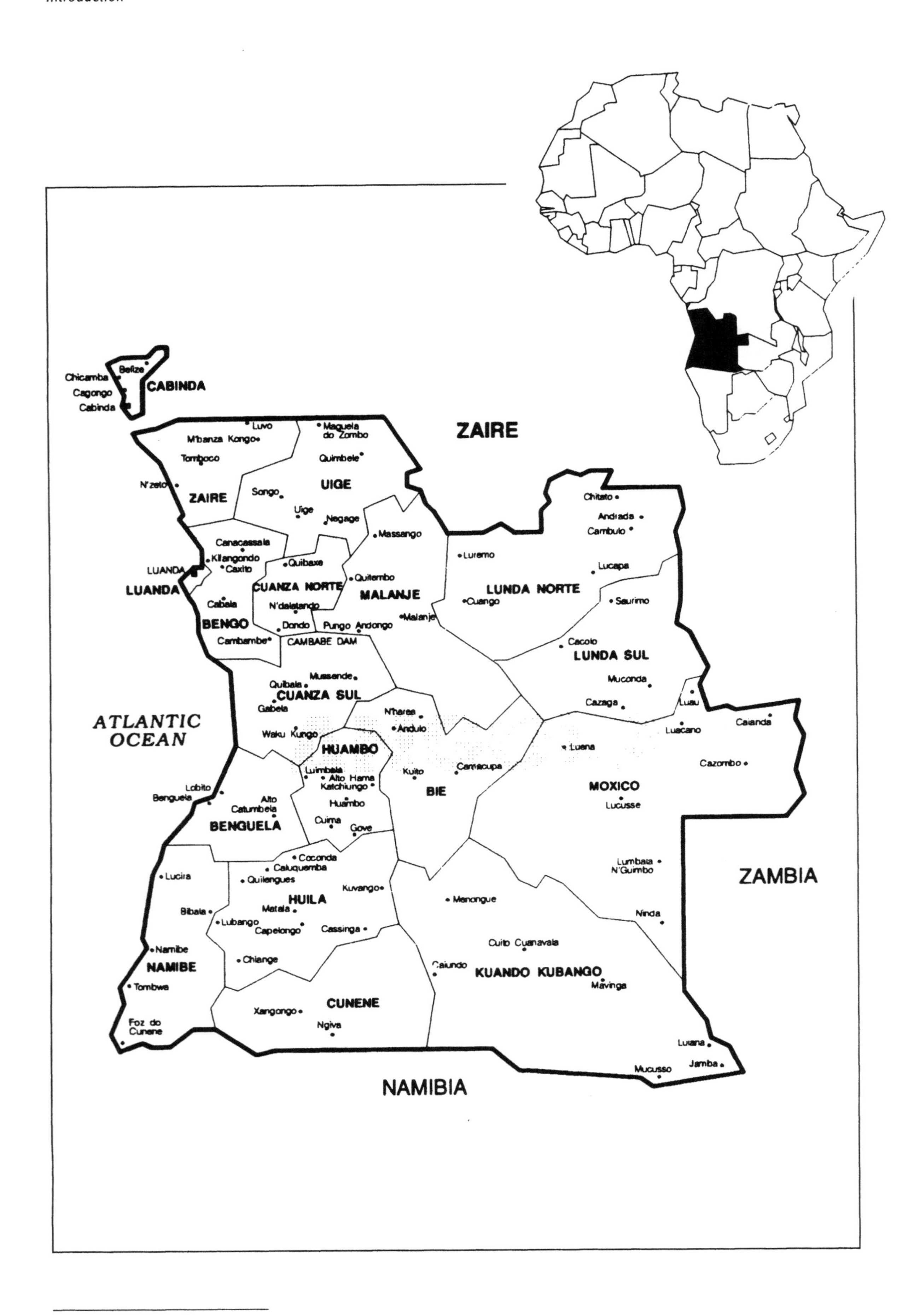
ZAIRE
ZAMBIA
NAMIBIA
ATLANTIC OCEAN
CABINDA
Chicamba
Belize
Cagongo
Cabinda
ZAIRE
M'banza Kongo
Luvo
Tomboco
N'zeto
UIGE
Maquela do Zombo
Quimbele
Songo
Uige
Negage
Massango
LUANDA
BENGO
Canacassala
Kifangondo
Caxito
Cabala
Cambambe
CUANZA NORTE
Quibaxe
N'dalatando
Dondo
CAMBABE DAM
MALANJE
Quitembo
Pungo Andongo
Malanje
LUNDA NORTE
Chitato
Andrada
Cambulo
Luremo
Lucapa
Cuango
Saurimo
LUNDA SUL
Cacolo
Muconda
Cazaga
Luau
CUANZA SUL
Mussende
Quibala
Gabela
Waku Kungo
N'harea
Andulo
HUAMBO
Luimbala
Alto Hama
Katchiungo
Huambo
Cuima
Gove
BIE
Kuito
Camacupa
MOXICO
Luena
Luacano
Caianda
Cazombo
Lucusse
Lumbala N'Guimbo
Ninda
BENGUELA
Lobito
Benguela
Alto Catumbela
HUILA
Coconda
Caluquembe
Quilengues
Kuvango
Matala
Lubango
Capelongo
Cassinga
Chiange
NAMIBE
Lucira
Bibala
Namibe
Tombwa
Foz do Cunene
CUNENE
Xangongo
Ngiva
KUANDO KUBANGO
Menongue
Cuito Cuanavale
Caiundo
Mavinga
Luiana
Jamba
Mucusso

Glossary

ACORD	Agency for Co-operation and Research in Development
ADRA	Accao para o Desenvolvimento Rural e Ambiente (Action for Rural Development and Environment)
FAA	Forças Armadas Angolanas (Angolan Government Armed Forces)
FALA	Forças Armadas de Libertacão de Angola (UNITA Armed Forces)
FCO	Foreign and Commonwealth Office of the U.K.
FRELIMO	Frente de Libertacão de Moçambique (Mozambique Liberation Front)
GATT	General Agreement on Trade and Tariffs
IDA	Instituto para o Desenvolvimento Agrario (Institute for Agrarian Development of Angola)
IDS	Institute of Development Studies, Sussex
IMF	International Monetary Fund
MPLA	Movimento Popular de Libertacão de Angola (Popular Movement for the Liberation of Angola)
MSF	Médecins sans Frontières
NGO	Non-governmental Organisation
OAU	Organisation for African Unity
ONUMOZ	United Nations Operation in Mozambique
RENAMO	Resistência Nacional Moçambicana (National Resistance of Mozambique)
SADC	Southern African Development Community
SADF	South African Defence Force
SWAPO	South-West African People's Organisation
UNACA	União Nacional de Associaos Campesinos Angolanos (Angolan National Union of Peasant Associations)
UNAVEM	United Nations Angola Verification Mission
UNITA	União Nacional para a Independência Total de Angola (National Union for the Total Independence of Angola)
UNO	United Nations Organisation
UNOMSA	United Nations Observer Mission in South Africa
UNTAG	United Nations Transition Assistance Group
WFP	World Food Programme

Session 1

The World Order

Keith Hart

Achol Deng

Jean-Emmanuel Pondi

George Wright

The opening session was one for the academics. In contrast to all the others, this panel was made up entirely of permanent or temporary Cambridge researchers; and it was chaired by the Director of our own African Studies Centre, filling in for a last-minute absentee.

It was eleven o'clock. We were all in our places, under starters orders; then chaos broke out. Papers were tossed aside in the spontaneity of the moment. Speeches were aborted. Panelists walked off the stage to be somewhere else. Cameras flashed whilst late arrivals scurried across the floor, blocking the view and interrupting the flow. Our careful plans to create in this session a path-forming precedent were rendered academic long before the lunch-time bell rang.

A lot depended on session one, or so we thought at the time. We needed to dismantle several barriers. First, we had to break down the separation of Africa from Cambridge; to show that Angola was not out there, that its problems were a symptom of a wider malaise, a malaise that touched us too. We also wanted to subvert the tyranny of the raised podium by making sure that the audience had a major say. And in a place where black figures of authority are extremely rare, we were bent on ensuring that this panel had a strong African component.

Keith Hart opened the workshop from the podium, welcoming participants to Cambridge and introducing the team. After enunciating the organising principle of Why Angola Matters, he made the on-the-spot decision not to give a summary of his paper as a panelist in the first session. So, with the collapse of the division between the introduction and the first session, we went straight into Angola and the World Order with a joint presentation by two experts in international law which produced some awkward moments. We then had earnest accounts of African diplomacy and American foreign policy.

When the audience was at last given a chance to make itself heard, the questions were few and not exactly animated. The academics has launched the conference with their customary deadening effect. But, as it turned out, this hardly mattered at all.

Keith Hart

Introduction

Welcome to Cambridge and to the workshop on why Angola matters. Welcome to Pembroke College on a beautiful spring day. It is of course, always like this in Cambridge, and I do hope you will see some more of the town before the conference is over.

My name is Keith Hart. I'm Director of the African Studies Centre. This session was not supposed to be introduced by me. I was to be one of the panelists but unfortunately, the Sudanese statesman, Bona Malwal, has been detained in an important meeting in Nairobi. So, I have two jobs. One, to introduce the conference and two, to summarise my talk, and finally to chair this session.

The point of the conference is, I think, more social than intellectual. It is concerned with making connections; with engagement, involvement; with developing networks and alliances across the division that separates us within our world. It is an attempt to bridge the distance, the gap, the difference, the ignorance that separate us from Angola, which turns Angola into some distant faraway place; an ugly civil war that the rest of us can happily leave behind. The purpose of this workshop is essentially to seek to bridge the gap between Cambridge and Angola which seems a fairly preposterous thing to do, especially given what most people think Cambridge is. But this is, nevertheless, the result of a human engagement I made in 1993 to Marco Ramazzotti, who was visiting Cambridge at the time, and who, in a very direct way, which I describe in my paper, touched my own humanity through his appeal for me to seek ways in which the African Studies Centre might play some part, however small, in the resolution of the Angolan conflict. Now I don't consider that this meeting is some kind of contribution to a political settlement, that would be absurd. But what I do hope is that participants will address the question, why should anyone else think that Angola matters to them. On the face of it, the fact that Angola is such a human disaster effects us all humanely. But what I want to establish to some extent is that the human connection we may feel is also part of an historically developed social connection, which is less visible, and which I hope this conference will help bring out.

The conference is called a workshop because originally I didn't think it would come off at all. But this is in fact an international conference of considerable stature and it has been made that way by the quality of the people who have chosen to play a part in it. Nevertheless, a workshop is about discussion and I hope despite the fact that we have so many eminent speakers, we will be able to create a discourse in the next two days, and that you the audience will be able to take part. I have been to so many conferences in my time where, as soon as the speakers get behind the microphone, they simply ignore everyone else and present their own prepared and often turgid and formal statement, without seriously considering whether they are engaging others or whether they are leaving enough time for the audience to participate.

So, one of the handicaps under which our speakers are going to be working in this conference is that they have been asked to swear they will keep their remarks to between ten and fifteen minutes. We have an hour and a half for each session although this one is large, and I hope that the time allocated for speech making from the podium and discussion from the floor will be roughly equal in each case. Although I am sure that the intellectual argument will be of a high quality, what I'm hoping is that this gathering will create new patterns of social connection and engagement and that the fluidity and the diversity of social possibilities that this occasion has brought about will be realised in some way. I don't have very fixed or clear notions as to what should come out of this conference or workshop. I hope there will be some kind of publication. But what matters to me is that people who do care about

Keith Hart sets the scene

Angola, who care about it across so many social, political and cultural divisions will find ways of collaborating through the African Studies Centre or with each other, establishing points of association, networks and communications, that will somehow feed their way into what ought to be a global involvement in the Angola question.

Angola is simply not some place over there. Angola is part of our world. What is going on there, as I try to argue in my paper, is very much an extreme symbol or symptom of institutional decadence that affects us all: it affects the world order as a whole. It is the institutional decadence of a world that was made in 1945 and I hope that Angola will be seen by those of you who have chosen to come here as one significant point of entry into addressing the issues that affect us all. I don't believe there is a popular government anywhere on this planet. And the fact that we are governed in a way that is so displeasing to so many people, is something that we all ought to care about. And the disaster that has occurred in Angola is in my view, simply an expression of it.

As I've said, I'm extremely grateful to those of you who chose to come. It's a gathering of enormous variety, extremely distinguished in all ways; but this occasion has come together in such a form so late that it can't really be well-structured. Wednesday last week, we had 50 people and when the dust had settled Sunday night, it was 120 and still rising. This sudden influx of energy - this precariousness and temporary structure of association - is something which has enormous dynamic potential and it is up to us not to snuff it out through boring speeches made from the platform, which should probably remind me that I ought to be terminating this part of my first speech.

I just wanted to say, in case some of you think that it is quite odd that Cambridge should be involved in a venture of this kind, that it is not new for Cambridge to be involved radically in activism concerned with African emancipation. In fact, two hundred years ago, Thomas Clarkson and William Wilberforce and others who were here were extremely prominent in launching the anti-slavery movement. And again, in the nineteenth century, various distinguished Africans came here: Alexander Crummel took a degree here in the 1840s while becoming one of the pioneers of Pan-Africanism; Joseph Casely-Hayford, the father of Gold Coast nationalism, was a student here towards the end of that century. And this tradition, though it could hardly be said to be the dominant political tradition of Cambridge, is nevertheless a continuing tradition that has seen anti-colonial, anti-racist movements, feminist explorers and ethnographers, and a variety of other people, including those who in more recent times have committed themselves to the anti-apartheid movement. And we, in the African Studies Centre, are hoping to engage with others who want to change the world, to contribute the research-based knowledge and privileges we have to all of you in government, in non-governmental organisations, in business, in journalism and so on, to try to build new patterns of alliance, across the divisions that separate the academy from the rest of the world; that separate Africa from Europe and from America; and separate the various professional interests from one another.

So I hope very much that this conference will act as a means for us to pursue what I see as our modern mission: which is to become engaged in questions that matter affecting Africans worldwide, and to bring the resources of this great University in a humble way to the service of causes and in the pursuit of knowledge that may benefit Africans everywhere.

That's the introduction to the conference. I was going to give an introduction to my paper but I won't because I think I've done it already, and I'll set.a good example by missing out one of my ten-minute speeches. *(Keith Hart's paper is reproduced below, pages 168-172).* When I say I've suffered from conferences so many times, as you must all have done, I've always felt oppressed by the table at the top; people who have the microphone, who actually symbolise the modern state, the way that they treat the audience as being there simply to listen, to take what's coming in whatever form it comes. I hope that we can begin to break down the barriers that people organising conferences retire behind in order to prevent themselves from becoming too closely associated with those whom they are seeking to impress. So I would hope that you will join me — all the chairs have been asked to do so, in the nicest way possible — in keeping speakers in line. I hope that as many of you as possible will be admitted. from the floor. I hope you restrict you comments to two or three minutes at the most, because if you go into a five-minute speech you are taking quite a lot of time away from others. And we can't ask you to do that, if we abuse our trust here.

I think the most difficult thing we have to achieve at this conference is not to bridge the gap between Cambridge and Angola, because that has already happened. What we have to do is to create the social milieu in which we can all explore our divisions in some mutual concern with Angola and its place in the world. So, thank you all very much for being here.

I would like to introduce some of the people that have been involved in making this conference possible. First of all

Marco Ramazzotti, whose passion, engagement and commitment launched this whole enterprise a year and a half ago. Joanna Lewis has been absolutely tremendous in the last couple of months. Without her energy and involvement it would not be the serene-looking gathering in this library that has been pasted over our chaos. Paula Munro — the backbone of the African Studies Centre, the Secretary — who will answer all your personal needs within reason. Salah Bander, my colleague and a pillar of strength in all this. I won't ask Sir Roger Tomkys, Master of this College to stand up, it would be undignified. He'll be here this afternoon introducing the second session and welcoming you to Pembroke College. So with that, I'll introduce our first set of speakers...

Achol Deng

(Achol Deng is a Research Associate of the African Studies Centre, Cambridge University. He was until recently Sudan's Ambassador to The Netherlands; and before that Deputy Permanent Representative to the UN. In 1988 he was Chairman of the Legal Committee of the United Nations General Assembly. He gave a joint presentation with Mark Weller, a Research Fellow at the Centre for International Law and a Fellow of St Catherine's College, Cambridge University.)

Peace-Keeping and Peace-Building in Africa

Internal Wars in International Law

International Law is mainly concerned with inter-state relations. Events occurring within a state prima facie fall within the domestic jurisdiction of the country concerned.[1] However "it has long been recognised that the dimension and duration of the civil conflict may affect the position of outside parties".[2] Thus apart from the 1949 Red Cross Conventions and the 1977 Additional Protocols [3] which enjoin the combatants to observe certain minimum standards of conduct, the international community has intervened in internal conflicts either to limit their adverse effects on other, particularly neighbouring countries to establish international peace and security.

One method the United Nations employs in controlling conflict is peace-keeping.[4] The United Nations tries to consolidate this through a number of peace-building measures. These include the promotion of a participatory electoral process, the encouragement of constitutional, judicial and penal reforms and the undertaking of large-scale measures to clear mines (demining).

In his "Angola for Peace",[5] Dr Boutros Ghali, the Secretary-General of the United Nations defined peace-keeping as "the deployment of a United Nations presence in the field with the consent of the parties concerned normally involving the UN military/and or police personnel and frequently civilians as well". According to the UN Secretary-General post-conflict peace-building means action to identify and support structures which tend to strengthen and solidify the peace in order to avoid a relapse into conflict.[6]

Bases of Jurisdiction

How does the international community, and in particular the United Nations, claim jurisdiction to get involved in the settlement of conflicts which are within the domestic jurisdiction of states? Firstly, as this Secretary-General mentioned in the "Agenda for Peace", the United Nations could rely on the consent of the parties. At times it could rely on the consent of one of the parties to a conflict.

Secondly, the Security Council could characterise the events within a state as a threat to international peace and security and could assume jurisdiction under Article VII [7] of the UN Charter. By definition, Chapter VII authority requires no consent of the affected parties.

Thirdly a dispute could be resolved through the efforts of a regional organisation under the provision of Charter VIII of the UN Charter. According to Article 52 of the Charter, member states have the right to establish original agencies to deal with matters relating to the maintenance of international peace. This is conditional on the matters being "appropriate for original action" and that such agencies and their activities are "consistent with the purposes and the principles of the United Nations". Indeed Article 52(2) places on members of regional agencies the obligation to "make every effort to achieve peaceful settlement of local disputes through such regional agencies before referring to the Security Council".

Fourthly, the United Nations could circumvent the application of Article 2(7) and intervene in matters that are nonetheless within the domestic jurisdiction of states. This could be on grounds of humanitarian intervention in upholding the provisions of the Genocide Convention or of the International Covenant on Civil and Political Rights.

In the Angolan situation, the attempts by the Organisation of African Unity (OAU) to contribute to a settlement were ineffective. The United Nations, for its part, did not intervene under Chapter VII of the Charter. It did not also characterise the situation in Angola as exceeding the parameters of conduct permissible under international law (violation of the Genocide Convention or of the International Covenant on Civil and Political Rights). It was on the basis of the consent of the parties that the United Nations intervened in Angola and it is to that we now turn.

United Nations Angola Verification Mission I (UNAVEM I) (Dec 22 1988 – May 1991)

Following South Africa's aggressive activities in southern Angola, the United Nations Security Council adopted Resolution 602 in November 1987. The resolution condemned South Africa and demanded its immediate withdrawal from Angolan territory. Meanwhile concern was expressed in western quarters that the government of the MPLA was getting support from Cuban troops based in Angola.

As a result the United Nations backed peace negotiations, and it was agreed that the Cuban troops would be withdrawn from Angola and that South Africa would end its support for União Nacional para a Independência Total de Angola (UNITA) and relinquish its rule in Namibia. The tripartite agreement [8] – involving South Africa, Cuba and Angola - facilitating Namibian independence was completed with a bilateral agreement between Cuba and Angola. This latter agreement catered for the phased and total withdrawal of Cuban troops from Angola. Both countries requested the Security Council to carry out the verification of the redeployment and the phased out total withdrawal of Cuban troops from the territory of the Peoples Republic of Angola.[9]

The United Nations Angola Verification Mission I (UNAVEM I) was created by Security Council Resolution 626 of December 20, 1988. Under its mandate "a group of unarmed observers were to verify the redeployment northwards and the phased and total withdrawal of Cuban troops from the territory of Angola in accordance with the timetable agreed between Angola and Cuba". This mission which became operative on December 22, 1988 and was to last till July 1991 was actually completed two months ahead of schedule.

Whereas the tripartite agreement facilitated the departure of the Cuban troops from Angola and ended South Africa's support for UNITA, it fostered the internal peace process which culminated in the Accordas de Paz para Angola of May 1991 between the MPLA, UNITA and under the auspices of Portugal. It was to assist in the implementation of the Accordas de Paz that UNAVEM II [10] was created and given a wider mandate.

United Nations Angola Verification Mission II (May 1991 – Sept 1992)

As we have noted above UNAVEM I was set up to verify Cuban troops' withdrawal from Angola. UNAVEM II was created by Security Council Resolution 696 of 30 May 1991 and was particularly aimed at fostering the Angolan peace plan. A Joint Political-Military Commission (CCPM) was established to ensure that "the peace accords were applied thereby guaranteeing strict compliance with all political and military understandings and to make the final decision on possible violations of these accords". The CCPM was composed of representatives of the MPLA and UNITA with the Soviet Union, the USA and Portugal as observers. Two Commissions, the Joint Verification and Monitoring Commission (CMVF) and the Joint Commission for the Formation of the Armed Forces (CCFA) were to report to the CCPM.[11]

Pondi, Wright, Hart and Deng absorb comment from the floor

It is worth underlining that the role of UNAVEM II was to "verify the arrangements agreed by the two Angolan parties" regarding the monitoring of the ceasefire and the monitoring of the Angolan police during the ceasefire.[12] As both the MPLA and UNITA had not worked out the details of the 1992 elections, the Accordas de Paz of 1991 merely referred to the prospect of the parties requesting international monitoring of the elections. It was not until November 1991 that the mandate of UNAVEM II was extended when Angola formally requested that the UN observe and furnish technical assistance for the elections. The United Nations Development Program (UNDP) covered the organisational and logistical aspects of the elections. A team of election observers was attached to UNAVEM II. Polling took place 29-30 September 1992. President Dos Santos won a clear majority and his party, the MPLA, won a majority in the parliament. The result as we know was contested by UNITA and civil war in Angola resumed with greater intensity bringing untold misery to many people.

Why Angola Matters

Despite the internal nature of the Angolan conflict, the international community has sought to alleviate the suffering of the Angolan people and to contribute towards the establishment of peace and stability in that country – it has done this by providing humanitarian assistance to Angola, and supporting the withdrawal of foreign troops from Angola and by monitoring the 1992 elections.

Indeed the verification and reporting mechanisms of UNAVEM II functioned well initially when the MPLA and UNITA worked closely. The demining sub-committee [13] of the CCPM did a superb job in clearing roads and farms of deadly mines. Subsequently as law and order broke down under the weight of ethnic cleavage, Jonas Savimbi, the UNITA leader, rejected the results of the internationally supervised election.

The international community gained an invaluable experience through its involvement in Angola. Members of the United Nations and various organs of the UN have engaged in imaginative methods of removing foreign troops from, and fostering internal peace in Angola. These are lessons that the international community can put to good use in other parts of the world. The international community can also learn from the omissions and indeed mistakes it made in Angola. It is contended that better international funding and supervision and a more forthright statement by the Security Council about the importance it attached to the election process might have deterred Savimbi from his decision to disregard the election result.

Angola matters because a stable Angola is essential for stability in Central and Southern Africa. Despite the welcome departure of foreign troops from Angola, events there remain a source of concern for its neighbours. The large exodus of Angolan refugees across international boundaries could create security and economic difficulties for receiving (neighbouring) states.

Angola matters because a rejection of the internationally monitored elections is a bad precedent. It could encourage any party that, in the future, is dissatisfied with the result of an internationally supervised election to ignore the results with impunity. As in Angola this would signal a resumption of hostilities with the resultant suffering to the people caught in the conflict.

Angola matters because success by the international community there could have been translated into success elsewhere. It is our hope that the parties to the Angolan conflict will have the foresight to give the international community the opportunity of assisting them in resolving their internal conflict. They should allow the international community not only to help in bringing about a ceasefire through peace-keeping but to consolidate those gains through peace-building measures. For its part the international community should show it can plan this twin role with efficacy.

(For endnotes see page 184 below.)

Dr Jean-Emmanuel Pondi

(Visiting Fellow of Cambridge University Centre of International Studies and Visiting Scholar of Pembroke College, Cambridge. He is normally a senior lecturer in international politics at the International Relations Institute of Cameroon (IRIC).)

Angola in African Global Diplomacy

Introduction

When the Popular Republic of Angola became independent on 11 November 1975, the configuration of the international system was strikingly different from what it had been fifteen years earlier, at the dawn of the first wave of African independence. The protracted guerilla warfare that had raged in the former Portuguese overseas territories had caused hundreds of thousands of deaths on the African side and 4,788 fatal casualties in the metropolitan armed forces.[1] The optimism that had greeted the accession of the first newly African independent nations had now turned to gloom and disappointment as one country after another fell under the rule of the generals instead of the general majority rule around which the campaign for self-rule and independence had been launched. The severe droughts of 1972-74 in the Sahel region exacted a heavy human and environmental toll on that region, while the first OPEC-orchestrated oil supply shock of 16 September 1973 contributed to further weaken the already fragile economies of the continent by quadrupling the price of oil in less than a year.

At the time of Angola's independence, the Organisation of African Unity (OAU), the principal continental organization in charge of harmonizing African multilateral diplomacy, was barely 12 years old. But well before the birth of Angola as a state, the real dedication of the OAU member-states to the issues of continental liberation and of apartheid in the Portuguese territories and Southern Africa (respectively) meant that Angola came gradually to assume centre stage in OAU diplomacy.[2] If diplomacy is the management of international relations through a process of bargaining among States [and other major international actors] with the view of narrowing down areas of disagreement, resolving conflicts or reaching accommodations on issues over which agreement cannot, otherwise, be reached,[3] it would seem understandable that the particularly eventful evolution of Angola should captivate the attention and whenever necessary require the action of the OAU.

The purpose of this talk is twofold: first, I intend to explore the reasons that account for Angola's importance in African global diplomacy. A convergence of interests between the preoccupations of African diplomacy and those of the Angolan State (which has since emerged as a symbol of Africa's triumphs, trials and tribulations) will be hypothesized.

Second, an attempt will be made to underline the reasons why, in turn, African diplomacy should matter to Angola if some of its long term concerns are to be addressed adequately. Particular attention shall be given to the recent rise of global diplomatic issues which can hardly be tackled by one country alone in this day and age. Some concluding remarks will focus on possible areas upon which African diplomacy might eventually concentrate if the plight of countries such as Angola is to be substantially relieved.

Why Angola Matters to African Global Diplomacy

From the standpoint of African global diplomacy, few other countries on the Continent have surpassed Angola in the unfolding of their national history as a classic textbook case study for the analysis of the defence of all that the OAU doctrine stands to defend: national liberation and independence (Article II 1(c) of the Charter): the pursuit of non-alignment (allusion in paragraph 6 of the preamble) and an enhancement of south-south cooperation. Whether these principles are upheld in the case of Angola has always mattered to the OAU, that country being, as it were, a key element in the Continent's overall diplomatic strategy both vis-à-vis the African continent (with its proximity to Southern Africa) and with respect to the Super-powers (with the possibility of seeing a proxy war being started in the heart of Africa for ideological reasons in the late 1970s).

A firm support of African liberation movements and a commitment to rid the Continent of all the remnants of racial segregation have always constituted the legs upon which the OAU has been able to stand for the best part of its thirty one years of existence. Indeed, the proceedings of the founding summit of Addis Ababa in 1963 indicate that a very profound disagreement existed between the two main factions of African States. These were known as the 'revolutionary' Casablanca group, which included Kwame Nkrumah of Ghana, and advocated an immediate continental integration, and the 'conservative' Monrovia Coalition which was led by Nigeria's Tafawa Balewa, and argued for the instauration of sub-regional economic cooperation. If the two opposing factions did not see eye to eye on the crucial issue of how to forge Continental unity.[4] Halfway through the conference, the continuing in fighting between them made it seem unlikely that a Continental organization might be created at Addis Ababa. It was only when Ahmed Ben Bella of Algeria made his passionate plea requesting the independent African States to support the total liberation of the Continent, that a common enthusiasm for that cause led to the ultimate signing of the OAU Charter.[5] Thus had the transcending interest of the Conference participants in the cause of African liberation and independence not been found and skilfully exploited, it seems very doubtful indeed that the OAU would have been created at all. Such is the 'umbilical' nature of the relation that links the OAU to the issue of African liberation, that the convulsions of Angola's fight for its sovereignty could only strike a very responsive note in the Pan-African body and place that country at the centre of its preoccupations.

There are some, however, who would readily challenge the characterization of the OAU as a liberationist body. In their view, Angola, Mozambique, Cape Verde, Guinea Bissau and São Tomé and Principe all owed their independence victories to a crucial change of government in Lisbon, Portugal in 1974, not to OAU diplomacy. Consequently, they have concluded that during the 1970s, the OAU was more a spectator than a director of the events that triggered the second wave of African independence.[6]

Though there may be some truth in the above argument, its basic flaw lies in the fact that it ignores the long term pressure that African diplomacy has put on non-African actors with important roles in the continuing struggle for continental self-determination. For instance on 31 March

1976, only a few months after the independence of Angola, the members of the security council and African bloc at the UN drafted a Resolution 387 which condemned South Africa for its aggression against Angola. Moreover, and perhaps more importantly, these had been the work of the OAU's African Liberation Committee (ALC) which was in charge of helping the freedom fighters of the territories still under colonial rule.[7]

Non-alignment was the second major principle which constituted a significant pillar of the African diplomatic posture and for the credibility of which the developments in Angola would provide a spectacular testing ground. The African States genuine attachment to the principles of non-alignment had been proven in their favourable predisposition toward that movement: that three out of the first five summits were hosted on African soil between 1961 and the time of Angola's independence stood as a testimony to that attachment. In turn, Cairo (1964), Lusaka (1970) and Algiers (1973) offered their facilities and hospitality to the conference participants. Despite their economic weaknesses, many African countries had attempted to toe the line of non-alignment, if only in public.[8]

The MPLA government took the decision to seek the military assistance of Cuban troops (armed with Soviet weaponry) in an attempt to consolidate its grip on Power in Luanda and to crush the other political and military factions in the country, mainly UNITA and the FNLA. Because that decision involved the movement of very significant numbers of Russian-supported Cuban troops in the region (30,000) on the one hand and the open involvement of the South African Defence Force aided by the United States and other Western Countries, on the other hand, the volatility of the situation could not be more obvious. From an African standpoint, the episode was made more confusing by the fact that several African countries (such as Côte d'Ivoire, Gabon and Zaïre) were openly seeking to enlist the military support of South Africa, an outcast then in African diplomacy.

Hence, barely into its infancy as a sovereign entity, Angola once against projected itself not only into the centre of the African global diplomatic scene, but in the heart of world diplomacy, raising many fundamental questions: why should the world (and many African states) worry about a deliberate act perpetrated by a sovereign state and well within its prerogatives? If this were against the principles of non-alignment, why have not the many defence pacts concluded between France and her former African colonies been denounced before? Furthermore, hardly a year later Paris intervened in Zaïre 'at the invitation' of President Mobutu and his government in what became known as Shaba I. Another military intervention by France was to follow in 1978 in the same region of Zaïre. The level of condemnation was significantly less then. Finally, were countries such as Kenya, Gabon and Côte d'Ivoire which had agreed to lease part of their ports to the US Navy in Mombasa and to the French army (respectively) well placed to condemn Angola and Mozambique before calling on South Africa?

What this episode clearly demonstrated was the extreme vulnerability of Africa in the face of Super-power and middle power rivalry.

On a more conceptual level, Angola has been and continues to be a very important focal point of African global diplomacy for at least three reasons: first, events in that country have contributed to enhance the overall mobilising capacity of African diplomacy. The issues that have been connected to Angolan emancipation (anti-colonialism vs. colonial oppression: South African aggression vs. right of exercise of sovereignty etc.) have been clear cut ones that have commanded the sympathy and support of the majority of States in the world: some Superpowers with other designs excepted.

Second - and here is another characteristic around which the convergence of the OAU and Angola have worked - Angola has provided African diplomacy with an unprecedented opportunity to materialize its south-south coalition-building potential. It is not well-known for instance, that it is only in the aftermath of the Angola-Mozambique independences that the US government decided to grant official status to the OAU's Executive Secretariat in New York.[9] The new facility allowed the OAU to better coordinate and harmonize its position with those of such Third World groups as the G77, or the league of Arab States etc. Moreover, the independence of Angola triggered a renewed interest of Brazil in Africa and that middle power opened a string of Embassies in the continent between 1975 and 1978, thereby putting south-south cooperation on a practical level.

Third, and of equal importance, the Angolan past episodes have also contributed to expose the limits of the capabilities of African diplomacy. It highlighted the extreme vulnerability of the continent in world politics in the face of militarily stronger entities on the one hand, and made clear the internal divisiveness of Africa along several ethnic lines.

Perhaps the most compelling reason why Angola matters so much to the African global diplomacy lies paradoxically in the fact that its many internal weaknesses and vulnerabilities to extra-African powers have called into question the very notion of 'sovereignty' in the context of an African state. If 'sovereignty is the political and legal autonomy of the state, (and represents) its capacity not to be subjected, except with its free consent, to any external direction, interference or control by any like authority',[10] one question must be asked: beyond Angola, is there today a single sovereign state on the Continent of Africa?

Dramatic as it may sound, the question is not as absurd as some might be inclined to think. On at least three levels, the exercise of the instruments of sovereignty has been withdrawn from African 'leaders'. First, the IMF and world bank programs dictate to national governments not only the terms on which their macro-economic aggregates should be managed, but also indirectly, these determine the sizes of the civil service, the armed forces, the diplomatic service, in each of the countries where structural adjustment programmes are run. This amounts to a renunciation of economic sovereignty and to its transfer to H street in Washington DC.

Second, the repeated inability of most French-speaking African states to pay the salaries of their civil servants at the end of the month and their subsequent dependency on Paris to perform that task has called into question the characterisation of those countries as 'sovereign states'. Unfortunately it is the majority of sub-Saharan African states that find it hard to make ends meet in terms of the state's responsibility towards its employees.

Third, on 11 January 1994, in Dakar, Sénégal, African members of the Franc zone had to witness a 50% devaluation of their currency which had been pegged to the French franc since 1945. Not much could be done besides swallowing their pride and attempting to explain these events back home. These were Heads of State.

These events should alert the analyst to the changing nature of the international system and to the real reasons behind Africa's increasing weakness. Real changes seem called for in Angola as in most African States. Angola will find it increasingly difficult to solve certain types of issues owing both to their complexity (for instance, global arms sales and the international refugee situation) and the changing structure of the global diplomatic scene itself with its new entities such as the strong EEC, and the North Atlantic Free Trade Area (NAFTA).[11]

Why African Diplomacy Matters to Angola

The scale and magnitude of the problems which Angola has to face will be less and less amenable to satisfactory resolution at the national level. For Africa, the end of the Cold War has meant a scaling down of its strategic importance and a dramatic weakening in its individual countries' economic capabilities.[12] In contrast, the trend in the Northern Countries has been towards a strengthening of their economic, political and structural capabilities.

To reverse Africa's decline and take the opportunity offered by the marginalization of the continent, priority should be given to increasing the capacities of the twin areas of peace and security building. In addition, African politicians should be led to see the glaring inadequacies of a diplomatic order based on the current 'sovereign' micro-state as its basic unit.

The Cairo Summit of June 1993 was the venue for the exploration of the new Mechanism for Conflict Prevention, Management and Resolution of OAU Secretary General, Salim Ahmed Salim.[13] From now on, the current chairman of the OAU, assisted by a Bureau, will be in charge of preventing conflicts, even if this means enforcing 'the right to intervene' in an African country. This, indeed, is an innovation.

Unlike previous attempts at OAU peace keeping where lack of funds led to the halting of missions (Chad for instance) Washington is prepared this time to contribute $ 300 million to the new OAU scheme, according to James Wood, the US Deputy Assistant Secretary of Defence.[14] Only by insisting on preventative diplomacy can African global diplomacy hope to resolve some of the problems on the continent.

As stated in the Kampala Document which was issued at the end of a meeting of experts on security and peace in 1991.

> The independence of African states and the link between their security, stability and development demands a common African agenda based on a unity of purpose and a collective political consensus derived from a firm conviction that Africa cannot make any significant progress on any other front without creating collectively a lasting solution to its problems of security and stability.[15]

One of the most practical ways to increase stability and security in Africa is to attempt to cut off the supply network of arms trafficking by applying a concerted diplomatic pressure at the source of the supply. Paradoxically, as a result of the end of the Cold War, Africa is now more open than ever to legal and illegal arms sales. "It is estimated that between 1990 and 1993, African countries spent a total of 70% more on their defence budget than on education and health combined. Furthermore, between 1960 and 1985, the USA supplied 45% of the 41.3 billion in total arms sales in Africa".[16]

Tackling the issue of arms sales is a prerequisite to the restoration of law and order on the continent. But how? By appealing to the constituencies of developed countries, prohibitive legislation could be passed in the parliaments of some of the Northern Countries.

Finally, African global diplomacy should work decisively towards the promotion of larger units over and above the micro-state whose record can be described as a failure, when all the other continents are regrouping into large, more efficient units. Africa, the weakest of the five, cannot afford to continue the folly of believing in 'the sovereign' micro-state. The future creation of a continental entity (maybe a generation or two from now) will release the sub-groupings – which will continue to exist as federated entities – from the very heavy burdens of defence and foreign policy making.

Angola will then be able to assume its role as an engine of growth in the Central African region relieved of the antagonisms which, in the final analysis, are created not by ethnic hatred, but by the rough competition for survival.

(For endnotes see page 184 below.)

Dr George Wright

(Professor of Political Science, California State University, Chico. He received his PhD from the Department of Politics at the University of Leeds. He is writing a book on the history of United States foreign policy towards Angola since 1945.)

United States Foreign Policy and Angola: The Prospects

Introduction

The people of Angola have experienced 41 years of peace since the Portuguese arrived in the 15th century. That state occurred during three separate periods: 1) from 1922, when the Portuguese Republican Governor-General Norton de Matos completed the colonial consolidation of the Angolan territory, until the outbreak of the anti-colonial war in February 1961; 2) immediately after the Portuguese coup d'état on April 25, 1974 until the outbreak of the internationalized war in March 1975; and 3) between the signing of the Bicesse Accords, which established the process for multi-party elections, on May 31, 1991 and late-September 1992 as those elections were concluded.[1] The conflict between the MPLA Government and UNITA resumed when UNITA's Jonas Savimbi decided he did not want to abide by the results of that election. The MPLA won a majority of the parliamentary seats, while incumbent-president Eduardo dos Santos and Savimbi would have to compete in a presidential run-off within 30 days. The scale of violence has become the bloodiest (and most tragic) conflict in the world. This paper sets out to address the following questions: How has the United States contributed to the violence in Angola? What is the current state of United States foreign policy towards Angola? What are the prospects for United States relations with Angola in the immediate future?

U.S. Involvement in Angola, 1961-1991

The United States has been involved in Angolan politics in some form since 1961. Presidents Kennedy and Johnson claimed they supported African decolonization. This was only as long as a neo-colonial regime was the outcome. After the anti-colonial struggle started in Angola the Kennedy Administration initially supported United Nations' resolutions to force Portugal to decolonize. The CIA also provided the Holden Roberto-led FNLA a small annual stipend. But Kennedy succumbed to the pro-NATO interests in the National Security Council and the Department of State and stopped pressuring Portugal, allowing Prime Minister Antonio Salazar to carry out a counter-insurgency campaign in Angola. Johnson also flirted with pressuring Portugal but quickly became embroiled in Vietnam. The Portuguese counter-insurgency also spread to Portuguese Guinea and Mozambique as national liberation struggles broke out in those colonies as well.

Since 1969 the United States has been directly culpable in the violence in Angola. The Nixon and Ford Administrations cajoled the Marcello Caetano regime, which came to power in 1968, while selling them 'dual purpose' items, such as helicopters and aircraft, which were used in the African wars. Nixon also terminated the FNLA's CIA funding. After the coup in Portugal Secretary of State Henry Kissinger provoked the 1975 internationalized war, undermining the Portuguese-orchestrated political solution. The U.S.-South Africa-FNLA-UNITA alliance was defeated by the combination of the Soviet and Cuban assisted MPLA counter-offensive and the passage of the 'Vietnam Syndrome'-inspired Clark Amendment by Congress, which terminated the U.S. covert operation. Angola became a symbol to neo-conservatives in the U.S. foreign policy establishment and the New Right of a 'Failure of Nerve' on the part of the United States, adding to their fervent commitment to 'roll back' communism.

The Carter Administration, influenced by 'regionalists' like Secretary of State Cyrus Vance and UN Ambassador Andrew Young, initially tried to normalize relations with Angola. The 'regionalists' viewed crises in the Third World in local/regional terms rather than East-West terms, nor did they advocate 'linking' those crises to U.S.-Soviet relations. But the 'regionalists' were quickly contained by a revived-Cold War militarist approach facilitated by National Security Advisor Zbigniew Brzezinski. This 'Right Turn', promoted by Cold War-policy planning organizations, such as the Committee on the Present Danger, and corporate interests, paralleled South Africa's new destabilization campaign in Angola. South Africa also resuscitated UNITA's military capability, which had nearly collapsed after the 1975 war. The destabilization campaign put the MPLA in a position where they requested from Cuba the recall of troops to help defend their national territory. Carter did not give encouragement to South Africa or direct assistance to UNITA, but Brzezinski did influence China to provide military assistance to UNITA.

The Reagan Administration accelerated the Cold War-militarist policies it inherited. In southern Africa the administration gave South Africa a 'green light' to expand its destabilization of Angola (and the southern Africa region). The Central Intelligence Agency and the National Security Council also set up a parallel covert foreign policy network which assisted UNITA, even though that assistance was illegal. The issue the Reagan Administration centered its Angola policy around was the demand that the Cubans had to leave Angola. Assistant Secretary of State for African Affairs Chester Crocker 'linked' this demand to the settlement of the UN-sponsored Namibian crisis. Congress repealed the Clark Amendment in June and July 1985, and in February 1986, the Reagan Administration resumed 'legal' covert aid to UNITA.

The reasons for the U.S. preoccupation with Angola since 1975 have been often debated. The most commonly cited reasons claim that the United States wanted: 1) to protect Western access to strategic raw materials (including Angolan oil) in southern Africa; 2) to protect the 'shipping lanes' around Africa; and 3) to prevent the 'export of communism'. These reasons do not apply to the Angolan case however. For example, the socialist-MPLA-Worker's Party had a 'mutually cooperative' relationship with Western oil companies (including Gulf/Chevron [Chevron purchased Gulf in 1984], Texaco, Total and Elf-Acquitaine) throughout the period when Angola was being destabilized. Those companies continued to expand their operations while providing the regime with 95% of its annual foreign exchange. The Western oil firms were in actual danger from South African commandos and UNITA and not the MPLA, Cuba or the Soviet Union. In fact, Cuban troops actually protected the oil installations in Cabinda. In the 1980s the United States also became Angola's largest trading partner, while Angola was the U.S.'s third largest sub-Saharan African trading partner.

The deeper reason for U.S. policy toward Angola has to do with the United States' post-World War II imperative to maintain global hegemony. In reference to Angola, Kissinger expressed that need at a meeting of senior State Department policy-makers in December 1975 [2] when he said:

> I don't care about the oil or the base, but I do care about the African reaction when they see the Soviets pull it off and we don't do anything. If the Europeans then say to themselves, 'If they can't hold Luanda, how can they defend Europe?' The Chinese will say we're a country that was run out of Indochina for 50,000 men and is now being run out of Angola for less than 50 million dollars.[3]

National Security Advisor/Secretary of State Henry Kissinger was trying to maintain U.S. hegemony in an emergent multi-polar world. The revived Cold-War-militarist strategy in the 1980s, in its attempt to beat back global 'obstacles' dusted off National Security Memorandum-68, written in 1950, and set out to 'roll back' 'communism' throughout the world. The 'obstacles' were 'communist' and 'nationalist' regimes. Even when the MPLA began to restructure the Angolan economy along 'market'-lines in 1985, that was not sufficient to the United States because the MPLA received Soviet and Cuban support and demanded its sovereignty.

International politics began to alter in the late 1980s to an extent because of the Cold War-militarist policies Reagan had overseen. In 1988, because of Mikhail Gorbachev's willingness to cooperate with the United States in resolving Third World 'regional conflicts' through negotiated 'national reconciliation' and the fact that South Africa was 'defeated'/'over-extended' by the MPLA-Cuban alliance at Cuito Cuanavale that year, rapid movement was made to settle the Namibian crisis and start Cuban troop withdrawal from Angola. Nevertheless, the United States and South Africa continued to provide military assistance to UNITA. Between 1989 and 1991 attempts at negotiating a peace settlement between the MPLA and UNITA occurred. On May 31, 1991, one week after the last Cuban left Angola, the Bicesse Accords were signed, calling for multi-party elections. Those elections were held on September 29-30, 1992. However, Savimbi avoided demobilizing his troops as required by the accords, and stockpiled weapons before the elections. Because of the failure of the Joint Political

Military Commission (the United States, Russia and Portugal) and high-level officials of the United Nations' Verification Mission to expose UNITA's violations and make it cooperate with the election process (and results) and Savimbi's motives and calculations, UNITA resumed the war. UNITA continued to receive weapons from South Africa and Zaire. There is evidence that UNITA also has received weapons from Russia,[4] China, and the Ukraine [5] in exchange for diamonds.

Clinton Reverses U.S. Policy, Recognizes Angola

On May 19, 1993 President Bill Clinton extended formal diplomatic recognition to the Angolan Government administered by the MPLA. This decision reversed the United States 18-year policy of refusing to recognize Angola. It was a decision the 'regionalists', either serving in the Carter Administration or posited on the edges of the Reagan and Bush Administrations had always wanted the U.S. to make. Gulf/Chevron had also lobbied the United States to recognize Angola. The 'globalists', who viewed geo-politics in East-West terms but were willing to deal with the Soviet Union from a position of superiority, claimed they supported that position as well, but they kept changing the conditions the MPLA had to adhere to. The withdrawal of the Cuban troops was always the main condition, but once that process began, the criteria became the establishment of a multi-party system; once that was agreed to the United States (the Bush Administration) declared it would recognize the government that won the election. When Savimbi resumed the war in October 1992, Bush still refused to extend recognition. Clinton broke that cycle; but why did he make the decision, what does it mean relative to current Angola realities, and what does Clinton's decision portend for the future?

The most obvious reason why the Clinton Administration recognized Angola was that the United States had achieved what it wanted in Angola. The Soviet Union no longer existed, the Cuban troops and advisors had returned to Cuba, the Bicesse Accords had installed a multi-party democratic process, and the MPLA had already agreed to drop its allegiance to Marxist-Leninism and support a liberalized economy. Moreover, the international community had declared that the September elections were 'generally free and fair' and should be respected. Furthermore, the United States could no longer be in open complicity with UNITA because of Savimbi's blatant disregard for the democratic process when he returned to the bush. Based on U.S. claims to support 'democratization', and what it had demanded of the MPLA, Clinton decided to extend diplomatic recognition to the MPLA-controlled government. There was also a Liberal-left lobby campaign, complemented by mainstream press editorials, which called for recognition. The Nelson Mandela-led African National Congress also used leverage on Clinton to extend recognition to Angola. When announcing Angola's recognition Clinton stated the decision reflected 'the high priority that our administration places on democracy'.[6]

Clinton's decision to recognize Angola was made while United Nations supervised talks were being held in Abidjan between the MPLA and UNITA. The decision was supposed to put pressure on Savimbi to compromise, but true to form, it did not. The new war became the most violent state of conflict in Angola since the anti-colonial war broke out in 1961. Ten-thousand Angolans, mainly civilians, were killed during the battle of Huambo in March 1993. The United Nations states that in recent months 1,000 people have died each day from war-related causes, many from starvation. David Sogge, an international aid consultant and a frequent visitor to Angola, said in January 1994, that for the first time one can see in Angola people who are 'living skeletons' like people in the Horn of Africa.

Further, the Clinton presidency represents an attempt to reform the United States. Domestically, Clinton is trying to install a 'neo-liberal' project to replace the 'monetarist'/'supply side' approach associated with Ronald Reagan. That project aims to have the government stimulate the economy rather than emphasize the 'market', while promoting high-tech production, civilian research and development and entrepreneurship. The intent is to reinvigorate the U.S. industrial base. Support for this new project comes from 'enlightened' elements of the U.S. business community who have recognized that Reagan's policies, even though they provided the top 10% of the society with enormous income, devastated the domestic economy. In the late 1980s and early 1990s the U.S. economy was plagued with no growth, a runaway budget deficit, huge public debt, a declining productive base, and a deteriorating infrastructure. The United States economy was also being overwhelmed by Japan as well as Western Europe. Clinton, as a member of the Democratic Party's corporate-leaning Democratic Leadership Council, adopted the 'neo-liberal' project and sold it to receptive business interests. There is no consensus corporate support for the project as of yet, but the belief is the United States economy will revive, and regain competitive advantage in the global economy. If that does occur Clinton's corporate support may become stronger.

Clinton's foreign policy complements the direction of domestic reform. This point is emphasized by the fact that many of the foreign policy-makers Clinton appointed are 'regionalists' who served in the Carter Administration. Most prominent are Secretary of State Warren Christopher and National Security Advisor Anthony Lake. (Lake even wrote a book on Nixon's Rhodesia policy entitled The Tar Baby Option.) The 'regionalists' in the Carter Administration stood for political and economic approaches, based on Human Rights criteria, to carry out foreign policy. Their ability to be effective, however, was undermined by the activism of 'globalists' and 'militant globalists' in, and outside, the administration. The 'militant globalists' were to the right of the 'globalists' and promoted 'roll back'. The result of this activism was the 'Second Cold War'.[7] But 'regionalists' still identify with those approaches.

Of course, the current world order is profoundly different to what it was in the mid-to-late 1970s. Clinton's foreign policy-makers have adjusted to the reality that the United States, despite the relative weakness of the U.S. economy, has unbridled hegemony over the world. Unquestionably the United States is still committed to being the global hegemon, but the means to maintain that status are being altered. For example, the use of 'unilateral' intervention or 'Low Intensity Conflict' to challenge 'communism' is no longer needed. The United States is shifting to a foreign policy which emphasizes economics; GATT, NAFTA, the OECD, 'Structural Adjustment Programs', debt rescheduling and relief are the policy instruments. This approach is underscored by a commitment to 'democratization' and Human Rights considerations. (Clinton's maintenance of a huge military budget is largely aimed to appease the military establishment, rather than using 'military Keynesianism' to stimulate growth.) This does not mean that the United States will no longer intervene militarily if it decides it is necessary, but multi-lateral structures (the United Nations) and alliances are/will be stressed whenever possible. President Bush shaped this framework during his 'transitional' presidency, now Clinton will attempt to fully implement it. Clinton's recognition of Angola should also be seen in light of this political orientation.

United States Policy Towards Angola Now

However, the political crisis in Angola is not resolved. There are talks between the MPLA and UNITA supervised by the United Nations going on in Lusaka at the moment (February 23, 1994), but the outcome is uncertain. Regardless, what is the stance of the United States towards Angola at the moment? One, the United States sees UNITA as responsible for the breakdown of the democratic process, but there is no vigorous effort by the Clinton Administration to stop Savimbi from being able to wage warfare. In September 1993 the United Nations introduced sanctions against UNITA for weapons and oil. However, UNITA is still procuring weapons. The United States knows the sources of those weapons and it has the ability to insist on the strict application of sanctions, but that has not happened. The Washington Office on Africa declares that if the Clinton Administration did make a stronger effort on enforcement that would place pressure on UNITA to negotiate in 'good faith'.[8]

Two, Angola is no longer important to the United States. During Reagan's 'Cold War' Angola was important in objective and symbolic terms because of the Soviet support, the role of the Cubans and the policies of the MPLA. That has all ended. Now there is very little mentioned in the media, public debate, and Congress concerning the tragic situation in Angola. Where is the Republican and Democratic support that championed Savimbi between 1985-1988, eagerly introducing legislation to help the African 'democrat' ward off 'communism'? Conservative Caucus-head Kevin Phillips stated in 1985 that if Savimbi was a United States citizen he would be the presidential candidate for the 'Conservative Party'. Why didn't that support push for adequate funding of the United Nations Angola Verification Mission (UNAVEM) in 1991-1992? Where are their condemnations of Savimbi and demands for mediation and peace now? The only important U.S. interest in Angola is oil. UNITA attacked the off-shore fields at Soyo in January 1993. But the Clinton Administration issued a very strong warning to Savimbi that UNITA should not attack any oil installation again. Edmund DeJarnette, the head of the U.S. Liaison Office in Angola, stated:

> The message is simple. These are our people [U.S. oil workers in Angola]. This is our property. Hands off Cabinda, Mr Savimbi.[9]

There was no mention of a military response, but the United States signaled to Savimbi that if he did not heed U.S. warnings he would become 'an international outlaw'.[10] This meant his international support as a legitimate participant in any negotiations would fade. David Martin adds that the oil companies have paid UNITA 'a considerable amount of money, presumably as "protection" against attacks on their facilities in Angola'.[11] Nevertheless, the Western firms are in no danger of oil production being disrupted.

Three, United States foreign policy towards southern Africa is focused on South Africa. The Clinton Administration is waiting for the results of the historic elections in South Africa in April. The new coalition that will administer the government (presumably dominated by the African National Congress) and South African capital will determine the persuasion of South Africa's regional foreign policy. That policy should emphasize economic and political approaches. But whatever form regional policy takes South Africa will continue to be the dominant state in southern Africa. The United States will rely on South Africa to do most of its bidding in that region, including dealing with Angola.

Issues, Questions and Concerns

The recent developments in Angola raise specific issues, questions and concerns that have to be seriously addressed by the United States (and the international community). The first issue has to do with the role of the United Nations in the democratization process. The implementation of the Bicesse Accords failed. The prevailing view as to why that happened is there was not enough money allocated for the UN mandate, nor were there enough UN observers on the ground.[12] Some critics also believe that the UN was openly biased towards UNITA. For example, Victoria Brittain points out the UN did not expose the fact that Savimbi refused to demobilize most of the UNITA guerrillas and had stockpiled weapons.[13] Could that failure have been rectified if the UN commitment had been larger? Are there technical and procedural things that could have been done which may have made the outcome different? Could guarantees have been made that all parties would abide by the election results? Or are there inherent political realities in the UN's relations with the United States which mean the UN could not have dealt with the Angola peace process any differently?

A second issue has to do with the tension between ethnic-defined opposition and the nation-state. This problematic is paramount throughout the world at this moment. The implication of that tension is violence, including forms such as 'warlordism' and 'ethnic cleansing', possibly leading to the fragmentation of the nation-state. The United States' project in Angola aimed to 'roll back' the Marxist-Leninist regime and incorporate opposition forces into the democratization process. However, as discussed above, that did not happen. In fact, the specter of the 'partition' of Angola, where UNITA would control the 'south', has become a possible scenario.[14] This problematic raises the questions as to whether the United States/West is committed to multi-ethnic societies in the Third World (and the former East European countries and the former Soviet Union) or is willing to accept the fragmentation of the nation-state in the name of ethnicity? And, if so, why? If the West accepts the latter position it could reverberate back to specific Western European countries, such as Spain and Belgium, which also face internal ethnic nationalism. Underscoring this issue is how will a civil society be created in Angola and what political interests will shape and influence that process?

Thirdly, when/if the Angolan political crisis is resolved will economic 'liberalization' policies be able to address the enormous problems that country faces? Or will interventionist policies promoted by the Angolan state play the dominant role in the accumulation and distribution of resources? The latter is likely because there is no national capitalist class (or even an articulate petty bourgeois) to counterbalance (and dominate) the state. Moreover, what will be the composition (and political interests) of the 'bloc' that will assume this function? The importance of this responsibility is amplified because of the relationship of the oil-sector to the rest of the economy and the amount of oil revenue available. Specifically, how will IMF/World Bank prescriptions intersect with the pressing economic and social requirements of the Angolan society?

Finally, there are concerns that the United States (and the international community) should address immediately. The first is the issue of reparations. The UN estimates that Angola has suffered $ 100 billion in infrastructural and property damage and lost revenues owing to the destabilization war since 1980. Moreover, the daily living conditions the people face are horrific, millions are uprooted and the countryside is in shambles. Surely, financial compensation is due to the Angolan people. The second issue pertains to the removal of land mines.[15] Nine million land mines were planted throughout Angola. At least 80,000 people have been injured by those devices already. Unless there is an international effort to remove these mines their existence poses a very serious problem into the next millennium.

U.S. Foreign Policy Towards Angola: The Prospects

Whatever the political outcome in Angola the situation is not promising for the immediate future. Certainly, if Savimbi refuses to accept a peace agreement and continues his 'warlordism', there will be more violence. But if new elections are held or a government of national unity is formed the possibility of another 'renewed' stage of violence also exists. There are already urban gangs and syndicates involved in criminal activities and violence which could easily expand. The social and human devastation will continue to feed into violence until the Angolan crisis is adequately addressed by a combination of international supported peace and aid, investments and/or reparations. Partition of the country does not assure peace either. There is large opposition to UNITA in the south-east and in the south-central urban areas. The prospects of another 'civil war' and/or widespread repression are probable. How will the United States react to whichever scenario develops? Will it commit, along with the international community, to enforcing peace? Will it intervene, either multi-laterally or unilaterally, or will it rely on the 'new' South Africa to 'police' the troubles. Or will Angola continue to live in its accustomed United States tolerated violence?

(For endnotes see page 185 below.)

Open Session

Keith Hart (Chair):

We have up to forty minutes so if anyone would like to open the questions.... I think unless anyone has a precise question they would like to address to an individual, I will ask that member of the panel to respond at the end.

Guus Meyer – International Alert – "Civilian-based initiatives to stop the violence"

Malik Chaka (UNITA Office, Washington DC):

I have three comments. One is about the use of language. Ambassador Deng said that President Dos Santos won the elections and he beat Dr Savimbi. There's a constitutional mandate that you have to get 50% plus one to win the election. There is a presidential run-off in the making if the constitution is to be followed.

Point two has to do with the demobilisation problem. If you look at the UN figures on demobilisation you had two things happening. UNITA troops were contained and were in cantonment areas. The MPLA army, which was very large, 120,000 people, did not demobilise to the same degree. Its crack units remained intact. Up to 30,000 troops went from the Army into what they call the Polico Anti Moti, the anti-riot police. They were not in fact demobilised but were moved from one unit to another.

The third point had to do with concessions. I have been following the talks in Lusaka. The point has been that they were talking about military concessions in return for political concessions. I think it's important to note that major progress has been achieved at the Lusaka talks. That peace is in fact possible and the two sides are much closer that when things started in November. If one doesn't look at that then all is lost.

Guus Meyer (International Alert):

I would like to express my appreciation and thanks for this conference and make three points. One is about the problematic aspects of the elections in Africa in general and specifically in Angola. Problematic in the sense that as a way out of the conflict, it seems to be an inevitable mechanism, but to resolve a conflict elections certainly don't work. So I would say that elections in Africa up to now in the last five years have proved to be a continuation of war by other means more than anything else like peaceful democracy.

Secondly, related to this, what do we do with the rights of non-represented parties which in Angola is the majority of the population? There are many parties in Angola that are not represented here. There were attempts to form a third force and for many reasons it failed and it is still very weak. But there are still contenders. The great majority of the people are out of any peace-making process and, even at the Lusaka talks, I wonder if the majority of the population who remain in Angola are in any way represented?

Thirdly I missed any reference to the incapacity or impotence of the international or interstate organisations like the UN or the OAU. There might be a little bit better prospect in Mozambique and one talks of thousands of troops for Angola but up to now the record of these organisations is rather poor.

I wanted to refer to my own organisation because I think one has to talk about civilian-based, people-based initiatives that, at least in the longer term (they won't bring peace tomorrow), can provide a great force for building peace after the settlement. We must look to civilian-based initiatives to stop the cycle of violence. *(Applause ***)*

Keith Hart:

Thank you. You have raised some very important points. I think that all institutions will have to play some part in this gathering. Many of us are disappointed with the kind of international institutions we have, but they will, nevertheless, have to be part of any solution in Angola.

Amir Attaran (Student, Oxford University):

I would like to address two questions which both relate to the same issue. How can we interdict the flow of arms into Angola? Ambassador Deng spoke about this very well but in consideration of what rights under international law and under what conditions powers outside of Angola might intervene. What if we entertain the opposite question: what can Angola do as a national entity to prevent the supplies of arms reaching there? How might it interdict the flow of arms to rebel UNITA forces, though we could ask the same about the MPLA?

Secondly, to Professor Wright, you mentioned that the UN was pursuing a policy of not so much interest in interdicting these weapons' flows, such as sanctions. Is that a possibility and could you say how that could be done if it were a goal?

Sisa Ncwana (London office of the ANC):

I appreciate the positions of the panel here but I have worries because what is the experience of Angola, it seems to me, will be the experience we are going to have in South Africa. To me Angola was a testing ground and I believe that if the international community does not learn from the experience of Angola, we are going to have the same situation in South Africa. And I wonder then if there is anything for instance that the UN is prepared to do in terms of adjusting its role in order to help stop the inevitable — another holocaust in Southern Africa. Thank you.

Keith Hart:

This will be one of the main topics of the fourth session.

Celestine Anasorro (Student,International Relations, Cambridge University):

I have a question for Ambassador Deng. Additional Protocol 1 of 1977 extended the scope of international armed conflict to include fighting for self-determination and freedom from forms of colonialism. As the retiring Portuguese left Angola in 1975, they left in such a way that no political group represented the people, and when the MPLA under Augustinho Neto got into power, they got into power, not by having it handed over to them by the Portuguese, but by fighting a guerilla war. So what I want - and the Angola case very well parallels that of Yugoslavia - is to find the international law governing the conflict in Angola. Whether it has to do with Article 1, 1977 or the additional protocol that applied during the civil war?

Marco Ramazzotti (Consultant):

Will Professor Wright mention South Africa as being a major player in the Angolan conflict? And I think we should not forget that the Angolan conflict was not a civil war. It was an international war. Another party in the war not mentioned is Zaire. It is important that we talk about this from a military point of view and from a diplomatic point of view. What has been the role of Mobutu and what will be the political implications of the South African elections on Zaire?

Sisa Ncwana

John Matthews (UN Monitor at the Angolan elections):

I was an observer in the Angolan elections about 18 months ago. I have taken part in the supervision of some 14 elections including Zimbabwe and the observation in Angola. I wish to question the assumption that all was free and fair, because of Miss Anstee's remark at the end of that election. We saw the voting at polling stations was very satisfactory and also the counting that took place there. But the correlation of votes, firstly at the principality then at provincial headquarters, and then sent through the Ministry of Security to the electoral commission by fax, left a very great deal to be desired indeed. This has been brought out in a book published by the University of Lisbon in December and an English translation will be available in a matter of months. While we are moving along from those elections to the next event in Angola it must not be assumed that these were in fact entirely free and fair, or nearly free and fair.

Guus Meyer (International Alert):

I was there for the elections as well. But I was in an American observer team of forty people. And what we did was to check after the elections in the central ward in Luanda and we checked out all the polling stations where we had observed and written down our accounts, and as they were faxed through, we found them all and, it was an arbitrary sample we had taken, all matched up to our own figures, sometimes out by only one vote.

Marco Ramazzotti – "Angola - not a civil war"

Rui Mangueira (Student at the London School of Economics and an Angolan):

My point is addressed to Professor Wright. I could never really understand why there is still conflict in Angola. The Angolan conflict since 1992 is simply Savimbi's war. *(Applause ***)*

Antonio Neto (Leader of the Angolan Democratic Party):

I speak as the leader of a political party in Angola that has been called a third force in Angola. I wanted to make two points. First, since 1968, the South African Defence force intervened in Angola and it intervened against the MPLA. But there was no legal basis of the MPLA government; no elections had taken place. Secondly, armed force seems to be the basis for legitimacy. What counts in Angola are those people who have weapons. We need to work to counter this hypocrisy and to counter the violence of the so called 'sub-contractors of the Cold War in Angola'; the MPLA and the UNITA. These are exhausted vehicles when it comes to moving forward to a new Angola. (*Applause* ***) What we have to face as leaders of a third force, when we want to speak out, is shall we use weapons or keep our mouths closed and thereby support the puppets of the Cold War since 1975?

Keith Hart:

I'd like to give some chance for members of the panel to respond, but I would like to make an observation first. I hope, and many people have expressed the hope here, including at the beginning Mr Chaka, that Angola does have a different future from its present. And that means that its past must be contested. Its past has to be changed in order to make it compatible with a different future. And I understand the tremendous importance of making an assessment of who did what, when and who was responsible for breakdown and aggression and so on. I am really not seeking to impose from the Chair a ruling on how the panelists should respond to this; but it seems to me not very likely that a constructive resolution will be available in the next ten minutes. (Mild tittering) So I would hope that those questions which were concerned with constructive issues, including armaments, international institutions, possible legal frameworks for doing something, might occupy the panelists in their attempts to answer what are too many questions to respond to effectively.

Replies from the Panelists

Jean Emmanuel Pondi:

I would like to answer first the questioner who raised the problem of the elections and the result of the elections being contested and the peace being 'a continuation of war by other means'. We have to understand why that is the case. We need to understand the political process inside Africa where participation in politics is often one means to apply distributive power. Those who are kept out in the dark, out in the cold and who have lost the election, whether truly or not, contemplate the next couple of years without anything at all. So the winner-take- all strategy which is enforced here cannot be accepted in the context of Africa because the state is a distributive instrument rather than a productive one. It does not organise or galvanise people into productivity but is perceived as something over which one has control in order to distribute and to take control of the other resources of the country.

Jean-Emmanuel Pondi – "The OAU is bankrupt"

About the OAU deficiencies. Well, of course, I think they are very glaring to anyone who has read anything on the OAU and that is why I did not dwell on them; it's a financially bankrupt institution mainly because African states themselves do not contribute, have always used double talk. They make discourses and nice speeches, but have not contributed to the funding of the institution for many reasons. The arrears are now in the region of $80 -$90 million and the budget of the OAU was $29 million only, and that has been scaled down to $26 million and even that is unavailable. When one looks at Western Sahara and the UN funds that were needed there were $200 million, how can an organisation like the OAU be expected to play a participatory role in the conflicts of Africa which are so numerous, when it has no money. But those who are supposed to give it money do not give it money and then blame the organisation for not performing its task. I think it is a question of being responsible which has not always happened.

Very briefly the flow of arms. One should look at the reason why arms are imported. The reason is political. So once you deal with the political aspect you have an impact on the arms area, but I think a structure needs to be put in place and legislation ought to be also, in order to prohibit and criminalise the sale of arms and to apply stiff penalities for infringing those rules. Just as we had the Clark Amendment during the 1970s. This is an example of what can be done.

Professor George Wright:

I'm not sure where to begin as there are so many things to come in on but I'll try to be brief. First remark goes to Antonio Neto who commented on the fact that both UNITA and MPLA were subcontractors of the Cold War. There's absolutely no question about that and I just wanted to make a historical comment. I'm a citizen of the United States and as I recall during the American Revolution, the US took arms from the French because the French were opposed to the English. Smaller countries perhaps have historically been sandwiched between inter-imperial rivalries. In fact, I personally think what the Americans call the French Indian War between the British and the Americans was literally World War One.

The election being bogus or problematic. I don't think there's any question about that. There are a number of ways of looking at the Angolan elections and at the general patterns of elections that have been applied throughout the world, in Third World countries and particularly in Marxist-Leninist regimes in Eastern European countries. Very quickly, I think there are two points that stand out in my mind. We are not talking about elections but a new stage in history. Thirty-five years ago one-party states were satisfactory in Africa to the former colonialists because those countries were stable and they helped to accumulate capital for the imperial interest. A number of things have happened over the last twenty-five years and one-party regimes are not viable in that sense. But an alternative in the 1960s and more importantly in the 1970s were more radical, socialist-orientated regimes - the MPLA, Ethiopia,

Mozambique, Nicaragua, etc. These regimes have been beaten back with a number of instruments: economic, military, political, ideological. Now what is needed at this stage of imperialism is a new process to co-opt and diffuse internal competition and opposition, as well as internal restiveness if not potential revolution, owing to the brutal results of structural adjustment programmes etc. These elections are problematic because they don't fit. They're not developed organically. They are simply applied like Cinderella and the shoe. What we see in Angola is that one party didn't like the results and decided to continue the war; go back to the bush more or less. And so it's not a matter of the elections not working in Angola per se or that international law has not been effective or applied correctly.

The other question is this. Is this model of democratisation going to work for imperialism at this stage of history. My reading of Angola indicates that it might not be viable but what are the alternatives? Barbarism may be a result. More specifically related to Mr Chaka's comment ' peace may be closer than we imagine'. I'm not privy to the results of the discussions going on in Lusaka; but I've two general remarks on that process. Clearly what has been shown in the last year and a half, related to the results of those elections, is that might makes right. If you don't like the results all you have to do is go back to the bush. Specifically related to the political concessions and military concessions, what I understood UNITA wants in relation to its definition of power-sharing is to control the Ministry of Defence, Home Affairs, Foreign Affairs and Finance. Well that seems to me to be the Government. This may be incorrect. I'm just basing it on the information I have available.

Keith Hart:

The point is I hope that you will talk to each other outside of these sessions and pursue these questions more informally and rigorously.

Ambassador Deng:

I would like to conclude on why Angola matters since I did not cover this in my presentation and it will, I'm sure, answer one of the questions which was posed by the ANC representative.

Angola is one of the few territories that achieved independence thanks to the support of the international community and it would therefore be a blight on the UN record that a country it helped to create in the first place remains in a state of chaos. Therefore it is essential that the peace-building process of the UN succeeds. The second point which answers the question of the ANC representative is that if the elections in Angola are to be a precedent, then it does not bode well for the UN since there are a number of other UN-monitored elections that are underway. So, I agree with him that the failure of the UN-monitored elections in Angola does have repercussions for South Africa.

One of the questions that was posed was by the representative from International Alert on the role of the NGOs in the peace-building process that has been offered by the UN. Particularly if you look at the integrated peace-building model in El Salvador where elections allowed UN monitoring, the UNISAR and UNCTAD in Cambodia, a comprehensive approach is envisaged which not only includes UN specialists but all the other NGOs that are in the field. So they are seen as an important contributor to stability and to the peace-building process.

There was a question posed on the additional protocols on the Red Cross Conventions which are not very clear to me because the purpose of the additional protocols is that governments and rebel movements conform to basic standards when they are in war. It doesn't matter what way you characterise the warring parties in Angola as long as they observe the additional protocols. He raised another point on the legality of the Government in Angola, regarding how the MPLA took over. To many people in the international community, it is a question of recognition. As long as members of the international community decided to recognise that government, it's immaterial how they took over in the first place.

Keith Hart:

On the principle of equal opportunity I will give one or at the most two members of the audience another chance.

Alain Aeschliman (International Committee of the Red Cross, Geneva):

I want to refer to the last statement from Ambassador Deng. In his first speech he mentioned that international law does not regulate international use of force in internal armed conflicts and civil war. I just wanted to make clear that there is no regulation concerning the so-called jus ad bellum. It means the right to start an internal conflict, to launch attacks, or to find ways to stop an ongoing conflict. However, there are very clear regulations in international law, namely in international humanitarian law, concerning the jus in bello. It means the rules and principles to be respected during an armed conflict. For

internal armed conflict, we have at least the third article to the Geneva Conventions 1949 which makes it obligatory to all parties of a conflict, either states, individuals or armed groups, to respect and protect persons who don't take part in the conflict: the civilians, the wounded, sick people, non-combatants etc.
Thank you.

Keith Hart:

I have some housekeeping to do. I'm overwhelmed by the desire to tell you what's in my paper, but I'll resist the temptation. You should all have access to a copy and there are three papers available at present.

This conference has been run on a shoe string but we are grateful to the Calouste Gulbenkian Foundation and the Smuts Memorial Fund, Cambridge University, without whose support the conference would not have been possible. We will have to try to work out some system whereby you can have access to papers and talks which have not yet been written on paper. I look forward to meeting you again after lunch when we are fortunate to be able to present a very high-powered set of representatives from Angola who will tell us what they think is the answer to why Angola matters to the rest of the world. (*Applause* ****)

Session 2

Angola

George Chikoti

Isaias Samakuva

Fernando Pacheco

This panel had assumed its final form five days before the conference began. We had been flung around a political arena and panelists had whizzed past us on a merry-go-round of intrigue over which we had no control. There were extremely complex political issues at stake. Whether the workshop was a success or a failure depended largely upon this panel. It was a tense time.

It was Keith Hart who bore the brunt of having to deal with a range of external forces that were potentially hostile, constantly shifting and sometimes unknowable. His task was to deal with the politicians; Joanna Lewis had secured the participation of the Director of an Angolan NGO for the panel on reconstruction; but the decision was made to offer him the opportunity to sit on the platform as a representative of civil society when leading Angolans would tell us why Angola matters.

Whether to include UNITA or not? That was the question. For if we did, then we ran the risk of upsetting the major lobbying groups in Britain who follow the politics of exclusion. According to them, UNITA ought not to be given any access to such a public platform for this would give them credibility; credibility that a military organisation which rejected the democratic process in favour of a return to war should not be given.

However, our view differed, a product no doubt of our institutional heritage at the African Studies Centre, which has always practised the politics of inclusion. UNITA is a force in Angolan politics. UNITA will be part of any settlement. They have some ground support. Let them be given the opportunity to account for their actions in public.

That's what we did. We invited Fatima Roque, one of UNITA's leading economic advisers, to speak along side Lopo do Nascimento, General Secretary of the MPLA. So far, so good. Our press releases were buzzing with excitement. Then disaster. No Fatima and no Lopo. We sat tight and carried on arranging the other panels in a state of constructive despair.

We were saved however, when news came through that the Angolan Government would send a representative. Then the Angola Emergency Campaign said they could come. We invited another alleged UNITA adviser and, at this news, we were told to expect a demonstration against UNITA's presence outside Pembroke College. However, Jaime Pinto declined to attend in such a capacity; so we went into the last week before the conference without UNITA. Then, almost at the eleventh hour, UNITA's London office made contact with their representative who was at the Lusaka talks. Quite suddenly the decision was made that he would fly to London on the Sunday to attend the conference the following day. We knew it would be a different conference from that moment on.

We were not disappointed. There was tremendous tension, not just among the organisers fearing the possibility of demonstrations, walk-outs and public brawling. The Government delegation was dominated by former members of UNITA. They and the UNITA delegates were wary of one another, but polite. How would they react to sitting together on the platform? Who would sit where? As it turned out, the Government Vice-Minister and the UNITA representative sat together on the Chairman's left.

Introduction from the Chair

Sir Roger Tomkys, Master of Pembroke College:

(Sir Roger retired from the diplomatic service in 1992 when he became Master of Pembroke. His last posting was to Kenya in 1990 as the British High Commissioner . Previous to this, his career had taken him to the Middle East.)

Sir Roger Tomkys introduces the belligerent parties

Can I bring us back to order after lunch? I think Keith Hart said this morning that those who sit upon this platform can be taken as a symbol of the modern state. I'm Roger Tomkys, now Master of this College, a former diplomat which is a suitable symbol of the modern state. I'm well suited to this session, however, because of today's three topics - the World Order, Angola and Britain. I would not pretend to know something about Angola. I have visited it once and am the least expert of those in the room, I suspect. This probably gives me a certain advantage as I will try to impose the sort of time discipline called for this morning; and, at least if I impose this time discipline on warring factions, you will all know that it is not because I am discriminating between one faction and another: I shall genuinely not know what faction it is I am addressing, so it shall all be strictly neutral.

I had a brief period in my time at the Foreign Office, before I went to Nairobi, dealing with African affairs; and in early 1989 I went to a conference on Southern Africa at Wilton Park and there was a wide range of opinion there, pretty well across the board. One session was on Namibia. There were lusophones and anglophones; there were National Party MPs, ANC surrogates, ministers from Angola and Mozambique and other front line states and they all had different programmes and objectives in Southern Africa. The only thing that they agreed on during the day was that it was going to be very difficult for anything satisfactory to come out of Namibia in the way of a settlement. But it did. And I do just wonder when we ask ourselves why Angola matters, whether we are not at the next phase of this situation, where once again, as with the Namibia problem, a satisfactory outcome in Angola might bring wider benefits throughout the region.

Now we are very fortunate to have with us this afternoon for this session, Vice -Minister for Foreign Affairs, George Chikoti. After he has spoken we will next have the UNITA London representative, Mr Isaias Samakuva; and third, we shall have Mr. Fernando Pacheco, a representative of ADRA, a non-governmental organisation concerned with development. Now sir, would you like to sit or to stand?

George Chikoti, Vice-Minister for Foreign Affairs:

I will respect my audience and stand. Ambassador?

Sir Roger Tomkys:

Ambassador, are you going to join us? Are you going to say something first, or are you going to leave it all to the Vice-Minister?

Ambassador Antonio DaCosta Fernandes:

I think the delegation has been introduced. It's alright.

(Well, actually we had all overlooked the fact that we ought to introduce the officials who accompanied the Ambassador and the Vice-Minister. In the chaos, Sir Roger had not received instructions to do so. However, we were fortunate that no offence was taken in this tense atmosphere. So our sincere apologies go to:

Dr Joao Mateus Bernado Antonio, Head of the Department for Analysis and Economic Studies, Ministry of Foreign Affairs; Silvestre Guido R. Castelbranco, Acting Head of the European Department at the Ministry of Foreign Affairs; Dembo do Amaral e Silva, Press Attache, Embassy of Angola; Dr José de Carvalho, Economist; Alice D. Da Silva, Vice-Minister's Private Secretary.

We were grateful to the Embassy for the collection of materials they brought with them on Angola for general distribution.)

George Rebelo Pinto Chikoti (Vice-Minister for Foreign Affairs):

(George Chikoti is one of the youngest members of the current Government in Angola. He is President of the Angolan Democratic Forum.)

George Chikoti – "Refugees in their own country"

Mr Chairman, allow me first of all thank you, for chairing this session on Angola. May I extend my thanks to the Director of the African Studies Centre, Dr Keith Hart and all those who have collaborated in the preparation of this event. My regards also go to Baroness Linda Chalker, Minister for Overseas Development for giving her support to this workshop.

Mr Chairman, Distinguished Delegates, Ladies and Gentlemen, when I was asked to come and participate in this workshop on 'Why Angola Matters', I was touched by the fact that there was such a strong desire among the British researchers, journalists, politicians and ordinary citizens to know more about Angola.

In fact I think that it will not be too much to stress that Angola is enduring at this moment the biggest tragedy of modern times, in a war that has been going on for 18 years and has caused the death of nearly 2 million people. Without forgetting the fact that Angola's ancient history is characterised by one of the worst and longest slave trades, since the very early contacts with the Portuguese, who later colonised that territory for more than four centuries, treating Angolan natives is a very inhuman manner. Even long after the abolition of the slave trade, hard labour continued in Angola in response to the needs of Portugal for some tropical products, thus causing a lot of death among native Angolans. It is not easy to estimate how many people died during the slave trade; neither is it easy to know how many died during the Portuguese colonial rule. But I recall that the Portuguese were the most cruel slave traders; and they practised it for a long period and were among the most ruthless colonial rulers.

Mr Chairman, Honourable Delegates. In these circumstances you will understand that in 400 years they have done a lot of damage. Our colonisation, compared to the average of most of our neighbours Congo, Zaire, Zambia, Zimbabwe, Botswana and Namibia, which in many cases did not go beyond 80 years, is extremely long because it started much earlier than 1885. This gap in the length of time between the British and French colonisation on one side and Portuguese on the other has an important impact on the political mutations inside these former colonies.

The British generally used the indirect rule system while the Portuguese used direct rule, thus leaving no chance for political and social emancipation. It is therefore very clear that after the Second World War, when the British and French recognised the right colonised people had to achieve independence, the Portuguese resisted, claiming that they were not colonisers and that Angola was part of Portugal; and they started repressing Angolans who contested their authority.

We can therefore understand why the Angolan liberation movements did not have any other alternative than to fight for freedom as early as the 1960s. My question here is why would the Portuguese deny freedom for native Angolans when the British could give it to the Ghanians or the Nigerians, or the French to Senegalese and Malians? This lack of vision and political realism among the Portuguese colonial authorities as far as independence and self-determination is concerned was a bad precedent and brought a sequence of tragic wars: firstly the struggle for independence, then the civil war between the major political parties, based on ideological rivalry with some slight ethnic and regional connotations. But, as the conflict became international during the 80s, it turned out to be a clear demonstration of the East-West confrontation of the Cold War era, with the Soviet Union backing the Angola government and liberation movements in Nambia, Zimbabwe and South Africa, while in Angola the USA were backing UNITA with the aid of the South Africans.

The short period of political transition to democracy between 1991 and 1992 is evidence that, beyond ideology and ethnic causes, there is above all the ambition of one man to become president regardless of violating democratic principles, human rights or ethical values. This ruthless attitude is the only one that can justify why a political party alone can go so far in a senseless war like the one that has been carried out by UNITA since October 1992, after obtaining more than 35% of Parliament seats in the General Elections.

Mr Chairman, Honourable Delegates, Ladies and Gentlemen, my country is undergoing one of the most dramatic movements of its history. In only 14 months of post-electoral conflict more than 500,000 people have died, 200,000 have been mutilated, more than 400,000 have become orphans and about 4 million people have been displaced from their original homes — this means they have become refugees in their own country. As many as 3 million people might starve to death if humanitarian aid is not increased, and if the war does not come to an end. The children, the women and the old are most affected by this tragedy. Material destruction and loss are as well very heavy and will need a Marshall Plan in support of reconstruction. The Economic Commission for Africa estimated in 1988 that about 60 billion US dollars were required for the reconstruction of Angola. I do not know how many would be needed now!

Honourable Delegates, can the international community allow that one party alone makes so much killing and destruction in a terrorist manner and yet can come and sit among us with honour and convince us that their struggle is for freedom or for democracy or for human rights? Are we not encouraging those who use violence to conclude that they can get away with it? Would it be reasonable if my country invited a member of the British government to a workshop like this one and invited as well one of the terrorist organisations like the one we all know here? When we all know that elections took place in Angola, under the supervision of the UN's 1,000 international observers and these elections were proclaimed free and fair by the UN representative, who ironically happens to be a British citizen, Miss Margaret Anstee?

Mr Chairman, my government is seriously engaged in the search for peace in Angola and that's why we did not hesitate to come here and meet our compatriots of UNITA and show our commitment to the peace process. They have only one alternative and that is to participate in the consolidation of democracy in Angola. This would allow them to explain to their fellow Angolans what their political programmes and ideals are. But making such a devastating war that kills so many innocent people after making them vote and choose freely, is a crime against humanity.

The international community bears major responsibility for the Angolan tragedy. We will all recall that most of the western countries — USA, Great Britain, France, Germany, etc. —supported UNITA, on the basis of East-West confrontation, on a rationale that UNITA was democratic and that the MPLA was not; and therefore on those lines nobody looked at what kind of damage UNITA was doing to the Angolan people, neither did people ever look at the dictatorial nature of UNITA, even when as early as 1989 serious violations of human rights were denounced within UNITA structures.

With the end of the Cold War era, most of the West forced the Angolan government of that time not only to negotiate with UNITA, but to hold elections in the shortest possible time frame just to satisfy UNITA, when we all thought then that we needed more time before elections could be held, as such an issue of democratic transition could not be limited to two parties only. The American President, Mr George Bush reacted very violently saying that, and I quote, "the United States will not allow that elections be held in Angola beyond September 30, 1992". This is a very strange diplomatic statement coming from a foreign country. What people were ignoring is that there was a multi-party democratic process going on in Angola and it was not a question of communists against capitalists. For some people in the West, democracy meant the victory of right wing over left wing, when we all know that in many western countries communists are represented in

Parliament. There are more than 25 political parties in Angola out of which 12 are now in Parliament.

Distinguished Delegates, is this not a paradox, when President George Bush himself addressed the American Congress on March 6, 1991 and I quote:

"Now, we can see a new world coming into view. A world in which there is the very real prospect of a new world order. In the words of Winston Churchill, a world order in which the principles of justice and fair play protect the weak against the strong: ... A world where the United Nations, free from cold war stalemate, is posed to fulfill the historic vision of its founders. A world in which freedom and respect for human rights find a home among all nations".

My question to this statement is, are we really protecting the weak against the strong with principles of justice and fair play, when UNITA can explode bombs against civilian targets in Angola and come to hide in London convincing the English public that they are fighting for democracy?

No, ladies and gentlemen, the truth is that the western countries have failed to admit UNITA's defeat in an election by a party considered communist; and, as long as this double standard situation is maintained, it will be difficult to understand the genuine intention that many European countries have as far as the progress of democracy is concerned, in Africa and the Third World. When we look at South Africa, for example, we quickly understand there again that the white minority has found a way to avoid ANC to rule in its full majority, even if it wins the elections in April, by forcing a government of national union, regardless of who wins.

After all, why would it be so important to fight against communism in Angola or elsewhere, when we have communists in Parliament in France and a Labour Party in England, even before the end of the Cold War?

In these circumstances, are we not allowed to doubt about the will that some people have to see Africans develop? We can all note very well that, in the name of the Cold War, everything was permitted to some African regimes. The West has created and tolerated some of the most dictatorial regimes in the world: look at Zaire today, Togo, Haiti and many other states that have not made serious democratic progress. I am convinced today that what existed in Angola was no different than any other one-party regime as in many other countries. So why so much concern with Angola? Are we not allowed to believe that someone wanted to justify the UNITA-South African engagement in Angola as a pretext to fight communism? Otherwise, how can we understand that most of the western countries mentioned earlier have always had UNITA representatives in their capitals, even after elections have been held? When are we going to be able to defend principle? Why talk about democracy when we can't defend its principles if our friends lose elections? Instead we hear statements like "Angola is not ready for an election."

Honorable delegates, I cannot end my statement without pointing out that it is high time we take action on Angola, otherwise it will be too late tomorrow, both on human and material grounds. Most of the economical potential has been totally ravaged, particularly the infrastructure which will need a lot of investment for its rehabilitation. This is where the donor community and private investors will have to help Angola reconquer its place in the sub-region. There is no doubt either about Angola's role among the SADC countries as the only oil producer with ports in deep waters and a transportation network that can be of great support to land-locked Zambia and Botswana.

But political stability is a must in Angola for a good economic environment. Thus elections in South Africa should bring us very quickly to the consolidation of a Southern African Community with solid institutions. Thus the creation of a Southern African Parliament, composed of member states who will have by now all undergone democratic elections, can be a very good way of developing trust and understanding in a region which has, for many years, been the theatre of hostilities, plagued by mistrust based on ideology, racism and ethnic differences.

Mr Chairman, as I end my speech, I wish to call upon Her Majesty the Queen of England, the British Government and everyone in this room to help Angola and South Africa find peace at last. Thank you very much. (*Applause* ***)

Sir Roger Tomkys:

Our next speaker will, I fear, be tempted to try to answer charges made point by point. It would be more helpful for us if he could forbear to a degree and tell us something about the future. Mr. Samakuva.

Isaias Samakuva (UNITA's Representative in Britain):

(Isaias Samakuva is a Brigadier in UNITA where he once fought along side the Ambassador Antonio Fernandes who left UNITA in 1992. He was currently involved in the negotiations taking place in Lusaka.)

Isaias Samakuva – "ethnic cleansing"

Ladies and Gentlemen. When on Saturday the chief of the UNITA delegation allowed me to leave the talks to attend this conference, I was wondering if it would be useful to debate our mutual accusation amongst ourselves. On the plane I thought that I should just outline my speech here by concentrating on the results we got in Lusaka which are leading to the peace. This is what I will do.

The geographical location of Angola makes it a country of strategic importance in Central and Southern Africa. Political stability, or the lack of it, in Angola may have direct positive or negative bearing on the other countries of the sub-region such as, for instance, Congo with repercussions for Gabon and Sâo Tomé, Zaire, Zambia, Namibia, Botswana and South Africa. For many years and for several purposes, Angola was considered by many departments in foreign ministries as belonging solely to the Southern Africa group of countries. However, many others have always considered Angola as part of Central as well as Southern Africa. In fact Angola has the virtue of linking the Western coast of Africa to the land-locked countries in the interior of the continent, and of establishing liaison between the English-speaking countries on its eastern and southern borders and the French speaking countries in the North, thus making an impact on the life of central African countries.

Angola has been at war for 33 years now. A war fuelled by fear and prejudice, sustained by lack of interest on the part of those who would prefer to see it ended and hatred and greed on the part of an unholy alliance of psychopaths, mercenaries and arms dealers, who benefit from it; a war whose origins are shrouded in lies transformed by repetition into received truths; a war whose origins have been disguised to protect the guilty and blame the innocent, especially those who are unable to speak out freely to defend themselves; a war sustained by a conspiracy, not only of silence but of deceit; a war whose continuation for well over a year, is a blot on the conscience of mankind. It started with the war against colonialism; but the struggle for national liberation was complicated by rivalry between the super-powers in their search for supremacy and influence beyond their own national borders. This Cold War was so vigorous and powerful in its expansion and dissemination of foreign ideology that Angola's national interests were relegated into second or third place.

Angola is a vast country with enormous economic potential. Its ruinous war is in some ways the result of colonial history and the way the process of decolonisation was conducted. In the meantime today, due perhaps to the same foreign interests trying to assert their influence or due to the lack of objective, non-partisan information, Angola's bloody war is explained in a simplistic way as being the product of the rejection of the election results by one of the parties.

The election victory of one party cannot in any way and, however presented, provide justification for the mass killing of tens of thousands of innocent people in a planned and systematic programme of ethnic and political cleansing. The racial, ethnic and regional differences of different groups of the same country are being exploited by hidden interests in order to create and fuel conflict and divisions that may destroy the country unless the country's leaders show the courage and vision to overcome party and group differences in favour of national interests and national reconciliation.

As far as UNITA is concerned, the war has to be brought to an end. This can only be achieved by addressing the fundamental issues that are the root cause of the conflict. Today, Angolans are divided by hatred and fear that this cruel and long war has created in their midst. For the sake of our own people, for the sake of our own children, this situation has to be brought to an end. 'Enough is Enough'. We have to look at the future and face it with courage and hope, based on the conviction that this conflict can be solved, and that this tragedy can be stopped.

We must create conditions and an environment that eliminate fear and hatred. It is of paramount important to devise formulas that can promote the sentiment of forgiveness. Confidence-building measures have to be found as necessary and indispensable means to achieve what has to be the main objective of all Angolans: National Reconciliation. National Reconciliation of course cannot be interpreted simply as the enforcement of laws or 'dictats' by the Government on other parties. Instead it must involve opening up a legal framework and agreements in order to accommodate the interests of other parties; to allow parties to participate freely (free from coercion and intimidation) in the political and administrative life of the country, thereby accepting peaceful coexistence and diversity. Where there is political will and commitment, coexistence must be possible.

At this stage, UNITA's vision of the country's future embraces the need to achieve and secure:

A. Dialogue and coexistence
B. National reconciliation
C. Social and economic development
D. Promotion of democracy

These issues have had a profound bearing on the UNITA agenda for the current peace talks in Lusaka, Zambia. These protracted talks have already resulted in significant achievements and can still be built on. UNITA has made important concessions to facilitate the talks and the search for a solution. It has agreed to surrender to the government the territory it controls, disarm its soldiers and demobilise them.

Now UNITA expects that the basic principle of a government of National Reconciliation coupled with regional administrative decentralisation, to allow time for the hatred and fear caused by the 'ethnic cleansing' to begin to heal, must be applied in the political negotiations. No other approach can succeed, given the fear and suspicion of each party for the other. There must be elements built into the agreement which will provide sufficient guarantees to each party that it will be able to protect the security and identity of its supporters.

The key elements should therefore be:

A Government of National Reconciliation

- Allocate seats in the National Assembly in accordance with the 'results' of the 1992 elections.

- Ensure joint political control by UNITA and MPLA of cabinet portfolios and ministries crucial to the success of the peace process and mutual security.

- The remainder of the portfolios in the Cabinet should be allocated on a basis which promotes National Reconciliation, much as South African parties have agreed to.

- Qualified supporters of UNITA and other political parties must be integrated into the civil service and parastatal institutions at all levels.

Regional Administrative Decentralisation

A variety of approaches can be taken to meet this need. The wounds of war and ethnic cleansing are still fresh and must be allowed time to heal. Confronting residents of a province who have recently suffered massacres of their friends and relatives by soldiers and riot police, with the prospect of the return of those who massacred them will obviously excite fear and violent resistance. At the same time, the geographical integrity of the country must be maintained.

It is also almost impossible to see how a stable peace can be achieved unless an 'arms embargo' is re-introduced and all prisoners and detainees are released without delay. Reconstitution of the National Armed Forces (FAA), as agreed in the Peace Accords and reintegration of the national territory within the framework of a Government of National Reconciliation are likewise essential.

Peace in Angola cannot be established on the basis of lies, military force or manipulation. Angolans have yet to find a common identity, to build a true Angolan nation; to put behind them the fear and the prejudice that is reflected in pejorative remarks about 'Bailundos', 'Zairenses' and 'Mulatos'; and to find and accept one another as Angolan brothers and sisters.

Perpetuation of the myths created by propaganda at the time of the elections in 1992 makes no contribution to nation-building. Indeed, its disastrous effect is clearly apparent in the vicious campaigns of ethnic cleansing which have marred our recent history. I hope that our discussions today will make some contribution to enabling Angolans to admit our faults and face the future as fellow citizens.

It is important to stimulate the public awareness of Angola's relevance to the future of southern Africa, the continent and the world as a whole. Press reporting should not concentrate on what divides the Angolan people but rather on what unites them; and there is much here from which to draw.

Foreign interest should concentrate on helping to rebuild confidence in our potentially prosperous country; to underpin national reconciliation and reconstruction; and to ensure that Angola can play its full part in the strengthening of the world economic order. What Angola does not need is self-serving, corrupt partners, pursuing their own agendas, undermining Angola's prospects of stability in the future.

Angola is not only a portion of territory in central and southern Africa, nor a country in the African continent alone. Angola is an important part of the international world. That is why it matters. We have made some contribution to face the future as fellow citizens. It is important to stimulate discussion and there is much we can do of that here. *(Applause **)*

Sir Roger Tomkys:

If I could just say that we've heard some hard words from our two speakers. I for one, and I'm sure all of us here, do not underestimate the advantage for Angola that they should appear here on the same platform and also outside the plenary session to talk over Angola's problems. Hard words are to be expected. I am grateful for the courteous way in which they have expressed them and I hope that example will be followed when we get to the discussion. Mr Pacheco please. There will be a consecutive tranlsation which inevitably takes a longer time.

Fernando Pacheco – President of Action for Rural Development and the Environment (ADRA):

(Translated by David Lehmann, Director of the Centre for Latin American Studies, Cambridge University. Fernando Pacheco is a trained agronomist. He lectures in rural sociology in the Faculty of Agriculture at the University of Luanda. He is also Director of ADRA, one of Angola's non-governmental organisation well known and respected by many British organisations for its work.)

Fernando Pacheco – "No space for civil society"

1990 was a hopeful year for independent Angola. It was at a cross-roads with a number of alternative choices before it. The long civil war appeared to be coming to an end, the political regime showed signs of opening up and of questioning the way forward. All in all it was a time for challenging, for change, that encouraged the making of plans and starting afresh.

It was in this climate, and certainly influenced by it, that a small group of people decided to set-up a non-governmental organization that would work for rural development. It would essentially have a challenging attitude towards the ways in which an understanding of the reality and development of the country were obtained. Such development should be appropriate, continuous, participatory and closely linked to the democratisation process.

In the short term ADRA wanted to help to heal the wounds of war, consolidate peace and help national reconciliation. It also wanted to take advantage of the spirit of change and general opening up at that time, so as to contribute through the organization work to the building (or strengthening) of an active and dynamic civic society. This wide reaching project took shape with the funding of ADRA (Accao para o Desenvolvimento Rural e Ambiente- Action for Rural Development and Environment).

It presented its objectives as follows:

- To work with local communities based on their needs and their aims, taking into account their ethnic and cultural diversity and plurality of ways of life, preparing and promoting participatory projects to help development;

- To support research into alternative development, based on Angola reality and to use practice, particularly in grass-roots projects, to develop adequate methods of work;

- Contribute towards the strengthening of civic society and the democratisation process taking place in Angola.

The projects that would put these objectives into practice would be based on certain fundamental principles that would constitute the moral axes of the organizations. ADRA became a non-governmental organization, independent, non-party, non-religious, non profit making; characteristics which completely describe it institutionally. But, perhaps more than this, ADRA is a social intervention project, with general objectives and working principles that are in line with a certain vision of society, of its history, its state and its evolution. These principles are expressed in the recovering of cultural values, the preserving of natural resources, in respect for diversity and pluralism, in the sharing of knowledge and understanding; in participation, in defence of human rights in the widest sense, in building a democratic culture. Flexibility, originality and the quality and relevance of its work are certainly the results of this critical assessment of situations, as well as the product of its creativity and innovative spirit in searching for solutions.

Its intervention in projects, studies and debates, and its relations with its partners (state, other NGOs, communities, etc.) are characterised by this critical attitude towards reality, by a profound respect for the "other", and by a willingness for building and for responsible social change, that will develop and democratise the country and create space for participation by its citizens.

As a result of this vision of the country, ADRA tries to establish links between the state and communities, without trying to substitute one or the other. Its activities give priority to those most in need, those who in present circumstances are most affected by the war, by economic inequalities and by social exclusion. They include displaced persons, who are suddenly bereft of their material goods (that were already very limited) and their identity and references, without the means to face a hostile urban situation, and the aggressive market economy that is developing so savagely; women, especially those who are heads of families, often with many children; orphans and abandoned children, with no points of reference except to struggle for survival, savage competition, speculation and delinquency; rural populations, affected in multiple ways, by the war, the drought, isolation, without the means of subsistence for numerous reasons and without ways to defend themselves from the aggressive nature of the market.

The ADRA project is not only concerned with practical activities on the ground with rural and community development. It is also active in the arena of ideas, trying to create opportunities for reflection, for understanding, discussion and debate of Angolan reality and of questions considered to be important in the national context. The organization tries to combine activities at two different levels. At the micro level, with its community projects at grass-roots level, at the pace and rhythm of people's lives, trying through practical activities to improve the quality of life and learn about the reality of the country. At the same time, at the macro level it creates space for discussion and debate of the questions that are challenges to the general dynamic of Angolan society.

To do this ADRA has organised two areas of intervention, which in fact are mutually dependent on each other, and are sometimes combined in practice. The first and foremost are the community projects at grass-roots level, involving local populations, discussing situations and finding innovative and appropriate ways to intervene. What is sought here is to strengthen the communities and have them take on responsibilities, through training and carrying out specific activities that help to make them self-sufficient, even in the context of the war. The identification of real life situations, always with active local community participation, leads to the development of programs to solve urgent problems such as food, clothing, water supply, medicines, and to developing small projects to generate incomes. In these circumstances training of the community is essential, because it improves local participation and allows for flexibility in the program. An example of this is the Huila-Peace and Development Project. It is financed by the European Union and involves demobilised soldiers, displaced persons and other vulnerable groups. With them it was possible to gain access to land for agricultural projects, to help the production of cereals, market garden vegetables, rabbits and poultry; to encourage the setting up of small scale workshops (mechanics, welding, carpentry, dressmaking, bakeries) and help the building of water wells, health posts and schools, sometimes in cooperation with religious organizations. At present 30.000 people are involved in these projects. All of them involve a high level of participation and creativity by the beneficiaries. They find original solutions (low cost water supplies and latrines) and they take the initiative in such things as self-build housing in residential areas. These attitudes show the appropriateness of the project and its search for self-sufficiency. Further projects of a similar nature are being developed in Malanje, Luanda, and again in Huila.

The second area of ADRA's work is in the "battle of ideas", where ADRA hopes to contribute to the promotion of debate, and to the opening of a space that will encourage and strengthen civic society. This is done by organising activities that stimulate discussion, around questions considered to be important for the country, and by broadening the discussion in the society. Relationships established in the communities where ADRA works are based on recognition of plurality and of the diverse situations existing in the country. They are based on the fact that it is essential to keep an open mind and have creative and listening attitudes. Conscious of this diversity

ADRA actively carries with it a concern for the development and strengthening of local institutions, for the decentralisation of power and strengthening of democracy. These are the two important themes for consideration, study and discussion, and the organization tries to impregnate its practical activities and relationships with its partners with the results of such discussions.

ADRA's strategy to strengthen civic society is based essentially on two main axes: the first, in the arena of the battle of ideas by organising debates and discussions around the grand questions of national dynamics. ADRA organises conferences, seminars and workshops on themes selected for their importance on context. As well as decentralisation and strengthening the democratic process, ADRA is also concerned to know the reality of the politics of development, economic reforms, gender problems, ethnic and cultural diversity, the production and circulation of information, among other questions. The second axis is support for strengthening and organising groups that constitute or potentially constitute civic organizations in society. That is it hopes to support the development of the Angolan associative movement, which will be referred to later in this article.

The early stages of ADRA's activity were not easy. Although ADRA's objectives were clear it did not have resources and its founders had little understanding of the working of such organizations. The lack of similar experience in the country meant that solutions had to be sought for questions of organization and institution, in terms of methodology and types of activity to be developed.

ADRA's form and structure are the result of discussion and debates among its members. It has adapted its work practices to its objectives and to the real day to day situations encountered. So, while right from the start of the organization rural communities were chosen as the priority target group, the reality of the evolving situation in Angola showed the depths of poverty of poor urban dwellers and the precarious situation of displaced persons. This justified, for example, the development of the Lubango Participative Periurban Development Program, where the influx of displaced persons aggravated the already poor situation of the inhabitants of Sofrio and Caluva boroughs, with lack of drinking water, basic sanitation, health posts and schools. These problems were tackled in a joint effort between the local community and state institutions with ADRA and ACORD (an international NGO supporting ADRA) acting as a link and a helper in training and the participation of the community. This program is also part of ADRA's history, and perhaps of the development of community participation in Angola, because it served as a laboratory for testing methodology and as a school for training cadres. It was the forerunner of later projects. For example it was possible there to adopt a system of secret ballot to elect different interest groups, something quite unheard of in these communities.

The civil war - apart from all the general instability it has caused in the country, all the limitations, social crises and crises of values - has brought thousands of displaced persons into the urban areas along the coast. They have settled here in a state of social and institutional emergency and are highly dependent on outside support. ADRA is aware of the particularly difficult situation of displaced persons, and they are one of the organization's special target groups. However, as ADRA rejects the idea of instant aid both morally and in practice, when projects must necessarily include an emergency component due to the weak and traumatized state of the people, the organization refuses to limit its support just to the distribution of food and other basic needs. On the country, its support is an attempt to respond to the urgency of the situation by creating conditions that will encourage the social and psychological stability of the communities involved. This is done by ensuring some continuity in rehabilitation, outside an emergency framework.

The Luacho Project in Benguela province is a case in point. ADRA began an emergency project there to support over two thousand displaced families, with financial support from the Swedish government. After carefully studying the situation to get a better idea of the community's problems, there was a careful discussion with the sponsor to allow the transformation of an emergency project into a rehabilitation project. It was soon clear that the displaced persons did not only want to be supplied with emergency food aid. They wanted to address the question of access to agricultural land and the opportunity to develop activities to produce income. They also needed to replace their identity cards that had been lost in their flight from the war. This showed their concern to maintain their identity and citizenship, aspects which donors don't give any importance to, and for which the official identification service was unable to provide help. Today Luacho is considered by several UN agencies and NGOs as an example of how it is possible to quickly move from an emergency situation to one of rehabilitation, by making the community responsible for itself. ADRA has tried to repeat this process in other areas where emergency action is required, in Huila, Benguela and Malanje.

At a national level, ADRA is now a structured organization with a certain executive capacity and enjoying considerable credibility. But it is no way ADRA's intention to become a powerful organization acting within a fragile and dependent institutional framework. On the contrary, as part of its second strategic objective to strengthen civic society ADRA tries to support the emergence and consolidation of other NGOs, community-based organizations (CBOS) and associations, which are organising individuals and groups in similar ways and with similar objectives. ADRA's final aim is to contribute to the setting up of a network of organizations and individuals that work in this way.

How does ADRA propose to achieve this strategic objective?

On one hand, every activity or project is a link in the making of this network of individuals and organizations. That is every project has as its prime objective to strengthen the institutions and communities involved in it. This is how it works from a methodological point of view. Thus, interest groups, associations and community organizations are strongly encouraged and activities in this area are especially supported. In this way partnerships are formed which are reflected in the network working to strengthen civic society.

This reference to "partnerships" brings us to the question of the agents who bring about ADRA's strategy: the "Creating Partnerships" program. We believe that ADRA has reached a point where it should organise and give structure to its strategic objectives. It has created a programme with the aim of helping the emerging national NGOs and CBOs and of strengthening them, and consequently strengthening the national associative movement.

How does the "Creating Partnerships" program work?

In the first phase the program is based essentially on ADRA's projects and on the work developed by its teams with communities and individuals involved in the projects. Its aim is to strengthen the communities and, with the organizations set up, find appropriate ways for them to achieve their own objectives. At the same time this program has more and more needed to put the different organizations in contact with each others' projects, and this is forming a network.

At the same time, and because ADRA has so often been requested to do so, the Creating Partnerships program establishes links between other NGOs, community organizations that are not directly involved in projects. This is particularly true in Luanda province, where in fact practical projects are on a smaller scale. This direct work with other organizations will become of greater importance in a second phase of a stronger program of Creating Partnerships. This will provide second links in the network, communication, solidarity and complementary links.

The role of this programme in relation to the institutions involved will essentially be done of training ("learning by doing"), by the development of means of communication and the promotion of adequate information.

The strengthening of community groups and their multiplication, allowing more and less closely knit and more and less specific networks to develop, could lead to the setting up of autonomous social movements with their own identity. In ADRA's view such movements would become actors in the democratic process, and they represent essential elements in the reconstruction of a society as splintered as Angola, the result of its own nature, the destructive actions of the state and the war. In this situation education and information play an important role and ADRA places great importance on them as ways of strengthening a civic society which, although still weak, has shown a great development potential. This is what is happening in the Catumbela-93 Project, where the movement demanding access to land may reach the proportions of a future social movement.

This represents a fascinating challenge, especially now that at the same time both the conditions and need for autonomous social movements in Angola have combined. (*Applause* ****)

Open Session

Sir Roger Tomkys:

With a translator it is very difficult to stay within time-keeping, even with such skilled interpreting as that. Thank you both. I would ask those wishing to make statements from the floor to keep them very brief indeed and to be as precise as possible..

Tony Fernandes (Angolan Ambassador):

I am Tony Fernandes, Angola's Ambassador to the court of St James. As such there are things that I can say *("briefly I hope" from Sir Roger)* and things that I cannot. If this conference was hosted by the British Government, I would be much freer to speak. But it is not, although we have members of the Government in this room.

I agree with Mr Samakuva when he says he did not come here to accuse the other side and vice versa, but I am concerned about **your** reaction, **yours** as British citizens, when Mr Samakuva says that the Government did not allow participation in state affairs by Angolan citizens free of coercion, when we all know that **they refused** to participate in the government before the elections, during the interim period, and more so after the elections. And the consequences of this you all know. I am concerned: what are **you** going to think of this statement?

Tony Fernandes – "they refused to participate"

And you know, ladies and gentlemen, history is not there to be interpreted. History is there to be told. Also, Mr Samakuva says that UNITA has accepted in Lusaka to relinquish its armed forces; to hand over territory and so on. What guarantees do we have now that they will comply? And what is your reaction to such a statement? This is what I am concerned with.

You all heard here this morning four statements from prominent professors, researchers and so on. Not one of them apportioned blame. You all heard the statements. We are here not to interpret history. We are here to salvage the wreckage that is Angola today. *(Applause ****)*

Patrick Smith, (Africa Confidential):

I wonder if Brigadier Samakuva could clarify UNITA's position in Lusaka now. Is this an unconditional acceptance of the results of the 1992 elections? And, if it is, what is their position on the first round of presidential elections in 1992? Does he envisage a second round being held immediately? And in the interim, what would be the position of the UNITA leader, Jonas Savimbi?

(Total silence as the answer is delivered very slowly and deliberately.)

Isaias Samakuva:

Firstly, I would like to answer his Excellency the Ambassador by saying that I would take his example. His Excellency the Ambassador and the Vice-Minister here are members of one party in Angola which won seats in the Parliament. And they have the Vice-Minister and the Ambassador here apart from the Minister of Justice in the country. UNITA has won 70 places in the Parliament and was given the place of Minister of Culture. That was it. *(Samakuva lowers his voice to almost a whisper at this point.)* What would you expect to be the reaction of UNITA?

To Mr Patrick Smith, what is going on in Lusaka? Yes, I think it was on November 6th 1992, contrary to what everyone says, a month later after elections, UNITA had written a letter to the Secretary-General to say that the election results had been accepted. Yes, however, we want a second round of elections as we only have an acting president at the moment.

Teresa Santana, (Student from Angola):

I would like to address some points to Mr Chikoti and to Mr Samakuva. The contentious position you both present is that Angola is a place given to you where you can do as much as you please without any regard to its people. The Angolan people do not want war. *(Enthusiastic applause ****)* You have all managed to reduce the Angolan people to a level of barbarity and the Angolan people do not want war. Nobody gave you a mandate to do this. *(More applause **)* And when Mr Chikoti talks of the Portuguese refusing to give up Angola, maybe it was because they thought it was given to them by God; an attitude which is perhaps being repeated right now.

Antonio Neto (Leader of the Angolan Democratic Party):

The Lusaka meeting has been going on for five months now. My own party has asked for a place at the talks, but we have been refused a place there. If national reconciliation is an aim, and if it is an aim that is to be realised, then it has to be recognised that this is a concern of a much wider political spectrum and more organisations should therefore be included in Lusaka.

There are five political parties made up of civilian people. Can both sides, the Government and UNITA, explain what is their position as far as this problem is concerned? Because what we need is national reconciliation. I have heard that you have enough weapons for another two years of fighting. Should we the people organise strikes and demonstrations? If Angola is going to be a democracy you cannot run the country as you do now. *(Applause **)*

Patrick Smith seeks clarification

Diana Miller (Retired Russian emigree):

If UNITA want peace, why are they in Yugoslavia with the South African Broederbond buying arms? *(Applause ***)*

Marco Ramazzotti (Consultant):

My question is to Mr Samakuva. UNITA refused peace and the election results as it only had one minister. Now you have three. How do you justify your actions? UNITA did not accept the presidential elections. So why should we believe that you would stick to any new agreement? What guarantees have we heard? *(Murmurs of approval)* . I wonder also what are the problems that we might envisage that would divide the major parties? What we have heard have been very similar in content and at this present time, I do not understand why there is still war.

Isaias Samakuva:

I would like to say that where there is war there are two contenders. War is not made by one party alone. To Professor Neto I would like to say that on May 14th 1993 UNITA's Political Commission issued a communique saying that it is time now for the political parties to come in and discuss national reconciliation. It was not possible to do it from the beginning because we were dealing with military issues between the MPLA and UNITA. At this stage when we are talking about national reconciliation, it is possible for other parties to come in.

To the lady who mentioned a meeting with South Africans. Sorry Madam, but I would say this is propaganda. What the South Africans are doing at this stage is to offer mercenaries to the Government who are at this time fighting in Angola. *(Dissent from the audience)* I'm sorry Sir, maybe it's my fault, but I did not understand your question.

Marco Ramazzotti:

I'll ask you again. You refused peace. You rejected the election results. You have one minister. Now you get three ministers more and one million dead. Is that accountable to a reasonable national party or is that accountable only to prejudice and a drive for power?

Isaias Samakuva:

Thank you sir. I would say that is a distortion of facts. UNITA has not yet rejected the elections *(groans of protest from the audience)*. UNITA contested the results of the elections and asked for investigations. And not only UNITA. Professor Neto, a leader of a party had also contested the elections. There were more parties that contested the elections. What we had asked for was just investigation. In the course of the investigation of the matter, people were killed. This is the reason for the war, not a rejection of the election. *(Widespread murmurs of discontent)*

George Chikoti:

I will help by not going into the rhetoric. It is an important issue. We made an agreement with UNITA in 1991 to go for elections regardless of who won. I have to say that myself and Ambassador Tony Fernandes were in UNITA at that time. We broke away from UNITA. Our strategy in the elections was to support President dos Santos because we didn't agree with Dr Savimbi. After the elections UNITA was beaten and then there was a government and this government has other political groups and I am from one of those.

I believe that UNITA has every right to be in Angola and oppose itself to the ruling regime, the government of which I am a member. But I do not agree with UNITA when it takes up arms because out of the 18 political parties in Angola, UNITA is the only one that went back to fight.

And the claims that UNITA bring up about the elections? UNITA started taking over cities even before the final proclamation of the results. There were about 17 cities and municipalities that were taken over. What did we do at that time? We knew UNITA was a stronger force. The Government had dismantled its army. We were faced with a situation, either we let UNITA take over or we defend ourselves. So we turned to the constitution which allows the government to protect civilian rights. And that's what we did.

Professor Neto brings up an interesting point. As a colleague I am President of the Angolan Democratic Forum. He is President of the Angolan Democratic Party. We have met several times before the elections and after. I think that the political parties in Angola have the right to demonstrate: the constitution allows that. If there is violence certainly the Government will intervene, just as happens in Britain, France and elsewhere. The Constitution allows demonstrations and strikes as long as they don't go against the public interest. So in my view, first of all UNITA should not create confusion whereby they reject elections and say our people were killed, that is why we were rejecting the elections. There is a framework worked out by UNITA and the Government and that's what UNITA should return to. The question of choices for ministries? UNITA can chose either to be in total opposition to the Government, which is its right, or to go into the Government, but not to fight.

Also UNITA has introduced the accusation of ethnic cleansing. Mr Samakuva and myself come from the same ethnic group. The Ambassador, Tony Fernandes comes from Cabinda. I do not believe that UNITA is a party based on ethnic lines. There are many people from other ethnic groups in UNITA, so these claims are inconsistent with what UNITA is saying and what is going on in South Africa. There was an agreement to hold elections. Only when UNITA lost the elections did we have all these sorts of problems. UNITA has never said anything about any other political leaders of other parties that were killed in other parts of Angola. Even during the political campaigning, neither I nor Mr Fernandes could go to Jamba to campaign. UNITA troops occupied the place.

So we are fighting here for democracy in Angola and we should not blame the MPLA for what is wrong at the moment. I think that the 16 years of war we fought were wrong. None of us agreed with the total occupation by the Cubans and the Russians when we were with UNITA at the time. Mr Samakuva knows this. What we agreed with was that people had to find other ways of contributing to the democratic process. We believed that a government of national reconciliation could come after the elections. UNITA had no right to reject this one democratic process in a country like Angola which has many problems that need to be addressed in peace. We desperately need that peace and stability.

To the lady who was referring to making Angola a toy, yes, I think that is an important point. I think that when there are principles to be respected we should not show doubt. That's what I've been saying to the Americans, to the western community *(interrupted by a heckler at this point)* that Angolans want democracy. Principles have to be respected. Professor Neto and myself said in 1991 that the time-frame of the elections was too short and we were ignored by UNITA, by the Angolan Government and by the US. I think we needed three or four years. Now UNITA realises they need this time to reconcile; to work out things that were not properly addressed at the time. And I think we need to address the issue of time seriously:

Kathryn O'Neill

time to allow trust to develop. Because the issue is having a democratic process and not a fight between MPLA and UNITA. This will always be the case. We need a total democratic society in which civil society can participate fully. *(Applause ***)*

Sir Roger Tomkys:

Thank you. I think there is time for two short and concise questions from the audience.

Kathryn O'Neill (Christian Aid):

I would like to ask Mr Samakuva about his use of the term ethnic cleansing. And to ask him whether he thinks the basis of the war, the internal conflict in Angola is ethnic or not?

Malik Chaka (Office of UNITA, Washington DC):

On ethnic cleansing, I have a number of articles here from the British press - the Times, the Independent - and they all talk about ethnic cleansing in Luanda and other cities *(he holds up the articles)*. And in respect of South African intervention, there are persistent reports in the press that a gentleman by the name of Edwin Barlow based in Johannesburg has been recruiting mercenaries from South Africa for the MPLA. Would the Vice-Minister comment on this?

(At this point the Angolan Ambassador jumps to his feet.)

Tony Fernandes:

This is nonsense. I'm sorry but it's nonsense.

Sir Roger:

Since we have had one extra question and a statement I would now like to ask Mr Samakuva and the Vice-Minister to respond briefly and then I would like three sentences from the person who does not come from either party. Would you mind taking ethnic cleansing first Mr Samakuva?

(Note how Sir Roger switches the order in which Chikoti and Samakuva gave their speeches, so that the Government would have the final say.)

Isaias Samakuva:

I don't mind.. On ethnic cleansing I don't need to say anything. I have British newspaper reports which say 'Ethnic Cleansing comes to Angola'. This is available here. *(Shouts from the floor: "What are the dates?")* They are from the Guardian, the Times and the Independent, November 1992.

As I said in my speech, it is impossible for people to know and to understand, for there is much distortion of facts. But I would like to point out that if this workshop is aimed at throwing accusations; if this platform is used to accuse each other coming from Lusaka where the talks are taking place, as I said, which are making lots of progress, then I would reject to participate in this debate. *(Total silence in the room)* As I have said, what we should do and I believe that is the aim of this workshop, is to find a way to solve the problem in Angola. Counter accusation is what is going on in Angola. It is useless to do it here.

George Chikoti:

I have been asked on ethnic cleansing and South Africa. It depends on who interprets what and what exactly we mean by ethnic cleansing. I don't think Angola is a society divided as such. You will find tribes structured on an ethnic basis and it is true, some of the leaders of the main parties come from different ethnic tribes, and there was in fact confrontation. But what we have to look at today is that Angola has developed towards functioning as a democracy, something we did not know before. We went into the elections with people from different ethnic backgrounds. In the MPLA there were people from different ethnic groups, as in UNITA. And it could have been true that what happened in October 1992 was a confrontation between sympathisers of MPLA and UNITA. That I agree and maybe we can't go into the reasons. But that is why I say that we are in a process that is interesting because today in Angola, Parliament is debating issues which are extremely complicated and everything is open. So we can say that we are not trying to evade issues. We are not trying to hide the sun with our hands. There are issues which have to be debated everywhere and we have to have the courage either here or elsewhere, or Lusaka. The truth has to be addressed.

Whatever we find in Lusaka will have to be respected, just as we needed to respect the agreement in 1991. I think it is very important that the Government makes extremely important concessions, as it has done, because we have now realised that the fighting was based on the number of ministries which we have accepted. And therefore we also know that the democratic process in Angola has changed. There is a parliament. There are many parties. Things will never be solely based on UNITA. The ethnic issues will be addressed in parliament just as they have already been addressed concerning the

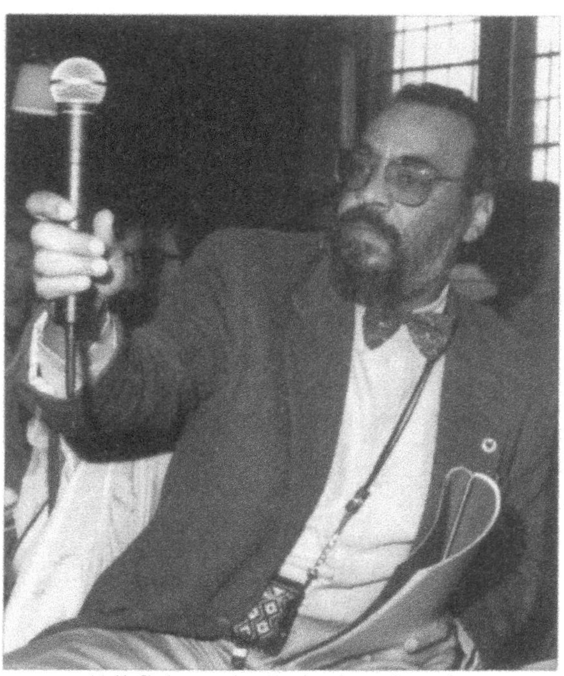

Malik Chaka provokes the Angolan ambassador

accusations. People can write whatever they want, but Angola is not divided along ethnic lines.

Secondly, the South African mercenary issue. We will need to investigate this. The Government that I belong to has not done any recruiting of mercenaries. What I know is that private companies which De Beers is involved with have recruited people to work in security. We expelled South Africans in December last year, as you know, who were in Angola with dubious visas, with a Security Company working with Angolan business men. The law in Angola allows that. The Government is not recruiting mercenaries and it is important that UNITA knows this. But private companies have the right to protect their own installations. Many of these companies have been constantly attacked in diamond mining areas for example. We, the Government, can't give them protection. The law allows them to organise their security. The South African government is not interested in sending troops to Angola.

Fernando Pacheco:

It is clear that here is a political problem in Angola which needs to be solved. Maybe it will be solved at the Lusaka talks, but it must take into account civil society. 1992 showed what Angolan society was capable of between the Peace Accord and the initiation of hostilities. What Angola needs is a common project which can unite all Angolans around it.

Sir Roger Tomkys:

No I'm sorry. I can't take any more questions. I would like to thank on your behalf all the members of our panel who have spoken very openly and fluently; to thank the questioners for putting their statements briefly and to thank those who have not succeeded in putting their questions for any tolerance towards me they have shown. Thank you.

Session 3

Britain

Richard Thomas

Victoria Brittain

Tony Hodges

Peter Brayshaw

The final session provided a fitting climax to the drama of the whole day. The Angolans in the audience were particularly highly charged after seeing UNITA and the Government together on a public platform for the first time in the previous session. After hearing what each side had to say, many chose this session to speak out, often in a tremendously personal way. Curiously, few British voices were raised during the time allowed for questions. It was Angolan women who now captured the mood of the audience by calling for an end to the fighting and restrictions on arms dealing.

The panel itself was evenly balanced between the right and left of the political spectrum. A diplomat and an economist were the more conservative elements who sat with a journalist from a left-wing newspaper and a Labour councillor. Originally, it was Baroness Chalker, Minister for Overseas Development, who was to tell us Why Angola Matters from the perspective of the British Government. Unfortunately, less than a week before the conference was to take place, she pulled out in order to go to Bosnia. This was a tremendous blow at the time, despite assurances of a significant FCO presence, as our press releases were focusing on her visit to Cambridge. The organisers and participants were thus denied the opportunity of witnessing together on the same panel Lady Chalker and Victoria Brittain, a well known critic of British policy on Angola.

Introduction from the Chair

Sir Hugh Byatt (KCVO 1985, CMG 1979):

(Sir Hugh's long and distinguished career in the diplomatic service took him to Nigeria, India and Kenya before he became Britain's first Ambassador to Angola in 1979. Now retired, he is Chairman of RTZ, a multinational corporation involved with mineral extraction in Angola.)

Sir Hugh Byatt opens the session

Ladies and gentlemen. I'm under strict orders from the Director to keep to time and we really do have very little time; so I wish to press ahead so that the floor may have its turn in due course. I'll just say I'm delighted to be here at this conference and my reason to be here is that I was the first British Ambassador to Angola. I went there in 1969 as a visitor, and then returned in 1978 and was there until 1981, when I then went to Portugal, where I continued to watch what was happening in Angola, as I still do, visiting Angola last year. And I have enormous sympathy for the Angolan people. I am personally convinced that they will reach an accord and that Angola will be a very important and prosperous country. I don't put a timescale on that, but I'm absolutely certain that will happen. Without further ado I shall turn to my successor, Mr Richard Thomas.

Richard Thomas – British Ambassador to Angola:

(Richard Thomas became British Ambassador to Angola in January 1993. His previous posts took him from Caracas to Budapest, Washington, Madrid, Johannesburg and Brasilia. In 1989 he became an FCO Counsellor.)

Thank you Mr Chairman, and good afternoon everyone. I'm very glad that the African Studies Centre has organised this workshop on a subject which I believe merits some attention; and I'm very glad to see how many people it has attracted. I'm also grateful for the opportunity to participate in the proceedings today. What I'd like to do is briefly outline present British policy towards Angola, and then to talk after that about the subject of the workshop, and say something about why the British Government thinks that Angola matters to Britain.

As a member of the Security Council, Britain's objective is to bring about a ceasefire and a comprehensive political settlement which reflects the wishes of the Angolan people. We see our role as being to support the efforts of the UN and the Bicesse Accord observers and not to launch initiatives of our own. At the same time, we are also concerned to lessen the suffering of the Angolan people through humanitarian aid. I would just like to say here that since the first UN appeal for aid or relief in May of last year, the British Government has pledged more than £15 millions and is likely to pledge still more at the end of this current financial year. And, if I might just mention, we are giving food aid and seeds and tools and various other types of food aid.

We give it through the United Nations and it is distributed through the NGOs. We also help NGOs, some of whom are represented here today directly. In view of what one of the previous speakers, Fernando Pacheco, said today, in the previous session, I would like to draw attention to the fact that we are giving seeds and tools. That's very important. All of the aid donors are conscious of the need to make the transition from pure relief aid to more developmental type of assistance; seeds and tools, as you can appreciate, are something that is community orientated. It's not depersonalising. Quite the opposite.

United Kingdom policy is based on a fundamental fact. The 1992 elections were deemed to be free and fair. That was not only the verdict of the UN Special Representative of the time. It was also the verdict of international observers who witnessed the election, including a group of British MPs. So, at the beginning of 1993, because those elections represented a watershed in the Angolan questions, and by extension, a watershed in British policy, the British Government made clear our full support. From the first, the UK condemned UNITA's rejection of the election results and its resumption of the civil war. We were not impressed subsequently when UNITA gave conditional acceptance to those results. In that spirit, we have been active in the Security Council with others to send clear signals to UNITA that the pursuit of power by military means is unacceptable; and, as long as it tries to set aside the decision of the Angolan people in a democratic election, it will be isolated and censored by the international community.

Richard Thomas – "motor for economic development"

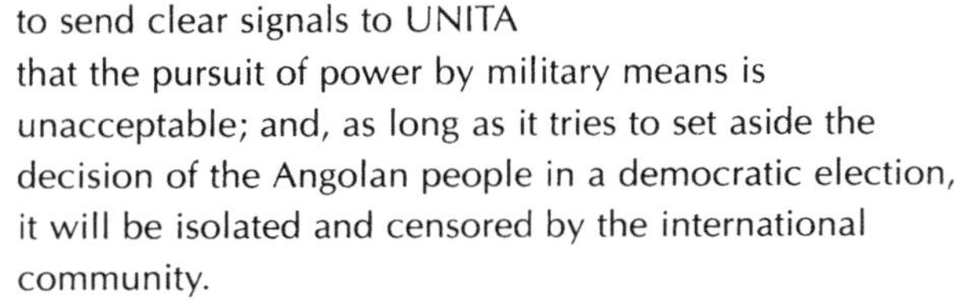

It's worth noting here that all the activities of the Security Council and the measures adopted have been set firmly in the context of the re-affirmation of the Bicesse Accord, which provided for the elections. We have also consistently supported all the efforts of the UN Representative to persuade the two sides to agree on a comprehensive settlement. We relaxed the UK embargo on arms supply to the Angolan Government in August 1993. *(Murmurings from audience.)* We were active in drawing up Security Council Resolution 864 which imposed sanctions on UNITA and I think it is interesting that UNITA's decision to embark on negotiations in Lusaka is attributable in part, in my view, to the imposition of those sanctions. It not only had a psychological effect but it actually had an effect on UNITA's political strategy. The Security Council has kept some additional sanctions in reserve. It has used the possibility of imposing sanctions as a spur to keeping UNITA's attention fixed on negotiations. This strategy seems to have worked so far; but progress in the talks has been very slow. But, if needed, the UK and the Security Council will not shrink from imposing further sanctions.

In all of this, ours and the Security Council's over-riding aim has been peace. We are therefore very concerned that both sides are continuing to attack each other militarily. Both parties seem to be pursuing a twin-track approach: using military attacks to improve their negotiating position and to try to influence the Lusaka talks. The British government believes that this puts the negotiations in danger and that it should be discouraged.

It is obviously not for the UK or any outsider to dictate the terms of the peace settlement. That would not result in a viable lasting agreement. The British Government welcomes the commitment from both sides to achieving a negotiated settlement. In line with the Bicesse principle, the British Government believes that that settlement should reflect the political reality; that the MPLA and the present Government won a clear majority and is the legally constituted authority in Angola. But along with other Security Council members and the current UN Special Representative as well as the Angolan Government itself, we recognise that a peace, a viable and enduring peace, is more likely to be obtained if UNITA is included, given a chance to participate in Government. And it is important to say here that the Angolan Government has shown flexibility and some generosity in this respect. And that is relevant to some of the things we were hearing this afternoon.

Now in our view, it would not be right for the Lusaka talks to make any agreements which in effect amount to a constitutional reform in Angola. That is obviously something which ought to be done ultimately by a freely elected national assembly. But these considerations aside, the form and detail of any peace settlement would be for the Angolan people themselves to decide.

One area which preoccupies us is providing the necessary UN backup, to assist the implementation of any peace settlement that comes out of Lusaka, which will not be easy. Very substantial resources will be required. UNAVEM II cost over $100 millions a day. I think we can anticipate that, before authorising another major operation, the UN and the Security Council will want to try to reassure themselves to some extent that both parties are showing a genuine commitment to working for national reconciliation.

So much for British policy. Now to the more interesting bit, why Angola matters to Britain. Angola matters to Britain because of what it is in itself and because of its significance within the Southern African region. I think this is very important and I hope that during the rest of the workshop we will hear more about that from other speakers also. We are all aware that Angola is very rich indeed in natural resources. If peace broke out and it began on the path of reconstruction, Angola would become the third biggest economy in Sub-Saharan Africa. Oil production, at the moment, even with the civil war, is likely to reach 600,000 barrels per day by 1995/96. The recently licensed deepwater sites look promising, so production could be significantly higher, by say 2010. We also know that Angola is very rich in diamonds. It is estimated that with full-scale mining, annual production could be worth $12 billion, something roughly the same as Botswana.

So with just the oil and the diamonds we could be looking at $7 to $8 billion per annum economy in Angola. But Angola has much more than oil and diamonds. It is vastly rich in other minerals; manganese, copper and other base metals. It has certain hydro-electric capacity and could top even more if a market were found for it. It has much fertile land and reasonable rainfall. It used to be a net exporter of agricultural products; the world's third largest coffee producer. Its seas are rich in fish and would be even richer with a bit of management and conservation. It has good timber resources and granite, marble and mercury. So, as Angola reconstructs and develops, it could become a very respectable market for industrial country exports. And there would be good opportunities arising for business and commerce from the process of reconstruction of Angola itself.

At the same time, Angola is crucial for the political and economic development of Southern Africa. And the UK has large investments in southern Africa, in South Africa itself, on which tens of thousands of British jobs depend. This means that the peace, development and prosperity of South Africa in particular are of great importance to Britain, and that South Africa is likely to be closely bound up with the future of the Southern African region.

So apart from the general interest which the UK has in political stability, peace and prosperity in Africa as a whole, there is a particular interest in the future of the Southern African region. Given peace, strong economic links between South Africa and Angola will develop naturally. It's already beginning to happen now, even with the civil war. There is a natural complementarity between the two economies. South Africa and Angola are set to be the motor for the future economic development and prosperity of the Southern African region. Both countries will also have a key role in the future integration of the region itself, a necessary factor in development. The present Angolan leadership are already highly conscious of the value of greater regional integration. Angolan leaders see the future of the region as lying in closer integration with the region. The present generation of Angolan leaders are now seeing English as replacing French as a second language. And they want to see that in order to assist in integrating more fully into SADEC. They want to see SADEC playing a more active and effective role. They have also built up some good relationships within the frontline state system and they much value those. And they want to see an expanded frontline state system, particularly after the constitutional reform process in South Africa, continue to play an important role in the region. They would like to see it develop into the political and security co-ordination network of the region.

Finally, Angola matters for two other reasons. Because as long as the civil war continues, Angola is a nuisance and a distraction for the region; an obstacle to its full integration. It is also a shockingly bad example of the consolidation of democracy for the rest of Africa. *(Applause **)*

Victoria Brittain – Foreign News Editor, The Guardian:

(Victoria Brittain has been particularly concerned with the plight of Angola for the last ten years. She has written many articles on the subject. Her book on Southern Africa, Hidden Lives and Hidden Deaths, is published by Faber and Faber. She is an active supporter of the Angola Emergency Campaign.)

The Chair of the last session urged the participants to look to the future. Ambassador Thomas has just looked rather nicely at the future. But I feel that you can't very well look at the future, without knowing the facts of the past. And earlier in the afternoon, we heard some very unhelpful versions of the immediate past and some myths which have a very important bearing on the future.

So, I will look very quickly at four aspects of the current situation. First the humanitarian and social which has been touched on already by the Vice-Minister who described the disintegration of a society. Because that is what is going on in Angola. Half a million people have died in the last year and a half. Tens of thousands are on the move. But the most serious thing, I think, is that the Government has been knocked out, not just by exhaustion, but by the logistical constraints of UNITA's denial of access to so much of the territory. I would like to quote Shawn McCormack, who has never been much of a friend of the MPLA, who described UNITA in a recent paper as "a military organisation with a human face". And I think that is a fact and not an opinion.

And the UN has found, when it has come to try to do something for the population in the areas occupied by UNITA, that there has been absolutely no alternative but to encourage NGOs to go into this area, because UNITA has no capacity. This entry of NGOs and also the UN into UNITA areas has a very serious impact on the political situation now, and is going to have an even greater impact in the future, because it has become part of the process of legitimising UNITA, by effectively providing it with administrative capacity which it doesn't have itself. At the same time, much of the UN and the NGOs are undermining the sovereignty of the Government by this process of dealing with UNITA as an autonomous power in its control areas. It's a very important point and I thought it was very interestingly put by Jean-Emmanuel Pondi this morning.

The second aspect is the military one. The military stalemate is sucking up all resources, both human and material, of the country. And another speaker this morning touched upon the involvement of Zaire. I think that in considering what has brought about this stalemate, the importance of both Zaire and South Africa in the continuing supply to UNITA is very important.

Thirdly, looking at the diplomatic side, the kind of deal being brokered at the moment in Lusaka essentially rests upon a proposal for a UN force to monitor a ceasefire. It is significant that the one thing the UNITA representative in the last session didn't talk about was a ceasefire. The whole question of withdrawal, disarmament and another chance for the military wing of UNITA to integrate its men into the FAA and also into the special police, rests upon the idea that there will be a substantial UN force; figures being talked about are 8,000 or 10,000 men. And as Ambassador Thomas said, there's a very serious question about whether those forces are going to be available and who on earth is going to pay for them. And then that brings us to the point made by speakers earlier on. Even if it happens, where are the guarantees?

The fourth aspect of the current situation is the political deal that is being brokered in Lusaka. Of course that depends on the diplomatic deal, the military deal, which I've already touched on. What it means politically – and previous speakers certainly won't agree with me – is the effective end of Bicesse. UN documents go to some lengths to obscure this fact. It means the end of the electoral process: a power sharing deal based on UNITA's military capacity. This negates the electoral premise of Bicesse in the first place: you don't really need to have elections. But you did have elections and there's a lot of lip-service being paid to all of that. The point I want to make about what is going on in Lusaka is that you can't have both. You can't have Bicesse and a deal that's being done on the basis of UNITA's military power as demonstrated over the last 17 months.

Another point I wanted to make about this is that one of the myths about Lusaka is that this is a deal between Angolans, which the outside world is looking for ways to support. In fact there have been, and there continue to be, huge pressures brought upon the Government, particularly by the UN in exactly the same way as they were throughout the very long process which those of you who followed the career of Chester Crocker will remember: the long negotiations which led to Bicesse in which the MPLA was forced to change its politics; send away its foreign defence forces, the Cubans and the African National Congress; dismantle its own army; and enter the electoral process with an organisation that never had any intention ever of being bound by that process.

So, that's the current situation. How did we get here? We are facing a situation in which the UN has been disastrously discredited in Angola. The deal being brokered in Lusaka makes a mockery of a democratic process which virtually everyone who witnessed it in September 1992 declared exemplary. The end of an elected government's sovereignty, or at least, a very serious erosion of it. In the end, a political deal which is unlikely to stick; and essentially a country that is destroyed.

The answer to how we got here is the folly and the dishonesty of the international community in which I regret to say Britain, as a member of the Security Council and with a fairly influential part within the diplomatic process, did play an important part. The most important thing it did, of course, was to keep quiet. There was, in a phrase which is not mine, "a friendly turning of a blind eye to UNITA". And to illustrate that, I want to highlight a dozen or so key moments of failure by the international community. These are all events that happened and none of them is secret. All of them are very well known to everybody within the UN.

The first was the killing of four tourists by UNITA in January 1992. Nobody ever said they were killed by UNITA. Secondly, a month later when General Nzan Puna and Antonio da Costa Fernandes (now of course, the Angolan Ambassador to Britain, who is present in the audience) decided to leave UNITA, they made a very clear description of why they were leaving, of which the essential part was that the UNITA leadership under Savimbi had no intention of sticking with the election, and in fact was preparing a secret army. The UN took two months to investigate and not surprisingly, when they got to the place where they had been told the secret army would be, it wasn't there any more.

Thirdly, they raised the very critical question of UNITA's failure to disarm or demobilise. In that period, (this was early 1992), this was raised again and again by ordinary Angolans and by many expatriates and by many people low down in the UN. Arms caches, arms "pilot committees", attempts by UNITA to gain footholds, for instance, when they tried to take over a hotel in Lobito and later when they successfully tried to make the whole area around Savimbi's house in Luanda a no-go area. UNAVEM met all these reports with irritation and hostility. Nothing was ever said publicly about them.

Victoria Brittain

Fourthly, in the same period, UNITA's failure to cede its territory to the Government as promised under Bicesse. For instance, Bie Province. In 10 of the 39 communas, there was no effective government presence by September 1992. In fact, about one fifth of the territory was under UNITA; and the UN, throughout this period, was already undermining the Government's sovereignty by dealing directly with UNITA in those areas (through the provision of food through Namibia for instance); and the use of inflated population figures provided by UNITA became an internal UN scandal which was to some extent hushed up.

Fifth, again in the same period, Savimbi declared publicly on more than one occasion that he was not disposed to accept any result short of victory. Publicly on the TV: it's not a secret. That was what he said. Meanwhile the most senior US official in Angola, Jeffrey Millington, was saying, and he continued to say it until two days before the election, that Savimbi "had the election in the bag". And the implication was, it didn't matter very much what UNITA was doing because they were going to win any way.

At this point, in view of the combination of factors which I've mentioned, and that's just a very very small amount of what was common knowledge at the time, it was absolutely clear that the situation was explosive; war was inevitable if Savimbi did not win. Nobody in the UN wanted to say anything about this. It was spelt out in the speech of October 3rd 1992, when Savimbi announced he was withdrawing his people from the FAA, essentially turning to war. That was, in my view, the last moment when the UN could have regained itself some credibility by denouncing what had been said, and facing up to what was going on on the ground.

By the last week in October, Western military attaches were reporting privately that UNITA had 11,000 troops and two armies outside of Luanda. In addition, as everyone knew, the armed pilot committees were more and more aggressive and this was what led up to the coup attempt of the last weekend of October. I think it's really very sad that in a meeting like this people are subjected to being told about ethnic cleansing, when what in fact happened was a failed coup attempt by UNITA which was met with an extremely fierce reaction by the population on the ground, aided by the Police.

During that period, the UN and particularly the Americans began to discuss power sharing as a way to appease Savimbi. It made a complete mockery of the election. And what became clear at that point was the historical weight of the description by Ronald Reagan and others of UNITA as "freedom fighters in Angola who deserve our support". Chester Crocker's description of Savimbi in his recent book, is very illuminating on this point: "a model leader for Africa and for democracy". And I'd just like to ask you to imagine for a second if things had turned out the other way around. Imagine that UNITA had won the election and the MPLA having had a secret army stacked away struck at the capital and three provincial capitals simultaneously. Imagine how the international community would have reacted. Would anyone have then called for power-sharing and for the MPLA to have been given a lot of important folios within the government? It's completely inconceivable.

As this appeasement of UNITA continued, UNITA in Huambo killed Dr David Bernadino and the Mascellinos. *(These were the friends that Marco Ramazzotti had lost which prompted him to demand of Keith Hart at the African Studies Centre Cambridge what he was going to do about this conflict in Africa, a conflict that had cost these and so many other lives.)* These were very provocative murders intended to test the waters for how far they could go. Nothing was said and throughout the end part of 1993, when five more cities came under siege, I think the manner in which the Secretary-General's Special Representative represented what was going on, was grossly misleading. The fact that the UN throughout 1993 failed to respond adequately to the attacks on UN planes and convoys, the killing of its various personnel. It never said these killings are being done by UNITA. They always urged both sides to turn to peace talks.

Ambassador Thomas has mentioned the sanctions. And, of course, the sanctions were an important psychological blow to UNITA. But they would have been a much more important psychological blow if they had actually been a practical blow. They weren't. They have not been the slightest bit effective and the repeated refusal of the proposal for more effective ones, I think has actually given a red light to UNITA.

I'm going to end quickly by answering the question of why all this matters. It matters for all the reasons that have already been said. I completely agree with them. But it also matters because Africa watched the international community cynically rejecting the alternative to the catastrophe which unfolded so slowly, and so visibly to everyone who wanted to look. That alternative was to face the failure of Bicesse from the start - it was obvious by March 1992 - it was necessary to start treating Savimbi then, as he was behaving - as a war criminal; and UNITA as what it is - a terrorist organisation; instead of allowing them to believe that their past history as a Western ally made them forever privileged; giving them a licence to destroy their own country.

The lessons for the region are being played out already in South Africa by Buthelezi right now. The lessons are that violence pays. That old Cold War friends can count on effective Western support, or at least a friendly blind eye. And that the UN is sadly just a front for Western policy. It is also a lesson that African lives don't weigh very heavy on the consciousness of the world. And that democracy matters so little in Africa that no-one outside can be bothered to defend it.

I think like the Congo, for a previous generation, Angola has become a symbol of why Africans distrust and hate the West. I'm afraid the effects will be very long-lasting. *(Applause *****)*

Sir Hugh Byatt:

I'd now like to call upon Tony Hodges who has served Angola for many years and has recently writen an excellent country profile of Angola for the Economist.

Tony Hodges – Econonomist Intelligence Unit:

Tony Hodges

(Tony Hodges is the author of Angola to 2000: Prospects for Recovery, published by the Economist Intelligence Unit in 1993. Since 1991 he has worked as an independent consultant and is involved with two programmes designed to strengthen post-graduate economics training in Africa.)

Thank you Mr Chairman. Let me too, like other speakers, congratulate the African Studies Centre for taking this initiative because, quite frankly, this is a problem which just by virtue of being the bloodiest of any in the world today, deserves a far greater degree of public attention than it has received to date.

This conference is about why Angola should matter to the outside world. Well, from a strictly moral and humanitarian perspective, there's absolutely no question about it. More than a thousand people per day killed; 3.3 million people, that's almost a third of the population, uprooted, dependent upon international food aid. And more people amputated per capita than any other country in the world. In fact, what is happening in Angola today, is worse by far than any of the dozen or so humanitarian crises generated by the conflicts that pock-mark our planet in the aftermath of the Cold War.

Yet, as we all know, and this is the great paradox we must confront, this enormous tragedy is being met by and large with indifference or silence. Angola is hardly ever in the newspapers or on TV. In the panel discussion tomorrow on media coverage, hopefully we will begin to understand better why this is, and perhaps even how to overcome the obstacles to bringing the reality of Angola to world attention. Is it poor media coverage, simple donor fatigue or attention diverted elsewhere that explains why donor nations have been tardy in providing emergency assistance for humanitarian relief in Angola? In May last year, the UN appealed to donors for $226 million; but by the end of the year only $93 million had actually been received. Good media coverage of foreign policy can re-focus attention where it is most needed and help overcome fatigue and indifference. This is important, not only for humanitarian relief but also for the big challenges lying ahead, if or when the Angolan Government and UNITA finally reach a new peace agreement.

The peace-talks have been continuing in Lusaka now for five months. Substantial progress seems to have been made on the arrangements for a ceasefire, on the disarming of troops, the forging of unified national armed forces, and on some of the political measures needed for national reconciliation. But a huge question mark remains. What will the international community do to help ensure that a second peace settlement sticks after the failure of the Bicesse Accords? It is recognised in hindsight that UNAVEM II failed in a large measure because of the restrictive mandate, miserable funding and very small size of the UN force sent to Angola in 1991/92. The agreement emerging in the Lusaka talks involves a wider mandate including probably control, rather than simple monitoring of some crucial steps in the peace process; and this will require a large international force of several thousand troops. But will the UN come up with the troops in sufficient numbers and get them to Angola quickly enough? And, just as important, will those troops have the mandate and the operational flexibility to deal effectively with ceasefire violations, and ensure compliance with other critical components of the peace agreement?

The prospects are not encouraging. UN peace-keeping resources are stretched to the limit, as the poor response to a recent UN appeal for more troops in Yugoslavia so graphically reminds us. An earlier experience closer to Angola was the long delay, more than six months, in getting UN troops to Mozambique. And the current withdrawal of US and other Western troops from the UN force in Somalia is further proof that peace keeping fatigue is a major new danger. It could be the fatal flaw in the peace-agreement that emerges out of Lusaka.

There will be, Mr Chairman, a second important challenge facing the international community after a new peace settlement: help to rebuild Angola's war-shattered economy. And this too, like the investment in peace-keeping will require a much heightened international awareness of the stakes involved. In his introductory paper for this conference, Dr Keith Hart remarks that while moral or idealistic arguments for assistance to Angola may be too abstract to lure most people out of their insularity, the most compelling arguments are economic, or as he put it, "an appeal to material self-interest". In Angola's case, if not Somalia's or Mozambique's, the economic argument is compelling. Angola is, as several speakers have mentioned, one of the best resource-endowed countries in Africa. It could one day be that rarest of economic phenomena: an African economic success story. And that means in the bluntest material terms that Angola could become a major market for British industry. Investment in peace and reconstruction will have a long-term return, not only for Angolans themselves, but for the outside world, including the UK. Because of its large oil resources, unique in Southern Africa, and its strategic transport links to Zambia and Zaire, post-war Angola could also contribute to a wider economic dynamism in the Southern African region economies, bringing further long-term benefits to countries like the UK.

But even now, despite the war, Angola has the highest foreign exchange earnings of any country in Sub-Saharan Africa apart from Nigeria, because of its oil, which has largely been unaffected by the war. If export earnings are a pointer to a country' s potential importing capacity, then Angola is not a market to be ignored. To give just one example, Angola's export earnings are roughly three times as high as Kenya's. Yet up to now Britain has hardly been a player in this market, with exports of well under $100 million to Angola over recent years (apparently about $30 million last year) compared with up to $400-$600 million for Portugal, which remains Angola's top supplier, or $200 million for France and the USA which have the largest stake in Angola's oil industry. Few British companies have yet invested in Angola. Lohnro is an exception. BP is hoping to start oil exploration on-shore in Cabinda; but on-shore operations can only begin when the war ends.

Talk of Angola's resource potential is not just a well-worn set of clichés. Let's look more closely at the oil industry. Despite the war, Angola is Sub-Saharan Africa's second largest oil producer now, with output of over 500,000 barrels per day. Nigeria is far ahead with about 1.5 million barrels per day but with a population almost ten times bigger. Per capita, Angola's oil production is three times higher than Nigeria's. At the current rate of extraction, Angola's recoverable reserves will last for 16 or 17 years. But with more than 30 international oil companies investing in the country, new discoveries are now adding to reserves at a faster rate than existing reserves are depleting. And given current oil development projects, Angola's oil production will rise to around 700,000 barrels per day by 1997: that's almost half Nigeria's current production.

In addition, as has already been pointed out, Angola is one of the world's largest producer of gem diamonds. Mining has been restricted to alluvial deposits up until now, but it is known that Angola has several kimberlite6 formations which, after large post-war investments will add enormously to Angola's exports of diamonds towards the end of the century. Angola has numerous other minerals which were mentioned earlier. One could add others: phosphate, gold, as well as an abundance of arable land. Several different climatic zones, generally good rainfall and the possibility of producing a wide range of crops in the north from tropical crops through to Mediterranean-type crops in the south. Angola was the fourth largest producer of coffee in the world and the third largest producer of sisal in the world before the war brokeout in 1975. And besides feeding its own population, Angola could eventually return to its traditional position of being a net exporter of food; it used to export maize.

But, as we all know, the past 19 years of war have devastated the economy, outside the enclave oil industry which is mainly sited off-shore. The war has uprooted much of the rural population, resulting in the dramatic decrease in production of other food crops. Cereal production for example, is estimated to have fallen from a little over one million tonnes in 1973, to around 320,000 tonnes in 1993, right after the resumption of the war. Nearly a third of the population are now dependent upon international food aid for survival. The coffee industry virtually no longer exists and cultivation of other traditional crops like cotton, sisal and bananas has likewise collapsed.

Transport infrastructure as well as dams and power pylons have been destroyed or severely damaged. Travel by road or rail is impossible across most of the country and there is almost no internal trade outside a few coastal enclaves. In addition, the main diamond mining sites in the north-east have been occupied by UNITA; and most manufacturing industries have halted or dramatically reduced production because of shortages of inputs. Angola in this context has become a macro-economic disaster story, as well as a human crisis of appalling proportions. There has been heavy military spending to rebuild the armed forces and face up to the threat from UNITA since the resumption of the war. But government revenues have been eroded by weak world oil prices in the last year and the collapse of the non-oil economy. There is a huge budget deficit which is being financed by printing money and inflation is running at over 1,800%. Despite its oil exports, Angola has been running a large deficit on the current account of its balance of payments for the past six years. The foreign debt has risen to an estimated $10.9 billions; about three and a half times more than annual exports of goods and services, putting Angola more or less on a par with most sub-Saharan African countries, in terms of its debt burden. Very little of the interest due on debts has been paid in the last few years, resulting in a build up of external arrears to some $4 billion.

The war has not been the only cause of Angola's economic decline. The loss of skills at the time of the exodus of Portuguese settlers in 1974/75; the failed attempt to institute Soviet style central planning in the late 1970s; and the Government's weak economic management capacity have also played a part. But the war, which is now worse than at any time in the past 19 years, must be regarded as the principal cause of the country's economic demise, and peace is an absolute pre-requisite for any viable economic recovery programme.

Mr Chairman, I don't have time to discuss in detail the points I made in the paper that was circulated, which is focused mainly on what it would take to rebuild the Angolan economy. I'll simply say that the paper does stress that while being a sine qua non for Angola's recovery, peace by itself will not be an automatic passport to recovery. Not even in peace-time conditions would rising oil and diamond exports be enough to restore health to Angola's debt-straddled balance of payments. Besides durable peace and rising oil and diamond earnings, a broad-based recovery will require other vital measures including: (1) progress in designing and implementing structural adjustment programmes, coupled with measures to alleviate poverty, create employment and resettle the displaced; (2) substantial international assistance, including in particular debt relief, as well as humanitarian and development assistance; (3) the rehabilitation of economic and social infrastructure; and (4) the strengthening of the country's skills base, including its economic management capacity.

It will not be easy to put together and implement such a broad ranging programme. It will be particularly difficult because of the shortage of skilled economists in the higher echelons of government, the scale of the imbalances and distributions to be corrected, and the serious social and political risks of drastic adjustment policies, unless adequate attention is given to safety-net and poverty alleviation measures in a post-war society, where much of the population is living on the margins of survival. Recovery in these conditions will clearly be a slow and gradual process, given the scale and complexity of the measures needed, and the time lag for the measures being implemented to bear fruit.

It is clear, however, that when a peace agreement comes, it must be accompanied by decisive international action. First, to provide sufficient UN forces and the necessary logistics without undue delay, and with a strong mandate in order to ensure implementation of the peace settlement when it comes. And second, to provide international assistance, notably debt relief, for economic recovery. Mr Chairman, thank you very much. (*Applause* **)

Peter Brayshaw – Chair, Angola Emergency Campaign:

(Peter Brayshaw has been the co-chair of the Mozambique-Angola Committee since 1990. He has jointly chaired the Angola Emergency Campaign with Robert Hughes MP since its inception. An economist, he has worked in consultancy, lecturing and local government and is currently a London borough councillor.)

Peter Brayshaw – "isolate UNITA"

Mr Chairman and colleagues. Angola matters because 1,000 people are dying daily. Angola matters because the international community has been standing idly by whilst an armed rebel movement has been insured against a government constituted by a democratic process. Angola matters because it is a tragic and dangerous precedent for the whole of Southern Africa and for Mozambique; and for the people there, for their aspirations for peace and democracy. Angola matters because if we let the tragedy continue, throughout the world, wherever people do want peace and democracy, they will be denied it.

We in the Angola Emergency Campaign believe that the actions of the international community throughout this process have been too little, too late. It gives us no pleasure to say with hindsight that we were right at the time. And those that we argued with, like Baroness Chalker who we met in January and last April - who were saying no, we shouldn't really have sanctions against UNITA; we should encourage both sides to be more flexible - were wrong. But we believe that it was those sanctions which we welcomed that did actually press UNITA a bit earlier to the negotiating table in Lusaka. I think without that the Lusaka peace process we are talking about today would not even have begun. The evidence for that is very very clear indeed.

It is UNITA that challenged the election results. Everyone else agreed that they had to be free and fair. It was UNITA that withdrew its troops from FAA and began to launch the war, using the reserve army that Tony Fernandes and General Nzan Puno warned of. It was UNITA that, as Victoria Brittain said, launched a coup d'état in Luanda. It was UNITA that broke the ceasefire agreement even before the ink was dry. It was UNITA that refused to turn up at Addis Ababa for UN-brokered peace-talks. It was UNITA too that refused to sign the key paragraph, paragraph 11, of the draft Abidjan Protocol, negotiated over a long process, which would have meant them relinquishing their armed control over areas they had seized.

All of this is tantamount to a generalised warfare inflicted on the people by one party, the militaristic wing of UNITA. For far too long, the UN has stood by and not taken action. We believe that, if they had acted back in November of 1992, the actions of UNITA could have been deterred. They would perhaps have accepted their role as the major opposition party. This didn't happen because, if the UN had acted sooner rather than later, the tragedy could have been averted, an estimated death rate of 1,000 per day. Every day that the UN delayed (in June for instance, in a major Security Council meeting; at the end of September – the only time Chapter 7 of the sanctions were first imposed in theory, not necessarily put in practice) 1,000 more people died.

We do, however, believe that this can be countered throughout the world. If governments are too slow, they can be pushed. They can be lobbied. They can be appealed to. There are no parliamentarians here today. We have officials from Government Departments. It is a shame we haven't got Baroness Chalker to talk to today. We have met with her on three occasions and made these points to her. We do believe that in political circles, where the power lies, in London, Washington, Brussels and Paris, these arguments should be raised.

It is good that academics and others are very deeply concerned about the tragedy of Angola. But we believe that those arguments must be taken into the decision-making circles, the political circles. We do what we can as a small campaign with limited resources to raise these issues in those ways. We are, as you will know from some documentation we put in the coffee room, lobbying parliament this Wednesday. We will be seeking to discuss these issues with Members of Parliament, making sure that Angola is not a forgotten war; that the British government does more than it has done so far. I accept what Ambassador Thomas said; that there are very clear positions at the moment. We believe that if those positions had been firmer and sooner, less people would have died.

There are five particular points that we believe should be particularly pressed at the moment. The first is the effectiveness of the existing sanctions. Resources need to be put into the monitoring of the flights that still reach UNITA from Zaire carrying fuel and arms for their war machine. That's got to be stopped. Satellite surveillance, a whole panoply of United States and Western technology could be put into that, if the will was there. The will must be generated. Secondly, the "reserve package", as the Ambassador referred to further sanctions, should begin to be implemented now. Restrictions on trade, on travel, on the profits of stolen diamonds that UNITA are using to finance their war machine. They must be on the agenda sooner rather than later.

Thirdly, Western governments should reaffirm, in even more clear terms than so far, support for the Bicesse agreement, support for the territorial integrity of Angola and not allow the Angolan government to be pressured, unfairly pressured, into more concessions than those particular processes should allow. It is outrageous in many ways that we are talking about an Angolan Government which was the elected government in elections deemed free and fair, that are giving more and more portfolios, giving in to yet more and more demands to a movement which lost those elections and resorted to war. And that outrage should stop.

Fourthly, we firmly believe that there is a need for more humanitarian aid and reconstruction aid for the Angolan people, through the Angolan Government, through NGOs, and through all those who can help in the reconstruction of this terribly war-ravaged country.

Finally, we do believe that action can be taken. We urge all of you to get in touch with political decision-making circles, starting with your own MP, or start by sending a letter to the press, not just talking in this room, in the library of Pembroke College, but going out as we have done. We have collected thousands of signatures. We have drafted memoranda. We have petitioned and placed adverts in the international press to draw attention to the forgotten war and put forward solutions to that war. And we believe that the key issue is the isolation of UNITA by the international community for as long as they persist in the use of war or the threat of war to gain more and more power. And we would say, and we would ask you to say, NO to UNITA's armed blackmail. (*Applause* ****)

(Peter Brayshaw received much support from the audience, though not quite as much as Victoria Brittain. Discouraging, from the point of view of the organisers at the time, was his apparent lack of enthusiasm for his audience, the forum itself and the initiative as a whole. The line appeared to be: you are amateurs, leave it to the professionals to deal with the politicians. The point of our workshop, however, was not to find a formula for Lusaka, but to bring together experts and activists and engage more people in the Angolan situation, to show how Angola's tragedy is a symptom of a wider sickness that people can relate to in their own daily lives and are therefore more likely to act upon.)

Open Session

Marco Ramazzotti (Consultant):

I will not ask a question. I will just say a few words about why Angola matters to me, as one of the people who helped organise this conference. I think everyone should be asked why Angola matters. I think it's important to underline that Angola is quite exceptional in its areas of wealth, its human and moral wealth. I think Angola is important because it's based on a multi-racial, multi-cultural and multi-religious system. And I find it strange that Mandela is now a national hero, an international hero, when Angolans are fighting for the same aims and objectives which moved Mandela. And finally I would like to say that there were friends of mine, friends....who were killed....by UNITA.

Ambrosio Calolita (Friends of Angola):

I have three points. First, you see, we Angolans, we don't want war any more. At the same time we want the arms going to UNITA to be stopped and the arms going to the Government to be stopped as well. In Bosnia, you have an arms emargo on the government and the Serbs. Why don't you do that for Angola, because people are being killed by both sides? It is not just UNITA. The Government is also killing our people.

Secondly, about the UN in Angola. The Government is spending more than a billion a year on buying arms. This billion should go to the UN so they can work in Angola to bring about peace. The problem here is not just UNITA. The Government is partly to blame.

And to Victoria Brittain. She is telling lies. Where she gets her facts from I don't know. None of the Government officials have said what she said. Her facts are based on naked lies.

Mario Cumandala (Friends of Angola):

My question this morning hasn't been answered yet; but moving to Mr Chikoti's speech and Victoria Brittain's, I don't find any difference between the two. And I would say they are very biased speeches, especially Victoria Brittain's, because I don't find anything I can identify with myself as an Angolan. I would like to comment on one point only. Today I am here. My mother is in Huambo and a lot of my friends have been killed in Luanda. For Victoria Brittain to come here and say there was no ethnic cleansing in Luanda, when after three months UNITA was not there and people were killed, that is a lie. Please stop furthering your interests in the name of Angola.

Fatima Pimentel (Angolan Community in the UK):

We want arms to UNITA and to the Government to be stopped. We need immediate action by the West. The situation is comparable with Bosnia and Serbia, yet the West has not acted in the same way toward Angola. Why is that? There has been an awful lot of killing on both sides. The Government spends one billion on arms, when all we the people want is peace. *(Applause and voices raised in agreement ****)*

Amir Attaran, (Oxford Student):

The Ambassador made the point that he felt that the UN had failed in some of the things it had done and I'd like to say something in defence of this. One thing I would like to make clear, and Alex Vines and others in this room know about this, and that is the mandate of the UN did not include all the powers the UN would have liked.

Let me support this point of view. Not wanting to offend representatives of the Guardian and the Economist, I want to cite the example of how much the world knew about the peace process as it was going along, by talking about the New York Times. In the sixteen months prior to the Angolan elections, the New York Times ran 20 articles substantially about Angola. Two of those warned that demobilisation was seriously behind schedule and that as well the peace process might fail because of that.

In the same 16 months, the Times ran 85 articles about Cambodia. This despite the fact that plans at that point were much more nebulous. It was only after serious disaster in Angola subsequent to the elections that the media really began to report this retrospectively. In the three months after the elections, the Times printed 45 articles: roughly an eight-fold increase in that time. Had we perhaps had more media attention focusing on the UN, the people on the ground feeling that disassembly targets weren't being met, we might have found out earlier that things weren't going well, and been able to avert the consequences.

Antonio Neto (Angolan Democratic Party):

(Like Marco Ramazzotti who spoke first, Antonio Neto found his words were soon choked by the pain and sadness his memories invoked.)

Mr Chairman, I live in Angola, I live in Luanda. I would like to contribute to this debate by drawing the attention of this audience about some misunderstandings of the Ambassador and the lady. I was jailed in October 1992 with other leaders of the opposition. The Police came to my place. They sent a bomb. I came out of the house and they put me in jail. And in jail I was in a security or military compound. I saw inmates from different political parties being killed by the Security Police.

This is why we pray for peace and reconciliation between UNITA and the Government. There was no coup attempt by UNITA in Luanda at all. This is a lie. We were in Angola and we were in Luanda. The Government is not dwelling on this as an argument. It is better to concentrate on the future. What can we do? We can also say for instance what UNITA was saying: that in the areas controlled by the MPLA there was a coup. But the Prime Minister, in an article published in a journal in Angola said that in areas controlled by UNITA, there was also a coup. Things like this, it is important to put aside, and to concentrate on what we can do from here. (*Applause* ***)

My party has struggled to have a ceasefire arrangement that will include a UN presence in Angola of around 10,000 to 12,000 people. This must be organised. Secondly, a government of national reconciliation and unity must be set up. Fortunately the MPLA is accepting this again. UNITA is accepting this again. Let us work as soon as possible to finish this war as there are a thousand people killed in Angola every day. There are murderers in Angola. There are thieves. For when we talk about diamonds, do you know how much money the MPLA has set up outside of Angola? What about the invisible Ministry of Corruption? (*Applause* **)

Teresa Santana (Angolan Student):

I wanted to make a point to the British Ambassador. I felt today as if I had been sold in a market. As if people here were saying: You're asleep! Wake up! It's time to go to Angola! There are diamonds and gold there. Let's all go! Quickly rush! Otherwise someone else will take them. Last year I heard a programme on BBC that Britain had nothing to do with Angola because it was so far away, so we have nothing to be concerned about.... Sir Hugh interjects:I think the fact that we're having this conference proves that Angola does matter to Britain.... Santana protests: Please, I am Angolan. I should have a chance to speak out. It's my country. Ask me why Angola matters. Why do I feel Angola matters to me? Because my children are living there. My family has been killed there. So it matters to me - as a people. There - are - people -in - Angola - now. Not only diamonds. Not only petrol. Peace matters to us. The main question is what - are - you - going - to - do - about - these -people - in -Angola - that - want - peace - and - who - want - peace - now? That is the message. We want peace now. We don't care that people are sitting in the United Nations Security Council, deciding for us what we have to do in Angola. It's time to change the policy...*(Enthusiastic clapping and voices raised in support drown out further remarks ****)*

Teresa Santana – "peace now"

Adao Alexandre (College of Ascension, Birmingham):

I am also Angolan and since this morning I have realised that the problem in Angola is an internal one as well as an external one. I think the democratic process failed and led to the war, because people were not educated to understand what democracy in Angola means. We have been educated for many years, but most people haven't been educated in what democracy is. There is a cultural lag. People like us who have never voted before, never been part of a democratic process before, have never been trained to listen to their enemy. What I want to know is if this conference will consider how you can teach people about democracy: how do you teach Angolans to listen to each other? Which implies teaching Angolans to accept an imposed political system in Angola. Democracy will fail unless people know how to listen to others.

Dylan Woods (British Defence and Aid Fund):

There has been a very great democratic process unfolding in South Africa, which is on a knife-edge and is something that could fail unless the UN gives it support. There was a great achievement in Angola but there is one clear difference, and that is the concessions being made by the right-wing in South Africa have not been made as a result of the UN, but were forced on them by liberation movements. This is the process we have going on at the moment. The right wing is being forced to take part in the democratic process. The right wing will take part in the elections and the majority will accept the results. De Klerk and the National Party will become a minority party in the new government. The lesson to learn for Angola is that it doesn't matter how many rounds of talks are going to take place. The bottom line is that UNITA has to be forced to make concessions and to stop the war: to come around to accepting democracy.

Clearly, comparing the situation in South Africa, the big difference is that Jonas Savimbi is not interested in the democratic process. He wants the number one job, nothing short. He has a bottom line of support and an end result and he wants nothing in between. The claim made about more portfolios is spurious. Savimbi wants the number one job and he won't stop until he gets it. It's important to have effective sanctions and it's about time the international community realised how many people are dying each day and every minute of delay will allow UNITA more power.

The Panelists Reply

Sir Hugh Byatt:

If I could ask panelists to pick up the questions that have been asked and I would like them to make time for me to invite the Vice-Minister and Mr Samakuva to respond to any particular points very briefly.

Richard Thomas:

I can't necessarily now remember who asked particular questions or made particular points to which I am going to reply, but I hope I will cover them all or the gist of what I say covers the questions.

First of all I would like to answer one point that was made, not by asking any colleague on the platform, but by asking you. Do you really think declaring Savimbi a war criminal and declaring the intention to try to convict him - and that would have to apply to UNITA declaring the intention to try to convict him, and other UNITA leaders, including some present here in this room - do you really think this will bring an end to the war and would help to bring UNITA to the negotiating table?

Secondly, would insisting on adherence to the strict letter of the Bicesse Accord, rather than the spirit, would that be likely to secure UNITA's agreement to a negotiated peace settlement? And make no mistake. There is no solution to the Angolan problem besides a negotiated peace settlement. There is no such thing as winning a military victory in Angola, a total military victory which would resolve the problem. Neither the Government nor UNITA can do that. So you must judge the actions of the UN and the actions of member governments always, always, by the criteria of will it help to get people to the negotiating table, and will it help to get the two parties to agree a peace settlement? Any other consideration is a waste of time.

Speaking about why Angola matters to Britain, I perhaps should have made it clear, that I was speaking about why Angola matters to Britain, and I was speaking as a Government representative. I have that disadvantage in relation to other speakers on the platform. I have to speak as an official representative. I was not speaking about why Angola matters to humanity. There are others here better qualified; but please, please don't misunderstand. I thought I had made it clear that the British Government is making an immense effort for humanitarian relief in Angola, second only to the humanitarian relief effort we are making in Bosnia Herzegovina. So be careful about accusations that it is because Angola is black and Yugoslavia is white. That is very unjust and unfair and I don't think it helps a rational debate..*(Murmurings of discontent eminate from a section of the audience.)*

Sir Hugh interjects:

Madam, I'm not taking any questions at the moment....

(Fatima Pimental had remarked on the arms embargo imposed on the warring factions in former Yugoslavia, but why not Angola?)

Richard Thomas continues:

....I hope I have covered all the points that have been made. The British Government does care about Angolans, about ordinary Angolans. I'm very happy that there were ordinary Angolans here, and that they spoke up. And the message that comes across is that they want peace. And that is what validates the efforts of the international community to achieve peace. Not to score points. Not to excoriate one side or another; not to anathematise it, because that will not help to bring peace. And Governments and the UN have to make a judgement about what is most likely to bring peace. It would give us immense moral satisfaction to be able to condemn one side or another when it has erred. But will that contribute to bringing about peace?

Victoria Brittain:

I will just take up three points from the floor. The first one from the student from Oxford who asked if the UN people on the ground had been warning more openly that targets like demobilisation were not being met, would it have made a difference? Well, I don't think you quite realise the constraints under which people were working. A lot of junior people were making these warnings privately; but, if they had been making them publicly, they would, of course, have lost their jobs. I did make the point in my presentation that there was a lot of hostility within

UNAVEM towards what was called rocking the boat; i.e. saying it wasn't going to work.

The second point was the speaker who suggested an arms embargo on both sides and he then made the suggestion that the Government be asked to pay for the UN. I'm sure this was a really disingenuous proposal which he must realise is clearly unacceptable and is a red herring.

The third point I would like to make is to the two people who criticised my presentation for speaking like the Angolan Government. I don't think they quite understand the role of a journalist. As a journalist you are free to make your own points. You are not responsible to any one side or the other, either to the UN or to the Angolan Government, or to the rebel movement, or any other individual. Your point is to make up your own mind and to make your own view of what happens. So it is clearly off the point to criticise someone for not representing or speaking like the Government. *(Murmurs from the audience.)*

Tony Hodges:

Very quickly. I agree with Ambassador Thomas that there isn't an alternative to a negotiated peace settlement ultimately. Neither side can win militarily. Both sides have some popular support, concentrated ethnically or regionally to some extent, particularly in the case of UNITA. Both have outside sources of military supply and, irrespective of sanctions, it's very easy for UNITA to continue to supply itself with arms across the border with Zaire which is a completely lawless place in current circumstances. So, a peace settlement, negotiated between the two sides is unavoidable and absolutely necessary.

At the same time, I think it's absolutely true and correct to say that sticks as well as carrots can be a very effective contributory factor in bringing a peace settlement about, and I think it's quite correct to make certain criticisms of the UNAVEM operation in Angola. To a certain extent, officials were so desperate for success, so afraid of the reaction of one or other party to criticism, that they tended not to criticise at all. And, as a result, there was a sense of appeasement, whereby violations to the Bicesse Accord were allowed to take place without much response. And this really did, I think, only encourage further violations and made it perhaps inevitable in the end, that the country should explode again when the elections were on, or after the elections.

I think in hindsight it's also possible to criticise the mandate under which the UN was there. It was restrictive. It was limited purely to a monitoring role. It had no role in controlling the confinement, the demobilisation of troops and the forging of a unified national force. It was also, as has been pointed out, extremely underfunded and very small. Election observers were a few hundred to monitor more than 5,000 polling stations. So I think we can learn from the past.

And that leads me to the essential point of looking forward to the future. And what we have to ensure is that, when this peace settlement does finally emerge, and I'm sure it will eventually, because there is no alternative to that, we do have to make absolutely sure that the UN is able to back-up the peace agreement effectively; and that must mean a much wider mandate for the UN mission in Angola: a direct participatory role in the process, particularly in controlling the withdrawal of UNITA forces from the cities it has occupied; the monitoring of the disarming of troops and the constitution of a new national force; perhaps a more direct role even in the election process itself. It must have a wider mandate. It clearly has to be a much larger force. One wonders whether 6, 7, 8 or 10,000 troops is enough in a country that must be twice the size of Yugoslavia, certainly twice the size of Somalia where the numbers of troops was very much greater. And we have to make sure that despite all the constraints on the international community, that that mission is properly funded.

Finally Mr Chairman, to go along with that, with a stronger UN mandate and a large rapidly deployed force, there must be international assistance for reconstruction in many many forms. Things like helping a large number of troops to be reinserted quickly into civilian society through various projects, and providing various alternative forms of employment. People, usually young people in many cases, have spent many years in the bush as soldiers. There needs to be put in place very quickly the same sort of projects for the displaced people, 3.3 million people apparently displaced or depending upon food aid. A large number of these need to be got back to their places of origin, mainly in the countryside, so they can start producing for themselves, as rapidly as possible. And that will require quick substantial international assistance, going along also with debt relief, in order to enable the Angolan Government to climb out of the big hole which it's in at the moment, where, even if the war stopped, and oil and diamond exports increased, without debt relief, it would be saddled with an enormous burden of debt around its neck. This would make it extremely difficult to overcome the economic problems which is essential, not just in their own terms but in order to underpin peace and stability with a more promising future for the country.

Sir Hugh Byatt:

Thank you. I seem to remember working out once that Angola, in terms of its physical size, is equal to France, Germany and the Benelux countries. It is a big place.

Peter Brayshaw:

I'll make one point only and refer to the document we put out earlier listing all the points that were made against UNITA's rejection of the elections. Following on from Ambassador Thomas's statement, what we must do at all costs is to take actions that do bring about effective and lasting peace. I believe that those actions should have been and now still should be firmer condemnation of UNITA; firmer and more effective sanctions against UNITA's armed machine and the denying of the means for UNITA to wage war; and I think that is still the argument that must be pursued. They have that war machine. It is still supplied from Zaire and elsewhere. They should be, as they are entitled to be, the major opposition political party in the Angolan National Assembly and in Angolan political life.

The Government and UNITA representatives respond:

(Clearly Sir Hugh had to gamble that if, as his own sense of official protocal told him, the Vice-Minister was given the last word, the UNITA representative would not take offence that their order of speaking in the previous sessions had been switched around to allow Chikoti the final say....)

Sir Hugh Byatt:

Thank you. Vice-Chairman would you like to have a word? I think the most polite thing for me to do is to hand the microphone over to Mr Samakuva, and for you to have the last word. I think we did it the other way around last time. I see your hands and we'll see if there's any time before we wind up.

Isaias Samakuva:

This time I will give priority to the Vice-Minister. He was the last one to talk. And he is the Vice-Minister and he deserves priority. (Delivered in a teasing tone) Any way I will accept this offer.(The room fell completely silent and remained in a state of hush throughout Samakuva's response).

What I would like to say here again is that it is very interesting to see here within this audience that a Presidential candidate who has been shown to have had 40% of support in a country is designated a war criminal by those who are foreigners. What about the people who support us? Do they deserve a right to have a say or should they abandon their rights to those who are not Angolan?

I will not be here tomorrow; but I would like to emphasise that what would be useful in this workshop is to devise solutions to the conflict in Angola. We make accusations. We may wish death to one another because he might have killed one of our friends in Angola. The Angolans themselves have lost their brothers, their sisters, their relatives. But if the case was to wish revenge, then we won't finish the war in Angola.

Thirdly, I would like to say that in fact I am telling you here that peace is within our reach, unless, while we are talking about peace in Angola, we are coming together among our brothers abroad, to fuel war in our country. I repeat. Unless this workshop concentrates on devising formulas to help to implement the agreement that is in our reach; unless it helps to devise formulas that will help to implement the process of democracy to avoid one party or another violating the process, unless we do that, I think we will not have contributed to the objective that the organisers had wanted to achieve. Thank you. *(Muted applause **)*

George Chikoti:

I will be very brief. I think that most of the comments made here have been very constructive. I would like to say to those who have been present since this morning that sometimes it is very difficult when you are on a panel like this one. There will always be people who think that they know more than others; they are more Angolan than others and they will try to intimidate and say you shouldn't have said this or that.

I think it is very important that everything should be debated and that people also learn to listen to things that they may not like to hear. I think that someone at the back spoke about educating people as far as tolerance is concerned. Somebody else who is one of our UNITA representatives from London, Mr Cumandala, who has been away from Angola for quite a number of years, certainly has his own point of view, and I agree, he has the right to criticise. But maybe some of the realities in Angola have changed today. I think that the approach that we have to have is in fact this one: to encourage those British citizens in this University to have the right to look at Angola, to bring about a number of things. I think each one of the sides here is furthering a point of view. I agree that the policies of the Angolan Government of the last 16 months, and those that are going on now, may not be perfect. But what we have been trying to show all along is that UNITA has to be part of this game. And this game is, and has to be, a democratic one.

So, I think it is a wrong approach to be saying, well maybe we can only talk if we contribute in this way and unless we do that. I think it is already very important that we have all come here to talk. But, if we start conditioning people, saying "don't mention that" and at one point my compatriot from UNITA said he would leave the meeting if this point is being discussed, I think this could have been wrong. I thank him for his time, for having stayed. He is leaving us now. Certainly he has a lot of work. I will stay a little bit more. I think it is constructive and I think it is necessary that we talk about the issues that concern us. And I think that even if UNITA can be here or not, the Government here or not, what is important about all the interventions I have heard is that people are concerned and most of the issues that have been addressed are extremely important.

George Chikoti argues for bringing UNITA into "the democratic game"

I was a little bit afraid that if we say we can't or shouldn't condemn what's wrong, it might affect us. The UN Security Council has passed a number of resolutions, at least five or six are important; and all of them have condemned UNITA for going back to violence, because we had an agreement. And what I feel about the future is that whatever might come from Lusaka will depend upon how much we fulfil this agreement; and that is why I think it is important to condemn when important aspects of an agreement are violated, while keeping open the possibility of negotiations. This has been the strategy of my government. We have been saying we are going to talk to UNITA anywhere and everywhere, and you know we met UNITA in Namibia. We made promises which they agreed to. Later on they broke them. But also we went to Addis Ababa and we went to Abidjan. And we will keep going wherever it is necessary. We have been in Lusaka for five months now. We should not forget that. We think that the only way to go about it is to talk to UNITA, to talk amongst ourselves to bring peace to Angola.

This is an issue that brings out emotions. People over-react sometimes. But I think we should not be here for that. *(Murmurs of protest from one or two in the audience.)* And I thank again people for intervening with points and say that they should not feel they can't say things about Angola because it might not please a number of people. I think it is important now and for the future. Thank you. *(Muted applause **)*

And finally Sir Hugh Byatt:

Thank you all very much indeed. I started by saying I had tremendous sympathy, learnt and acquired over the years, for the people of Angola. I would like to congratulate both sides in the debate and the African Studies Centre for assembling us in this way. I hope the discussion will go on further. (attempts to speak are made from the floor) It seems to me that.... I see one hand raised. I think you must continue afterwards....

I personally take away from this session great encouragement, that what has emerged very very clearly is the extent of the wish for peace; the extent of the war-weariness; and certain indications that perhaps the Lusaka process is moving forward also. And the only thing I would like to leave you with is one thought. I do, as I say, greatly admire the Angoglan people and all that they have been through in the last thirty years and they deserve much better than they have had so far. But the sea is changing, as various speakers have said, and now I think we are reaching a point at which a certain responsibility passes to you, the Angolan people, to make this work, and to take your due and right place in the evolution of Africa. I'm sure that you will and I'm sure that those of us who live here in this country wish you tremendously well. Thank you very much. *(Applause and discussion amongst the audience breaks out ****)*

Keith Hart:

Please everyone stop. Please don't go away yet. I don't have a long speech. Participants may like to think about a short statement to be agreed upon at the final session tomorrow. I would be happy to discuss this with anyone during this evening. Thank you.

(The end of day one of Why Angola Matters. A number of important points had been raised. The British Ambassador unwittingly made a remark that would be carried over to the next day. He had talked of ordinary Angolans in the audience and day two of why Angola matters would see a powerful display of defiance against the view that Angolans anywhere had ordinary, normal lives.

He had also unwittingly staked out the division of the two days in a profound way. If day one was the day of parliamentarians, politicians and government representatives, the men in the suits talking about negotiated solutions to the problems made through the established institutional networks, then day two was the triumph of those outside these structures, the people for whom Angola matters because it shows up the decadence and inadequacy of these structures for solving the problems Africa and the world faces in the 1990s. For the Ambassador had said in reply to one question that he was not sitting on the platform to talk about why Angola matters from a humanitarian perspective, but rather from the perspective of government. Why Angola has been allowed to happen is because we live in a world where those in positions of power find it easy to separate the former from the later. This point would be played out on the second day.)

Media Coverage

Monday Evening, March 21st 1994, 10pm
The World Tonight, Radio 4

While the prospects for peace in Bosnia seems to have been improving over the past couple of weeks, so too have the prospects for the equally war-ravaged Angola. We have seen far less of the Angolan war on our TV screens; but since elections 18 months ago which the rebel UNITA group refused to accept, tens of thousands of people have died in a merciless war.

Over the weekend, it has been reported that the two sides in the war may be approaching agreement. Today in Cambridge leading figures from both sides appeared on the same platform at a conference on why Angola matters. Maurice Walsh was there.

(Sound of a man speaking in Portuguese gradually fades)
"He says in Angola what you can see can be compared to Sarajevo but you have many Sarajevos because you have many towns that are completely under siege now for one and a half years, and the situation in these places is very bad. The situation is such that in extreme cases some mothers even sell some of their children to support the rest of the family." Fernando Pacheco, the head of an Angolan aid agency, describes the horrors he has seen in his own country. According to the UN, the latest phase of the Angolan Civil War is claiming over 1,000 lives a day. Many die of shell-fire. Many are killed by landmines as they forage for food. Many die of starvation.

Now after all this fighting there is new talk of peace. The Angolan Vice-Foreign Minister, George Chikoti, himself a defector from UNITA to the Government side, brought optimistic news to his audience in Cambridge: "Quite important and significant steps have been made and we are still waiting. We made an offer to UNITA and UNITA has made more demands. We have given about four ministerial positions. There will be about as many as ten governors and municipal administrators."

And with an extraordinary degree of civility, Chikoti was sharing a platform with a former comrade-in-arms in UNITA and now his sworn enemy, Isaias Samakuva. Mr Samakuva had arrived at the weekend from Lusaka where he has been negotiating peace with the government. He was optimistic too. "I would say that at this stage we have overcome lots of issues: there is progress on lots of issues and we are optimistic about the agreement."

So far so good. But the Angolan hopes have been dashed before. The world wanted to believe that the last peace accord had worked, when President José Edwardo dos Santos and the UNITA leader Jonas Savimbi were electioneering up and down the country in 1992. When the war started again, the United Nations and the international community was ill-prepared to stop the slaughter. Saving Angola from communism was a popular rallying cry in the United States during the 70s and 80s. But Professor George Wright of California State University says that, with the end of the Cold War, Angola and its peace doesn't matter to the US and its allies any more. "It doesn't have the same significance. The Soviet Union no longer exists. The Cubans are not there and the MPLA regime which was committed to a socialist project has committed itself now to a multiparty system based on market based ideas. So the symbolic and objective concerns of the US prior to the '91-'92 period no longer exist."

Many of the participants in today's conference wanted the international community to cast aside realpolitik and take a moral interest in guaranteeing the peace in Angola. The journalist and campaigner, Victoria Brittain, argued that since 1992 the international community had even facilitated UNITA's offensive, by being weak-willed in enforcing the sanctions supposed to stop weaponry and fuel from reaching Savimbi's troops. "What happened at the end of 1992 was that one party in an internationally supervised election chose to completely ignore the results; go back to full-scale war; get aid in that full-scale war from several countries including South Africa, Zaire and a number of other African countries; and to try to overturn what had been an internationally supervised election. What Savimbi showed himself to be in this last year and a half of war, in which incidentally, half a million people have been killed, he has just shown himself to be what he always was throughout the two decades before: a terrorist who happened to be supported by the West."

The Angolan Government believes there is one event that may turn the international tide decisively against UNITA. Next month's elections in South Africa could end the rule of the white government that has consistently been one of UNITA's most important backers. George Chikoti believes this could severely undermine UNITA's ability to prosecute the war. "How can you explain that UNITA sustains offices in London, Washington, in France and in Portugal? Who pays for that? We know that everything is supported from South Africa. So what we think is that a democratic situation and transformation in South Africa will bring a new situation, whereby maybe the new government will better control some of these mechanisms for supporting UNITA both financially and militarily."

Talk of international pressure or indeed a change of wind from South Africa provokes a posture of defiance from the UNITA negotiator, Isaias Samakuva. He protests that it's the suffering of the people trapped by war which has brought him and his comrades to the peace talks. But he hinted that if UNITA is not satisfied with what it gets, that suffering might have to continue: "If what the international community says threatens my life, I think it is logical and natural that I will try to leave as much time as I can, and will defend myself." "If these talks break down for any reason or there is another hitch, how long could UNITA prolong this war?" "I can't say how long. What I can say is that UNITA would have the capability to defend itself."

That was Isaias Samakuva, of UNITA, speaking to Maurice Walsh in Cambridge today. ... The Annual Oscars bash will soon be in full swing, another opportunity for the brash and beautiful to look good and pray hard to make lots and lots of money. Winning an Oscar means instant success. Instant success at least in the movie business means instant wealth. Instant wealth means power. Power means money. Money means more movies ..."

Suburban security in Luanda Photograph by Zed Nelson

Session 4

The Southern African Region

José Campino

David Birmingham

Reginald Herbold Green

The first session of the second day was more restrained in comparison to the mood at the end of the first day. Our aim was to place Angola in a regional context to explore why peace required a regional input and would deliver a regional dividend: Angola matters because it could bring a new economic and diplomatic cohesion to the whole of Southern Africa.

Perhaps our audience was on its best behaviour in light of the range of heavy-weights we were lucky enough to gather together on one platform. We had the godfathers of Lusaphone studies in Britain. Professor Reginald Green from Sussex towered over the audience in a fetching Tanzanian hat. Professor David Birmingham spoke with the eloquence of a true historian, whilst Professor Patrick Chabal ruled serenely from the Chair. Also José Campino, Desk Officer for Angola at the UN Secretariat came to Cambridge for the second time to address the conference on UN involvement in the region.

We were indebted to Professors Green and Birmingham for having been among the very first to agree to speak when the conference was a mere twinkling in the Director's eye. Both escaped from the intellectual straight-jacket we had placed on them by adapting the session's theme to their own: Professor Green spoke on rehabilitation; Birmingham on language and regional politics in Angola. Both talks covered extremely important issues. Campino could be relied upon to stick strictly to the mandate given him and much interest was shown in the UN's role in the region, particularly in terms of UNAVEM I in Angola. Although the topics were too big for one session to really open up an indepth debate, the discussion certainly produced a lot of African responses, especially in relation to the role of international forces in Southern Africa and the balkanisation of the region in the aftermath of colonialism and apartheid. A collective sense of regional wrongs clearly united many in the audience.

Introduction from the Chair

Patrick Chabal (Chair):

(Patrick Chabal was Reader, now Professor, in Lusophone Studies at Kings College, University of London. He has written widely on former Portuguese Africa and was one of the first to join the African Studies Centre's Angola initiative.)

Welcome to this the fourth session of Why Angola Matters which will consider the regional dimension of this conflict. As there are many issues and aspects to cover, let us begin immediately and I would like to call on our first speaker, Mr Campino from the United Nations to begin proceedings.

José Campino

(José Campino joined the United Nations in 1982. Currently, his duties include those of desk officer responsible for Angola in the Africa Division of the Department of Political Affairs and, in this connection, he attended the Abidjan and Lusaka peace talks. The views expressed here are personal and do not necessarily reflect the position of the United Nations.)

José Campino – "shoestring operation"

United Nations Involvement in the Southern Africa Region

Thank you very much. It is a great pleasure to be here in Cambridge and share some thoughts with you regarding the United Nations involvement in Southern Africa. For many years the Organisation has been concerned about the situation in the region. Yet, it is only in the last five years that the United Nations has had a political presence and played an active peace-making and peace-keeping role in some Southern African countries.

It was indeed in the very first General Assembly, back in 1946, when the delegation of India put forward a resolution deploring the discrimination that the Indian population of South Africa was being subjected to. Beginning in 1952, the wider question of the policies of apartheid followed by the South African government was included in the General Assembly's agenda. Since then, and until recently, literally hundreds of resolutions were adopted by the United Nations condemning apartheid and its effects not only on the majority of the South African population but also on the region as a whole. Thus, while the physical presence of the Organisation in the area is relatively recent, the United Nations has been at the forefront of the struggle against apartheid for many years and it has tried to sensitise world public opinion about the injustices of the South African system and the consequences of its acts of aggression and destabilisation against a number of countries in the area.

Namibia

After many years of negotiations, the United Nations Transition Assistance Group (UNTAG) was deployed in Namibia in early 1989. The Organisation had been dealing with the situation in this former German colony since the late 1940s due to the refusal by South Africa to place Namibia under the Trusteeship system of the United Nations. The question was brought before the International Court of Justice which rendered a total of four advisory opinions and two judgements on the matter. By 1971, the Court, as well as the General Assembly and the Security Council, had condemned South Africa's continued occupation of the territory and had requested the withdrawal of its military and administration from Namibia.

The operation which led to Namibia's independence was one of the most complex undertaken by the United Nations in recent years. Although in the beginning UNTAG experienced some difficulties, the transitional process was soon back on track. Under the supervision and control of the United Nations, a number of delicate tasks such as the liberation of political prisoners, the return of thousands of refugees, the electoral registration and then the elections themselves, were successfully accomplished. Before independence on 21 March 1990, SWAPO and the conservative opposition, which until a year earlier had been fighting a bitter war, were also able to adopt a Constitution noted for its democratic principles and its clauses containing safeguards for the respect of basic human rights.

South Africa

In South Africa, the presence of the United Nations Observer Mission (UNOMSA) lasted for a relatively short period, from August 1992 to May 1994. Following the massacre of ANC supporters at the Boipatong township in June 1992, the Secretary-General of the United Nations dispatched to the country Mr Cyrus Vance, a former Secretary of State of the United States. After consultations with the Government and the ANC, Mr Boutros Boutros-Ghali decided to send to South Africa ten Secretariat officials to monitor the week of mass action planned by the ANC and affiliated organisations in protest against what was generally perceived as Government's connivance with the security forces in the repression in the townships.

Since the work of this small team of Secretariat officials proved to be useful in defusing potential violence during the week of mass action, it was agreed by all concerned that the United Nations presence in the country should be expanded and made more permanent. Together with observers from the OAU, the Commonwealth and the European Union, UNOMSA was thus established in South Africa to monitor the political violence, to facilitate the transitional process and to strengthen the structures set up by the South Africans to bring about a united, non-racial and democratic society in their country.

With the establishment of the Transitional Executive Council in early December 1993, UNOMSA's mandate was extended to cover the observation and monitoring of the electoral process. During the elections, held from 26 to 29 April 1994, the United Nations deployed over 2,000 observers who were able to visit 7,430 of the 8,478 voting stations established throughout the country. Despite some delays and technical difficulties the Special Representative of the Secretary-General, Mr. Lakhdar Brahimi, as well as most other international dignitaries, agreed with the Independent Electoral Commission that the elections had been "sufficiently free and fair".

Mozambique

After many years of a brutal war, Mozambique has enjoyed a period of relative calm since the General Peace Agreement was signed on 4 October 1992. Shortly afterwards, the United Nations Operation in Mozambique (ONUMOZ) was created to assist the Government and RENAMO in the implementation of the comprehensive settlement signed in Rome. Its main features included the assembly into quartering areas and the demobilisation of more than 70,000 Government and RENAMO troops, the formation of a new Mozambican army, the return to the country of over 1.5 million refugees who had fled to neighbouring states and the holding of presidential and legislative elections.

By and large the United Nations tried to avoid in Mozambique some of the shortcomings it had confronted in Angola. While in the latter the Organisation was simply invited to observe the proceedings of the mechanism responsible for the implementation of the Bicesse Accords, in Mozambique the Special Representative of the Secretary-General and other senior officials of ONUMOZ actually presided over the Supervisory and Monitoring Commission and its three main subsidiary bodies. In Angola, the Security Council only authorised the deployment of 350 military observers, augmented by some 400 electoral observers during the elections of September 1992. In Mozambique, the total number of civilians, military and police personnel of ONUMOZ reached 7,000 and during the elections from 27 to 29 October 1994, the Organisation was able to use the services of approximately 2,300 electoral observers. The United Nations was also able to exercise a much greater degree of flexibility in Mozambique than in Angola. The General Peace Agreement stated that the elections should take place within one year after it came into force. Yet, due to the delays experienced in the implementation of almost every major aspect of the peace settlement, all concerned agreed that it would be advisable to hold the elections one year later. Such considerations were not entertained in the case of Angola where elections were held according to schedule but without the proper fulfilment of key aspects of the Bicesse Accords.

Angola

Since Angola is the main subject of this conference, I will attempt to examine in greater detail United Nations involvement in that country. After years of laborious negotiations in which the former Assistant Secretary of State for African Affairs of the United States played a key role, the United Nations Angola Verification Mission (UNAVEM I) was originally established by the Security Council on 20 December 1988 at the request of the Governments of Angola and Cuba. Its creation was part of the larger package negotiated by Mr. Chester Crocker and others which led to the departure of the South African administration from Namibia and the deployment of UNTAG in the territory. The task of UNAVEM I was to verify the phased and total withdrawal of Cuban troops from Angola in accordance with the timetable agreed upon by the two Governments. Given the friendly relations between Angola and Cuba, there were no major difficulties in the implementation of the mandate of UNAVEM I. The withdrawal was completed by 25 May 1991, more than one month before the scheduled date.

Meanwhile, in April 1990, the Government of Angola and UNITA had begun a series of talks which eventually led to the signing of the Bicesse Accords on 31 May 1991. One day earlier, the Security Council had adopted a resolution entrusting a new mandate to UNAVEM (thereafter UNAVEM II) which included the verification and monitoring of the ceasefire and the demobilisation arrangements agreed to by the Government and UNITA as well as the observation of the electoral process.

The Electoral Process and its Aftermath

The electoral campaign was conducted without major violence, although there were reports of intimidation by some political parties as well as difficulties of access to certain areas, particularly those controlled by UNITA. More serious were the complaints about continued delays in the demobilisation process and the fact that the new army never really became a reality. The new Angolan Armed Forces were only formally established two days before the elections and for all practical purposes the Government and UNITA troops were never integrated into a joint army.

Despite these shortcomings, the elections were held as scheduled on 29 and 30 September 1992. The following day, the then Special Representative of the Secretary-General for Angola, Ms. Margaret Anstee, issued an interim statement in which she noted that the great majority of the 4.83 million registered voters had cast their ballots in peaceful and orderly conditions. Similar to other electoral processes where the United Nations has been involved, UNAVEM II carried out its own "quick count" of the presidential election at a selected sample of 166 polling stations where its observers remained throughout the count. The "quick count" proved to be a valuable tool for the verification process since its outcome (within 0.3 percent of the final result for President José Eduardo dos Santos and within 2 percent of that for Mr. Jonas Savimbi) turned out to be an accurate forecast of the final results and thereby contributed to the eventual United Nations assessment that there had been no conclusive evidence of major, widespread or systematic fraud.

Complaints by UNITA of widespread, massive and systematic irregularities and fraud began on 3 October. During the following critical days, the Secretary-General and Ms. Anstee repeatedly urged Mr. Savimbi not to reject the results of the elections. On 6 October, the Security Council, expressing its concern that one of the parties to the Bicesse Accords was contesting the validity of the elections, decided to dispatch to Angola an *ad hoc* commission composed of representatives of Cape Verde, Morocco, the Russian Federation and the United States. The National Electoral Council established four investigative commissions to examine UNITA's complaints. On 16 October, in a meeting at which all political parties were represented, it declared that the investigations conducted in the 18 provinces of Angola had not revealed any conclusive evidence of electoral fraud.

On 17 October, the President of the National Electoral Council announced the official election results. More than 91 percent of those registered had voted. The MPLA had won the legislative elections, with 53.7 percent of the votes, against UNITA's 34.1 percent. In the presidential elections, a second round would be needed since President José Eduardo dos Santos with 49.57 percent of the vote (versus 40.07 percent for Mr. Savimbi) fell short of the required majority. Later the same day, Ms. Anstee issued a statement declaring, *inter alia*, that despite a number of deficiencies which did not significantly affect the results, the elections had been generally free and fair.

Immediately after the results of the elections were announced, increased movement of UNITA troops was reported in various parts of the country and UNITA launched a nationwide operation to occupy municipalities and other towns by force and remove the Government's administrative structures. In some cases administrators were killed and in others they were forced to flee to the nearest locations controlled by the Government. On 31 October, heavy fighting broke out in many major cities, particularly in Luanda. By the time a tenuous and short-lived ceasefire came into effect on 2 November, several thousand persons had died, including a number of prominent UNITA leaders such as Vice-President Jeremias Chitunda and Mr. Salupeto Pena, a close relative of Mr. Savimbi who had been the UNITA chief representative at the Joint Political-Military Commission, the body responsible for the implementation of the Bicesse Accords.

Attempts to Restore Peace

Soon after the outbreak of the hostilities, the first high-level encounter between representatives of the Government and UNITA took place on 26 November in the southern provincial capital of Namibe. This was followed by other meetings, organised under the auspices of UNAVEM II, in Addis Ababa and in Abidjan. Such efforts were not successful mainly due to UNITA's reluctance to abandon the military option and to withdraw from the cities and other localities it had occupied by force. The Security Council, particularly after the failure of the Abidjan talks, held UNITA responsible for the continuation of the hostilities in Angola and, on 15 September 1993, the Council adopted a resolution under which it not only strongly condemned UNITA for the refusal to abide by the provisions of its previous resolutions but it also imposed a number of measures against UNITA, including an arms and oil embargo.

Meanwhile, the Secretary-General had appointed a new Special Representative for Angola, Mr. Alioune Blondin Beye. Since his arrival in the country in early July 1993, this former Foreign Minister of Mali conducted intensive negotiations aimed at the resumption of the peace talks. With the active support of a number of leaders from the region and the three observer States to the Angolan peace process (Portugal, the Russian Federation and the United States), he succeeded in convening from 25 to 31 October in Lusaka an exploratory meeting during which UNITA reaffirmed its acceptance of the results of the elections and agreed to withdraw from the locations it had occupied since the hostilities had begun.

The way was thus paved for the formal peace talks to resume in Lusaka on 15 November 1993. By 11 December, agreement had been reached on all the military items on the agenda: the re-establishment of the ceasefire; the withdrawal, quartering and demilitarisation of the UNITA army; the disarming of all civilians; and the completion of the formation of the Angolan Armed Forces.

Following the agreement on the military items, the discussions moved to the political issues on the agenda: the police; the completion of the electoral process; the new mandate of the United Nations and the role of the three observer States; and the question of national reconciliation. By 31 January 1994, agreement had been reached on the police and by 5 May on the completion of the electoral process, involving the holding of the second round of the presidential elections. The agenda item on the new mandate of the United Nations and the role of the observer states was the last to be considered and was completed on 17 October. Finally, the question of national reconciliation proved to be the most delicate and difficult issue since it comprised matters such as the allocation of senior Government posts to UNITA, including the governorships of provinces. Following long and laborious negotiations, agreement was reached on this question in October, when important issues pertaining to the number and particular posts to be headed by UNITA in the national, provincial and local administration were agreed upon. In early September, after more than three months of discussions, UNITA had dropped its insistence that one of its members be appointed Governor of Huambo. According to the compromise proposals put forward by the United Nations and the observer States, UNITA would be given instead the posts of deputy governor of the province and mayor of the municipality of Huambo.

Throughout 1994, the Security Council regularly extended the mandate of UNAVEM II and repeatedly urged both the Government and UNITA to make every necessary effort to conclude the Lusaka peace talks. The Council also condemned the intensification of military actions throughout the country and demanded that the two sides cease all offensive operations. With respect to humanitarian assistance, the Council appealed to all states, United Nations agencies and non-governmental organisations to provide relief aid to the estimated three million Angolans severely affected by the war.

Conclusion

Given the existing time constraints, I will be brief and confine my concluding remarks to Angola. However, before doing so, I would like to note that although the United Nations political presence in some Southern African countries has come to an end, the Organisation's involvement with these states is likely to continue for many years to come in the form of a variety of economic and social assistance programmes administered by the different agencies of the United Nations system.

With respect to Angola and the position which the United Nations has been called upon to play in the peace process, it should be clear that while the United Nations is willing to continue to chair the peace talks and can eventually assume a prominent role in the implementation of the Lusaka Protocol, it is primarily the responsibility of the Government and UNITA to muster the necessary political will to ensure the successful implementation of the different provisions of the Protocol. Such realism and political commitment will be particularly necessary during the first months of the ceasefire when the number of United Nations forces in Angola will still be rather thin and the Government and UNITA troops will be expected to disengage with minimal international supervision from all areas of contact.

Closely related to the capacity of the United Nations to monitor and verify another complex and expensive peace-keeping operation in Africa is the resolve by the international community to provide a sufficient number of troops and other qualified personnel for such an operation, as well as the willingness to pay for it. In recent years, as the Organisation has been called upon to perform increasingly challenging tasks, the availability of troops, particularly in such specialised areas as transport and communications, health services and engineering, has become a severe problem. At the same time, many member states of the United Nations continue to fail to pay their assessed contributions in full and on time, as they are required to do under the Charter. In the case of Angola, it is evident that if some of the shortcomings experience in the past are to be avoided, the international community will have to commit the necessary human and financial resources in order to ensure that an expanded United Nations operations in the country can properly fulfil its mandate. *(Applause **)*

Patrick Chabal:

Thank you. There may well be people in the audience who might want to ask further questions, but not now, about the future of the UN involvement in Angola; but let us continue.

David Birmingham:

(David Birmingham, who presented a paper he wrote with Sherilynn Young, is Professor of Modern History at the University of Kent, Canterbury. He has taught at SOAS and in several African countries, including Angola. He has served as an editor of the Journal of African History and as president of the African Studies Association of the UK.)

Language is Power: Regional Politics in Angola

I am the odd man out in this conference because I am an historian. I do not look at politics and I do not peer into the future. So in ten minutes all I can do is to come along and ask you one simple question to which I would like some answers. The question is what is the importance of language in the politics of Angola? It seems to me that it is potentially a question of some interest. But since I was put on a panel which dealt with regional politics, it seemed to me that I was being asked to direct my question in a regional context. And therefore I decided that I would look at two neighbours of Angola, one to the north called Zaire, and one to the south, called South Africa, to see if they gave me any clues to the answer to my question - what is the importance of language?

David Birmingham – "demilitarisation of politics"

Angola has, for the last 100 years, been divided between the people of the city who speak Portuguese as their native mother tongue and the people of the countryside who speak various dialects of Bantu and use Portuguese only as their vernacular language of wider communication. In the last 20 years these two traditions have been at war with one another. In the city the term of disparagement used by black Angolans for the equally black people of the countryside has sometimes been 'Bantu'. One is reminded of the term of opprobrium lately used by white South Africans for their rural co-citizens; the 'Munts' (a corrupt European plural for the singular form of Bantu).

A 100 years ago the great black families of the Angolan coastal towns – many of whom bore Portuguese and Dutch names such as Dos Santos and Van Dunem –called themselves proudly the 'Natives'. They looked down on Africans, Angolans and Indigenes, though they were themselves African, Angolan and Indigenous. They bore with pride the cultural legacy of Europe that gave them their names and their mother tongue and yet they saw themselves as the true sons and daughters of Africa, the heirs to the future. They became known as the 'Old Creoles'. Their roots lie in many cases in the army and their language was the language of army command.

The destiny that the old creoles envisaged for themselves in the late 19th century, during a semi-democratic period of colonisation by the 'bourgeois' Saxe-Coburg monarchy, was to be thwarted. When the republican regicides seized power in 1910 they introduced half a century of enhanced racism and gave preference to colonial immigrants to the detriment of culturally assimilated Africans. The desire to exploit the colonies to the benefit of Portugal was further heightened when the republicans were overthrown by a dictatorship backed by catholic army officers. An almost fascist-style of authoritarianism followed the Wall Street 'crash' that had bankrupted Portugal. The old creoles of Angola only re-emerged in the 1950s when they became co-founders of a new political party, the Movement for the Popular Liberation of Angola (MPLA). In the process they formed an alliance of convenience with another Portuguese-speaking urban community, the 'New Creoles'.

The new creoles had emerged during the half century of old creole eclipse and themselves had two strands. One was the 'coloured' (to borrow a South African concept) strand of mixed-race peoples and the other was the 'acculturated' strand of assimilated black urbanites. The mixed-race creoles had white fathers (or more rarely mothers) who gave them privileged access to education and jobs and who protected them partially from the clamorous demands of less skilled white immigrants who insisted that purity of race be the over-riding criterion for preferment in the Portuguese colonial world. The assimilated new creoles came predominantly from the Methodist mission fields of the city hinterland and shared their educational attainments as well as their church affiliation with some of the mixed-race creoles. They were more distant from the equally black old creoles of the great bourgeois families of the 19th century, but they shared with them the power conferred by command of the colonial language, the language of power and authority.

When looking comparatively at regional politics among Angola's neighbours one must immediately ask questions about the power of language in the two neighbourhood states that have played – and continue to play – an intrusive role in the politics of Angola. In the case of Zaire the language of power is the language of the army, Lingala. In the case of South Africa the language of power was until recently Afrikaans, the language of the white and coloured creoles. In Angola army power is a factor that needs to be analysed as carefully as it has been in Zaire, and creole power needs to be critically assessed in comparison with creole power in South Africa before reform began in 1989.

Zaire collapsed after independence in much the same way that Angola did because the frail new political institutions of the post-colonial state were unable to moderate the competition for resources between regions and more especially between town and country. The only over-arching institution with a semblance of national cohesion that could link the towns and quell the countryside was the army. It used the old languages of long-distance trade and of Christian and Muslim evangelism – Lingala and Kiswahili – as the languages of national unity with which to transcend several hundred ethnic identities. After the failure of United Nations efforts of the early 1960s to create an inter-regional political equilibrium in Zaire, the late 1960s saw the creation, financing and arming of a military regime which crushed regional and rural political aspirations. The army gave power and prosperity to its own personnel and sided with the towns against the countryside in the great rebellions. Rural rebellion, which cruelly invaded the cities and crucified the petty bourgeoisie, was crushed by the army and its mercenary recruits in the 1960s. Regional rebellion was similarly crushed in the 1970s by the army and by international supporting regiments of paratroopers. One may ask how illuminating these Zairean events are to an understanding of the politics of Angola.

In Angola the national army uses Portuguese as the language of national unity. Conscripts may have been very conscious of their diverse regional origins and used vernacular languages in the bars and during leisure hours, as suggested in Pepetela's novel of guerrilla experience, Mamba, but army discipline through the Portuguese command language was a factor of growing national identity. It was also, however, an alienating experience. To conscripts who saw the war drag on for 30 years, the colonial war, the war of interventions, the civil war and the election war, military service became irksome rather than fraternal and demobilisation or escape became an obsession. The role of the army as a means of creating a trans-ethnic national consciousness was flawed by the fact that the army was used by the political authority to maintain control over civilian society during times of austerity and crisis. The army was no longer seen by all as the defender of liberty and the hammer of the South African and Zairean invaders, but as the agent of control, the defender of wealth in the possessing class.

The army command became increasingly identified with a privileged political elite. The army general staff and the old creole bourgeoisie came closer together and the new creoles were periodically marginalised from power although preserving their social and economic stake in coastal and urban society. The wealth of the townsmen and presidential courtiers of Angola was not as obscenely affluent as that of the Zairean elite of Kinshasa in their high-living, palace-strewn enclave of North Zaire, but the differentials of wealth between town and countryside in Angola sat uneasily with the egalitarian rhetoric which had accompanied decolonisation. Rural disaffection and the political mobilisation thereof was not to be wondered at and the repression of such disaffection brought Angola into yet closer parallel with Zaire.

A minor strand of the language of power in Angola has been the use of French. In 1975, when the petty Portuguese traders who ran the consumer economy and distribution networks of the metropolitan area of the Angolan capital withdrew, they were replaced by an influx of returnees who had spent the colonial war in exile. During this Zairean exile across the northern border the Angolans had learnt French and the younger members of the community had been born, brought up and educated in a French-speaking environment. French was the language of Zairean business and, since they could not – as foreigners – gain access to state employment, it was in commerce and industry that they made their living. By the time they returned to Angola they had acquired financial skills which were much needed and very scarce in the newly decolonised Angola. They had also developed a political ideology of entrepreneurial capitalism which was in sharp contrast with the ideology of state service that was adopted by Angolans who had remained at home during the colonial war and aspired to step into the shoes of fleeing Portuguese bureaucrats rather than into those of fleeing Portuguese peddlers and merchants.

The problem of the Zaire returnees was whether they would form a 'fifth column' that might be used by the government of Zaire in the event of any attempt by outsiders to impose a Zairean model on the politics of Angola. The similarity of the two economies did not make the thought of such an imposition wholly unlikely. Both countries depended to an overwhelming degree on the export of extracted minerals in order to finance the institutions of the state and pay the salaries of its politicians, bureaucrats and soldiers. In the case of Angola the export was oil rather than copper and its dominance in the export earnings probably exceeded 80%. Both countries neglected peasant producers and made up the urban food deficit from the export account.

The pain that rural neglect inflicted on Angolan peasants in the 1980s was probably as severe as the pain inflicted on Zairean peasants in the 1960s. Angolan farmers had been harshly integrated into the agrarian market economy of the last colonial years as cheap labour and as producers dependent on an exploitative network of rural white traders who had the backing of the state. The collapse of the system, the ending of the opportunities for migrant earnings, and the closing down of the rural markets meant that they were wrenched from their limited colonial opportunities and given little or no post-colonial alternative means of wealth creation. Many moved from colonial semi-poverty to autonomous sub-subsistence of a very low level. Despite the normal peasant reluctance to destabilise the known world, some were ready to be mobilised by the leaders of protest, be they local politicians or the agents of foreign interest. Peasants who refused to support the rebellions were threatened, their footpaths were strewn with land-mines, their children were marched off to join the armies of the war lords and the survivors fled into impoverished exile in Zambia.

Chaos in Angola seemed to suit Zaire well. At the very least it prevented Angola from emerging as a role model for its oppressed peoples; but it also minimised the likelihood of Angola being capable of supporting regional rebellions as had happened in 1977. In a reverse process the army regime in Zaire permitted its military bases to be used to supply the rural rebellions in Angola with the essential tools of war, discreetly condoned if not partially financed by the United States. The longer the war lasted, the more the Angolan government depended on its army and the more the country came to resemble its northern neighbour. Angolan unity, like Zairean unity, was held together by an army, by a command language, and by a network of transport planes that overflew the abandoned roads and railways to link an archipelago of provincial towns to the expanding capital city.

The links and parallels between Angola and South Africa are no less interesting than those between Angola and Zaire. In South Africa the power of language was for long the power of Afrikaans. In 1948 the Afrikaner capture of the state gave a virtual monopoly of state employment to Afrikaans speakers in the army command, the police, the railways, the post office and many branches of administration. The English-speakers were temporarily left to control the economy.

The Angolan parallel occurred in 1975 when the Portuguese-speaking creoles acquired a virtual monopoly of state employment and protected their position not only by running the army and the police but also by preserving often redundant bureaucratic positions and salaries for themselves and their clients. They also controlled the 'command economy' of state capitalism but the real, or parallel, economy was in the hands of French-speaking Angolans who could not obtain bureaucratic sinecures but were very skilled at recycling the payments in kind that were given to office-holders and in preying on the export-import trade that went through the city harbour. The challenge to the Portuguese-speaking black creoles of the coast of Angola, and of the satellite towns that were linked to it by air networks that overflew the disaffected countryside, came from the rural explosion of spontaneous or inspired rebellion. The challenge to the Afrikaans-speaking, and predominantly white, creoles in South Africa came from a very different quarter, from the English-speaking blacks of the cities.

In South Africa, as in Angola, language was a feature of power and black urban dwellers refused to allow themselves to be cornered into a controlled world in which their only language of wider communication was a local Dutch patois that was easily subject to censorship and supervision and which denied them privileged access to the English-language community of business opportunity, let alone to the worldwide community of ideas. Urban revolt began in the mid-1970s, intensified in the mid-1980s, and spearheaded a reform movement in the 1990s. As in Angola, however, urban power – albeit black power – appeared to threaten rural interests and South Africa found itself encouraged to examine parallels and links with Angola.

Rural society in South Africa was harshly exploited by the economics of apartheid. The Bantustans – the old breeding and dying grounds of South Africa's black labour – were turned into areas of low-cost production. The system was designed to force women into performing nearly all household maintenance and agricultural labour necessary to sustain home and family. This work provided a subsistence subsidy to men who could then be paid less than a family wage for their labour down the mines and in white-run manufacturing. A political elite was created in each Bantustan and the rulers gained power and wealth from the apartheid status quo. This elite was willing to fight against reform and against the transfer of power from their armed rural barons in their fragmented fiefs to the urban politicians of national unity.

The reluctance of those who had gained regional, local, rural and provincial power to throw in their lot with those who had gained national prominence highlighted the similarities between South Africa and Angola. Zulu leaders in particular realised that, even if they created a political party that appealed to all their Zulu-speaking brethren, they would still not command more than a tiny fraction of the national vote. They were therefore reluctant to step onto the national stage. In Angola the Ovimbundu may possibly have had greater ethnic support than the Zulu in South Africa, many of whom probably preferred the national to the local agenda. But the Ovimbundu also had political and ideological agendas rather than ethnic ones. Their leaders, like the Zulu, had to resort to threats in order to mobilise support in what they had deemed to be their natural constituency. But the white-inspired regional and ethnic loyalties which divided South Africa and helped Afrikaner politicians minimise the appeal of national unity were not the only problems that the South African reform movement faced.

In South Africa, as in Angola, the national politicians were supremely ignorant of rural realities. The potential conflict between town and countryside which had torn Zaire apart in the 1960s and had torn Angola apart in the 1980s was also a real threat to South Africa in the 1990s. Urban politicians entered the 1994 elections making promises about land redistribution and water allocation which may have seemed reasonable in a city planning office but which were wholly unrealistic in rural situations. The expectations for a new future that decolonisation had brought to Angola had led to bitter rural disappointment and eventually to prolonged civil war. Similar expectations may now be escalating in South Africa. The grumbling of Bantu-speaking farmers in South Africa could become as loud as that of their kinsmen in Angola. And the political acuity of the post-apartheid Afrikaans-speaking creoles of the Transvaal and of the acculturated English-speaking citizens of the Eastern Cape may have proved to be as insensitive as that of the Portuguese-speaking creoles – both old and new – had been in the coastal towns and urban enclaves of post-colonial Angola.

Another parallel between South Africa and Angola concerns army power. In the 1980s South Africa and Angola were at war and in both countries covert political power effectively passed into the hand of the military. In both cases the reason for this hidden agenda was primarily internal rather than external; but in both cases the foreign war was a live and costly political issue. In South Africa the army surreptitiously took command not only of foreign policy, controlling the peace and war agendas for its own reasons rather than those of the electorate, but also took control of the home agenda and placed its appointees on cabinet committees that had previously been under parliamentary control. The army replaced the securocrats as the privileged recipients of funds for social control and for the internal repression of dissent, including white and coloured dissent as well as black dissent. The army in South Africa, unlike the army in Angola, did not, however, long survive in this position of de facto power.

In the late 1980s the South African army lost the war in Angola when it failed in its endeavour to defeat Soviet-supported government troops, to ensure the continuation of Angolan disorder, and (possibly as a surrogate for the United States) to install a new Angolan government with an ideological and regional agenda congenial to South African and Western interests. The army also failed to end violent protest inside South Africa or to restore worldwide business confidence in the security and profitability of the economics of apartheid. Hence reform was undertaken in South Africa in the light of the army's failure. In Angola, by contrast, the army seemed to have won the foreign war and embarked on negotiating an end to the civil war in a mood of optimism. Peace was signed, the election was held, and the government won – freely and fairly. The losers went back to seeking power through the barrel of the gun since their ballot agenda had not been sufficiently attractive to win them power. New and disturbing questions about potential future parallels with South Africa arose.

In order to conclude one must return to the Cambridge conference agenda. Why does Angola matter? In particular why does it matter in a regional context as opposed to a humanitarian or a global context? Angola may have lessons that the other countries of the region can learn. If Mozambique, with rather more help from the United Nations than was available to Angola, can complete the process of demilitarisation before its ballot takes place, it may have a better chance than Angola of avoiding a return to war after the elections have been held. But demilitarisation is not the only key to success. The political process also requires that each and every section of the society feels that its interests have been fairly presented, heard, and incorporated into a truly national agenda.

Reginald Green

Perhaps Africa will try to re-invent the single-party-state in which competition over resources and priorities can be moderated within the framework of an overarching political party where compromises have been reached before the chips are down in a 'winner-takes-all' election and voters choose the representatives they think most likely to carry out the promises made. Losers cannot be allowed to feel too harshly betrayed. If Mozambique can demilitarise its politics and give a voice to those who cannot master the old language of command, then perhaps there is hope also for South Africa. The demilitarisation of politics, the reconciliation of the ethnic segments partially created by the white minority in order better to divide and to rule, the calling in of the weapons which were secretly awarded to those factions most vehemently opposed to a national unification, and the continued broadening of the democratic process will lower the temperature of confrontation in South Africa.

There may not be such thing as a clean slate in South Africa, but if the recent darkness can be toned down, and if the growing dialogue between groups which previously had no venue for communication can be enhanced, each section of society may come to feel that its interests can be catered for in nationally cohesive politics. If the lessons of Angola are learnt and it proves possible to demilitarise the politics of Mozambique and South Africa perhaps it will eventually be possible to demilitarise the politics of Zaire and bring peace and prosperity to that anguished land. (*Applause* ***)

Reginald Herbold Green:

Angola Through A Cracked Glass Dimly: Peace, Reconstruction, Rehabilitation, Regionalism

(Reginald Green has been a Professorial Fellow at the Institute of Development Studies, Sussex since 1975 and he is currently Senior Social Policy Advisor to the National Directorate of Planning in Mozambique. He worked on Angola for UNICEF over 1986-1988. His paper was circulated to conference participants beforehand. It went on to form the basis of a discussion by the Board of Trustees to the Bank of Angola. For reasons of space, we have omitted his oral summary. The paper is reproduced below, pages 173-180.)

Open Session

Patrick Chabal:

The floor is now open for questions.

Amir Attaran (Student):

I'd like to address my comments to the official from the UN who spoke today. I'd like to place your comments in contrast to some that were made last year, when Marrack Goulding, the former Under-Secretary for peace-keeping operations, spoke at Oxford and gave us what I felt was a touching analysis of what happened in Angola. He called it "an unmitigated failure" and one which he took personal responsibility for. What I find different between your discussion and his is that he feels the UN was wrong in the first instance to accept the weak mandate, and that once in Angola, with a weak mandate, grossly neglected

Amir Attaran

its opportunities to communicate the failure of the incipient peace process to the outside world. That being the case, it makes it a bit difficult to swallow when you say that some things about the peace process are substantially improved in the case of Mozambique; but, when Lusaka and the role of the UN in any agreement that emerges from Lusaka is discussed, you mention that at present the UN won't be undertaking any role that might even be called 'peace-making'. You won't for instance tell us what role you envisage for the UN in UNAVEM III. Marrack Goulding did mention `peace-making'; he called it a viable alternative option to war. I would hate to see it slide away from us. Perhaps we can now entertain a notion of what might happen, when the UN, if the UN ,does get another opportunity in Angola. (*Applause* **)

Unknown Angolan man:

I am from Angola. I just want to comment on Professor Birmingham's speech. It's a very important speech that he made which I agree with completely because in Angola there is a problem. There are for example people in urban areas and people in rural areas and these provinces are neglected and underdeveloped. A lot of oil and diamonds come from Cabinda for example but Cabinda itself's been neglected, underdeveloped. And the people are not stupid; they know who's to blame - people from the coast areas more especially. They are undermining the ethnic population there and this is causing a big problem. In Angola up until now the people who are controlling want power and power alone. Thank you very much.

Unknown Angolan man:

My first question is to the UN official. Is the UN aware that the USA is a big brother within the community? I want to know if the UN representative is aware of what is the attitude of the USA towards the Angola situation. The second question is this. We all know that the process of 'enlightenment' from the West has created a division between rural and urban, between the civilised and the primitive, between the democratic and the non-democratic. If the language of man is the main problem then the division of Africa as carried out in 1885 is the main problem and the main cause. Do you suggest that the reorganisation of Africa, the reordering of Africa according to its previous kingdoms, is a solution for the concept of the nation, for how we understand ourselves as Angolans? Thank you.

Sisa Ncwana (ANC London Representative):

I'd like to comment on the question of the militarisation of South African politics and the language involved. My main view on this is that language is only an aspect of the division. In 1948, when the National Party got into power, it set out to divide our people; and out of this divide-and-rule policy came Verwoed's policy of balkanisation and the bantustans. He said he'd rather have eight different black states than have to deal with one black nation. Now here we see a continuation of the struggle that is an economic struggle between the indigenous black people of South Africa and the colonials.

However, I do agree that the official policy was to divide and give privilege to the white over and above the people. That they successfully did; but, unfortunately for them, the people themselves were bound to win their struggle eventually, because it is not possible, however strong they might be, that they could subdue for ever the fact that people want democracy. Now this has been proved by our own struggles, mass action etc. coupled of course with external economic action which brought that government to its knees. Therefore, I'm pointing out, their reform movement, the late meetings that took place, was not exactly a reform movement within the white community. It was not a reform movement but a crisis of politics and economics which brought South Africa to its knees. De Klerk himself said in 1990 that he was not going to devolve himself out of power.

However, what I want to say on the question of the division of the urban and the rural, is that the division is so intermarried over such a long time. But if we look at the official pronouncements contained in the new bill of rights, designed to redress what the Nationalists put in place, do you think it is possible that a manifesto of the type used by the ANC can address this problem of the urban and rural division in Angola?

Tony Hodges (Economist Intelligence Unit):

Word has been spreading around the corridors that one of the proposals put forward in the framework for the Lusaka peace talks is that the Angolan government itself should pay for a substantial proportion of the peace-keeping operation that is proposed for Angola. I would like to ask José Càmpino whether this is true and to make a brief comment. I think this is something that this conference should pay particular attention to because it would be a really quite astonishing precedent for a peace-keeping operation launched by the international community to be paid for, for the first time in history as far as I know, by the country that has suffered the conflict that the peace-keeping operation was designed to try and help her resolve.

Now I know it's argued that Angola is a rich country with substantial oil and diamond resources; but, as I tried to point out yesterday, its economy outside the oil sector has been devastated over the last 15 or more years. It's also now a highly indebted country partly because of its murky purchases in the past; partly because of accumulation of interest very little of which has been paid over the last few years. It is now suffering a debt burden which is as great as in any other country in sub-Saharan Africa. We have already had discussions elsewhere in Africa about the economic situation in some middle-income countries which also have very heavy debt problems like Congo, Cameroon or Côte D'Ivoire. These problems are not being sufficiently addressed in the discussions on debt relief in Sub-Saharan Africa. Angola is perhaps another case a little bit like the so-called middle income countries; but in this case they're scarcely recovering from a war that has devastated the economy, where the mass of the population is literally on the borderlines of survival, a very large part of the population barely even surviving in fact.

I find it quite astonishing that there should now be a discussion of the Angolan government, considering this very serious economic situation, helping to contribute to the cost of the peace-keeping operation. I think if this is being proposed, it also in a way risks holding the peace-keeping operation hostage to the frailty of the Angolan economy. Can you imagine what would happen if, as a result of the economic situation in Angola, a peace-keeping operation came unstuck in some way? Or perhaps it would simply add to the very substantial debt level, which I don't think is quite as easy to resolve as Reginald Green implied.
Thank you

Rajah Jarrah (ACORD, UK):

In reply partly to Tony Hodges' comment, I would like to remind everyone of the situation in Iraq and international intervention there. The Iraqi people have been made to pay for the humanitarian costs of that intervention, which I don't think we should forget.

The other point I wanted to make is that yesterday we heard about the cost of the Mozambican UN intervention as being a million dollars a day. That is nothing compared to the million dollars an hour that was spent by the UN during the Gulf War. If the international community were prepared to invest as much in peace as they have been over the past decade in promoting war in Angola, then I think that this idea of money being a constraint to the UN intervention in Angola is a complete red herring. We heard from Margaret Anstee, after she left her post last year in a speech she gave at the House of Commons, that in Abidjan she was very close to securing peace between the two sides; and it was not the MPLA position or UNITA's position that frustrated that deal, but it was the refusal of the UN to guarantee the necessary UN troops to secure disengagement of the two sides at that time. So, if the UN is now putting the worry of finance as the only reason why they can't intervene assertively in Angola today, then I think that poses a very serious precedent for the rest of the world.

Dr. José de Carvalho (Angolan economist):

First I would just like to point out that we have do not have any border with the South Africans. In terms of the comparison between the ethnic, language and the structure of society and so on, this happens because the colonialists wanted to divide the people. This is the root of the war situation and don't forget that these elites, after the 1960s until the late 80s, were created as a policy of the West which has led now to the new disorder. We have a UN with a role in Angola. It is not the objective that all Angolans want. The US is the number one power in the UN and anything happens if the US wants. (*Applause* **)

Marco Ramazzotti (Consultant):

To Campino, I would like to say these negotiations have been going on for such a long time, we should get to what is the real basic issue. I suggest the nature of UNITA. It always felt it was a quasi-government in exile. UNITA wants to be recognised as an equal partner to the Government. Let us remember that the Peace Accord did not have UNITA as a member. Only states were members of the peace agreement.

To David Birmingham, I fully understand this question. Who has power? Where? One of the major problems of teaching in Angola was that teachers didn't speak the local languages. In schools obviously you speak Portuguese. But in the Army the majority of the people did not speak Portuguese. They spoke Nguno at least in the south, the majority language spoken by UNITA.

To Professor Green, for reconstruction there is a model which can be followed. After independence, the Marxist/Leninist economic development model was implemented only in part. The colonial model still existed outside of this model. In fact the government always wanted to revert back to the old system of production; they loved the market system that was before independence. I would like to ask what would be the role of government, in an economy which should be controlled by a new state?

Patrick Chabal fields questions to Reginald Green, David Birmingham and José Campino

Malik Chaka (UNITA Office, Washington DC):

The remarks made by Professors Green and Birmingham were very provocative and they have had an impact today. Once peace is achieved, I think the question of instability is going to have to be addressed by developing the rural areas. In terms of access to schools, credit and roads, the countryside will come to the city. So rural development has to be a priority after peace. (*Loud murmurings ripple through the audience*)

In terms of language policy, I think this is very important. Portuguese will have to be the official language; but then what will be the national language? Will other languages be made national as part of the rural rehabilitation programme? I believe that the learning of different languages by people from different parts of the country can help to rebuild national solidarity.

Replies from the Panelists

José Campino:

Before providing a reply to some of the questions and comments which we have just heard, I think it would be useful to make a few general comments regarding the financing of the United Nations and about what we in the Organisation understand by such concepts as peace-making and peace-keeping. I find it necessary to do so since I have noticed some misunderstandings in the media, and indeed even here, regarding the meaning of such concepts.

Who pays for the United Nations? The Organisation is totally dependent upon its member states for the payment of the regular and peace-keeping budgets. If member states do not pay, the United Nations cannot deliver. It is as simple as that. At the moment we are in arrears of about $1.3 billion, just on the peace-keeping budget. And most specifically, in the case of Angola, what would have been adopted if Abidjan had succeeded a year ago, and what is the mood now of the majority of contributors to the UN, that provide about 30% of the peace-keeping budget, are completely different. In Abidjan then we probably could have got 15,000 persons to try to implement the peace process in Angola. We probably will not get 15,000 soldiers, if an agreement is reached within the near future. We at the Secretariat, including the UN in general, are very pressed, particularly by the US, to produce an operation which will be feasible to implement, but will not cost 3 or 4 or 5 million dollars per day, as Yugoslavia and Somalia did.

I completely agree that the international community was paying over a billion dollars per day in the Gulf War; but the Gulf War was not conducted by the UN. It was authorised by the Security Council, but it was conducted by a force which had no direct UN connection. But I completely agree with you that it is much much cheaper to do peace-keeping than to wage war.

Turning to the question of whether what we are doing in Lusaka is actually peace-making. The Secretary General has defined it in several documents since the Security Council meeting in January 1992: preventative diplomacy, peace-making and peace-keeping and peace-building. But preventative diplomacy is like preventative medicine; trying to prevent a conflict from erupting. Peace-making is clearly what is happening in Lusaka, contrary to what has been said here, with the emphasis on trying to find ways of preventing conflict. Peace-keeping is the deployment of forces in the field, usually after an agreement has been reached. And peace-building is the process that can take place after demobilisation; the elections etc. All these are part of the peace-building mechanism. These processes can co-exist. In Angola we have a small peace-keeping force, but we are engaged in Lusaka in the peace-making process.

The specific question regarding Mr. Marrack Goulding and his remarks in Oxford. He is my current boss. He was Under-Secretary General for peace-keeping operations. He is now the Under- Secretary General for Political Affairs. I will ask him this question. I did point out that UNAVEM had a weak mandate. It was a shoe-string operation. We hope, despite short-comings with resources available, the UN will be able to deliver, once an agreement is reached in Lusaka.

On the question of the US being the big brother, of course, the UN is a mirror of reality. Although all states are sovereign, some states are more sovereign than others. And these days we have just one superpower, that, as I have mentioned, pays for most of the peace-keeping expenses. So obviously, what they say is a little bit more important than most of the other members of the UN. This is reality.

Regarding the rumours about the US wanting the Angolan Government to meet some of the costs. They are just simply rumours. It is true that the US has approached the Secretariat and possibly approached member states to try to find ways and means to help defraying the costs in the future of UNAVEM III. But at the moment these are rumours. I don't think it will actually happen. I think all of the peace-making operations of the UN, we have about 17 at the moment, with the exception of Cyprus, all of them have their own peace-keeping budget and I will find it quite surprising if these proposals which have been ventilated in a very preliminary state will actually come ventilated in a very preliminary state will actually come into fruition.

David Birmingham:

Thank you all very much for your comments which have been extremely helpful. Let me briefly say, yes of course, the regions of the country where the major extractions take place need to get some benefit from this. One cannot see a secession of Cabinda, but the people of Cabinda should benefit. Of course it must be integrated into the national economy; but the people of Cabinda should benefit as well.

Secondly, as a member of the ANC recently said, there is no such thing as a clean slate. I think this is something we should take on board. We cannot go back to a pre-colonial past. We cannot erase the colonial experience. We have to go forward.

Thirdly, the ANC according to its manifesto does think that it is vital to get integration of town and country interests. The agenda of the MPLA was exactly the same. It said that one must have an integration of town and country interests. The peasants too are heroes of the revolution. So far they have found it difficult to implement that policy, but the policy is there.

Fourthly, I stand corrected on my geography. Of course Angola is not an immediate neighbour of South Africa, as next-door neighbour. They are simply neighbours in the way that they live in the same region of Africa. But I do take the point that was made by the speaker. The new elites created by colonialism do have exceedingly difficult choices to make.

Fifthly, I was very interested in the answer to my question does the army act as an agent for integration by creating a common language and the answer was that in the bars where the army congregated, Ovimbundo is still spoken by the infantry recruits.

Reginald Green:

Very briefly, first Angola is not at present a middle-income country. It is very difficult to estimate GDP per capita as above the $400 to 500 range, which makes it below the eligibility range. If you look at my paper, you can see this point in more detail. Probably about 60% of the population lives in absolute poverty. 30% are vulnerable to demobilisation or bureaucratic reform, so you have 10% to 20% that are safely above the absolute poverty line, while one tenth are above the absolute luxury line as well. So we are certainly not talking about a rich country. As to debt, I didn't say it would be easy. But there is nothing much you can do if rouble debt is paid in roubles. There's no future economic interest in Angola if there's no leverage.

Secondly, if the Angolan economy, on the basis of peace, is moving forward, the interest in rebuilding markets will mean that the Egyptian/Latin American kind of settlement, in which you have 40-50% of the debt to the West in one way or another de facto written off, is possible. All this is difficult, but it is more boring and tedious than impossible, if one has peace and a situation in which people think it is worthwhile making an investment. In terms of models, turnpike models, simple rapid growth models are much of a muchness, whether they are Leninist New Economic Policy models or the old joint venture colonial models. This applies to all growth models whether they are by Feldman, the intellectual side of the Soviet five year planning or by Harrod-Domar, who certainly could not be accused of being Marxist in the normal sense, or by Mahalanobis which is in between.

But what none of them do is show the slightest interest in the livelihoods of the absolutely poor people. That is their one common characteristic. Rehabilitation, in the sense of livelihoods as opposed to the reconstruction of physical assets, remains an oddity. You might get certain aspects of this mentioned in a fairly straight-forward economic policy model; Bukarin and Lenin were at least interested in fair numbers of the peasantry because the opposite policy was so disastrous. And you might get something out of the World Bank neo-liberal model. The only snag is that, when you put them together, the particular ways of dealing with the absolute rural poor cancel themselves out, so you get the worst of both worlds. You end up with looking at things like the Bank's long-term perspective study for Africa - its poverty reduction handbook, or the papers of the Government of Mozambique - that are simply not models for raising rural livelihoods. You might claim that you have one in Botswana, but this is unhelpful because in Botswana the elite is rurally based; so it is prudent to follow a livelihood model: the macro-economic policy is always shaped by social and political reasons.

So, quickly, today Angola is not a middle-income country. It could get back to it after two or three years of peace, yes. Secondly, there just aren't any functioning rehabilitation-orientated models going; Leninist and neo-liberal models are much of a muchness. They all think that the rehabilitation of the poor people, especially in rural areas, is irrelevant. It was once said "what was wrong the potato famine in Ireland was that it did not kill enough Irish people to make the place viable"! Growth models are like that. So the greatest challenges to the Angolan economy, from the point of view of whatever government emerges in peace, is what their view is on rehabilitation, as opposed to maximisation of growth; and regional involvement outside, as opposed to from within, is a couple of years down the road from that, and really does turn on the energy sector, petro-chemicals to hydro-electricity.

Patrick Chabal:

Thank you all very much. We must break for refreshments now and we are due to restart at 11.30 for the next session.

The youthful face of the informal economy

Photograph by Zed Nelson

Session 5

Rebuilding Community at War: a Test Case

Catrin Schulte-Hillen

Rae McGrath

Sue Fleming

Teresa Santana

Reconstruction and the role of non-governmental organisations in this process was the organising theme of session five. It was a huge area to try to break down into three topics. We approached this problem by settling for one speaker who would talk on immediate humanitarian relief in Angola; we were lucky to get the globe-trotting and immensley busy Catrin Schulte-Hillen from Médecins Sans Frontières, an agency with a reputation for fearlessness and going it alone. One speaker would talk about a huge obstacle to the reconstruction of communities in Angola – the problem of unexploded mines. After watching a recent World in Action's programme we contacted Rae McGrath, Chairman of the Mines Advisory Group; a charity involved with sending experts around the world to defuse mines and to train local people in this difficult and dangerous task. A third speaker would then address the question of long-term development projects in Angola and the need to safeguard this type of work despite the conflict. Sue Fleming, an anthropologist agreed to cover this topic, having had experience of working in Angola with ACORD, a British NGO pioneering participatory local development schemes.

We had always intended that this session would open with the testimony of an Angolan who could tell the audience about Angolan initiatives in this broad area, so that there would not be just white representatives from the Western liberal humanist elite. On the advice of Raja Jarrah from ACORD and Paul Robson, from One World Action, we contacted Fernando Pacheco, Director of a small Angolan NGO. He found the means to travel to Cambridge but we later made the difficult decision to give him a higher profile slot with the politicians in the hope that he would represent civil society and say from the perspective of a person involved with development, why Angola mattered. So, it was unsurprising therefore, that on the eve of the first day of the conference, when we talked with some of those people who were Angolan and heard about the conference only days before but had immediately put everything to one side to attend, they complained that they did not have a voice and found it difficult to articulate their views from the floor, and we both agreed to give one person a slot in this session, in place of Pacheco. It was a decision that provoked criticism but it did nevertheless transform this session and even the rest of the workshop into a forum where the people could speak.

One very important debate surfaced. The previous day, Victoria Brittain had criticised some NGOs for being tools of a war-machine; for allowing themselves to be the life-blood of UNITA by providing aid to people under UNITA control when UNITA was incapable of doing so. Her argument was that this gave support to this organisation and therefore enabled it to carry out more violent acts against innocent civilians in the long-term. Chris Aldrige, at that time working for Save the Children defended the NGO right to humanitarian intervention wherever lives are at risk.

Clearly, as Angola illustrates, NGOs are now involved with political disasters in Africa. Their privileged status from their traditional roles as emergency relief organisations has enabled them to amass new functions, from shaping international public opinion to lobbying governments and the UN to take political action. But as Angola illustrates, they are being drawn into the cycle of violence on the ground. Now that NGOs have taken over many of the functions which were previously the exclusive monopoly of governments, it becomes more urgent than ever to identify and confront the contradictions involved in humanitarian intervention.

Introduction from the Chair

Joanna Lewis, Chair:

(Research associate at the African Studies Centre, conference co-organiser.)

I ought to start as Marco Ramazzotti urged us all to do yesterday, by saying why Angola matters to me. On a personal level, I have been moved by the plight of ordinary Angolans and repulsed by the horrors modern warfare inflicts upon civilian life. On a professional level, Angola matters to me as a historian of colonial empire researching rehabilitation strategies during the Mau Mau uprising in Kenya. I believe Angola stands as a crucial test case in rebuilding society and in remaking communities during and after prolonged violence and civil conflict. Our next set of panelists will, I am sure, illustrate this point by talking about different aspects of this challenge.

First, we are extremely fortunate to have with us today, Catrin Schulte-Hillen from Médecins Sans Frontières, who was in Angola as recently as January. Secondly, we have Rae McGrath from the Mines Advisory Group, an NGO whose work was featured in a recent World in Action programme. Thirdly, we have Sue Fleming, a rural development consultant. And, in a late change to the programme, Teresa Santana wants to tell you, as an Angolan living in Britain, why Angola matters to her.

Obviously there are problems in trying to cover in 90 minutes a topic which could legitimately devour a single workshop in one go. And this is something NGO representatives here today may like to explore with us later. *(Angola 95: the road to peace, a seminar hosted by the African Studies Centre on 7th April 1995 was largely a continuation of the concerns expressed in this session)* At one end of the spectrum of recovery in Angola, we have long-term issues of reconstruction, rehabilitation and demobilisation which Professor Green raised in his paper this morning. How to set in motion a self-sustaining programme of livelihood reconstruction that will lift 6 million Angolans out of absolute poverty? And such a policy in Angola has an extra set of constraints, among them war, an elitist oligopsony, and enough primary source wealth to ensure an immediate GDP recovery that does not require initial livelihood recovery. Somewhere in the middle of this spectrum of recovery, we also have efforts needed to rescue civil society, which Fernando Pacheco from ADRA told us about yesterday. And then there is the more abstract issue of how to nurture democracy and tolerance.

Finally, at the opposite end of the spectrum in Angola, we have the brutal reality of a conflict which produces victims like 10-year old Wilson Msungo, featured in Jenny Barraclough's recent documentary for Channel Four entitled Angola's Lost Children. We watched Wilson languishing in a hospital that has no drugs, no anaesthetic, no blood, often no electricity; bodies putrefy on the wards. Angolan Save the Children workers manage to trace his mother who travels to Luanda for the first time only to find her first-born son with barely enough energy to die. He has anaemia, under-nourishment, severe osteomyelitis and now septisemia, for when she gently lifts the sheet that covers him, she finds that what remains of her son's legs lie in makeshift splints with a crude catheter in between. And Wilson has to endure his pain for another eight cruel weeks. I have not seen anything quite so upsetting.

But providing so-called humanitarian relief in similar situations in Angola is not above criticism as we heard yesterday. So I would like now to ask Catrin Schulte-Hillen who works for an organisation not unused to a bit of controversy, to begin this session.

Catrin Schulte-Hillen – Médecins Sans Frontières:

(Since October 1992, Catrin Schulte-Hillen has held the position of Project Manager for MSF-Spain's programmes in Kenya, Somalia, Tanzania and Angola. She trained as a midwife in Germany and the United States, holds a Master's in Public Health and is a qualified epidemiologist and statistician.)

Catrin Schulte-Hillen – "solidarity with victims"

I would like to give you a very brief description of the organisation and then enter into the necessities, possibilities and difficulties of humanitarian aid in Angola. MSF was created by doctors who had been working with the Red Cross looking at the possibility of creating a structure independent of government: to create an NGO that is in some ways private but does not look for any profits. We have been in existence for 23 years now. MSF based its principles of work on operational independence and political neutrality. One of our main aims is to create solidarity with victims.

MSF has been working in Angola since 1983; and since then it has been working in zones controlled by the MPLA government and by UNITA. The main activities I supervise in Angola are medium-term programmes, which deal with a range of medical structures that give basic medical care to a large population. These medium-term activities also allow a monitoring situation which means the teams in the field are capable of seeing what is going on on the ground, and are then able to intervene in emergency situations such as malnutrition, epidemics, outbreaks etc. MSF has as its speciality and is very well-known for emergency interventions. During the last year we have worked a lot on that and given a lot of attention to detail. Just to give you a short update: at the moment there are about 80 expatriates working in Angola, who work in 10 provinces in about 15 different projects. These are quite equally distributed between areas controlled by the MPLA and by UNITA. Today, I will concentrate on giving an analysis of the difficulties that we encounter even working in Angola as an NGO; as an organisation which has as its principle, political neutrality and the freedom of action to decide where to intervene.

The organisation chooses its intervention sites according to the needs of the population, which means the population that is most affected, that has the most problems is the population we aim at. This has a considerable amount of operational problems which can be summed up in terms of access to the victims. I will summarise the main factors that intervene in this access. First, access can be viewed as a problem in terms of security. Access in Angola is nearly impossible on the road, which means that everything has to come by plane; but there are not airports everywhere. The roads are mined and many roads are in such a state that you cannot pass them even in a four-wheel drive vehicle. Too many places nobody has gone to in the last years. Access is possible to a lot of cities but there are still problems.

Apart from the security problem, the logistics also create a financial problem. Flight is extremely expensive. Going from the capital Luanda to the southern part of the country, just one flight, a plane with six people costs about $ 9,000. So the financial aspect is extremely important in this. Another aspect to the accessibility of a place is the permits, or the possibilities both the government and UNITA have in these countries of handing out flight and landing permits. Security in this sense is a major problem because the expatriates that we send into the field are running major risks not only because of mines, not only because of attacks, but also because, once working in the field, neither of the two sides that are implicated in the conflict in Angola, care if this humanitarian work is being carried out in the field: if a military attack is planned, it will go ahead anyway. So, on the operational side, these are the most important factors we have to contend with.

The accessibility of the population, accessibility in terms of security, finance and logistics, depend on three main factors. First, the opinion of the international community. Secondly, the government and the rebels. And thirdly, the relationships our organisation has with international agencies. Taking these one by one, the opinion of the international community is extremely important in relation to both the financial and political aspects. On the financial side up to now, there has not been a major problem in getting funding for humanitarian, especially emergency work in Angola. So until now, we have only run into some problems. In the future I'm not quite sure about it. On the political side I'm probably not the person to talk about this, so I'll just refer to what's been said before. The intervention that had been planned in the implementation phase, during and after the elections, clearly did not get the support it would have needed to have had a successful outcome. I think everybody agrees on that and it's a pity that the international community did not get involved to support longer-term work on Angola; a country that by that time had been at war for 16 years and had been under Portuguese control before. It needed more than one and a half years to establish its democracy.

The second factor I mentioned is the relationship an NGO has, or has to have, with the government and the opposition to call itself neutral. If we want to reach a certain population that is the most needy, we treat both sides in a politically neutral way; but it is not easy. To work on both sides is like walking on a razor blade. It presents a lot of security problems for the teams in the field, but it is also important because at this time in Angola the zones that are the most isolated are the zones that are under the control of UNITA. If we want to reach them, we need permits to fly out of Luanda from the Government and we need permits to land from UNITA, which means we need field contact. This field contact is always being misconstrued by the Government as taking part in the war. So even if we try to be present on both sides because both sides of the population have incredible needs, we're constantly being accused of not being impartial. Last month in the press, MSF Belgium was accused of forming part of UNITA, of working together with UNITA, which is not true. Their work at that moment was with UNITA because it was a very important intervention to help the Cuito area which had been isolated for eight months. Because of the relationship between the Government and UNITA over many months, a lot of the NGOs were not able to intervene because they didn't have the contact. Contacts with UNITA are difficult and you have to know them for a long time.

The third feature which influences operational factors is the relationship with the international agencies. In Angola this means the relationship with the UN agencies. A branch of the UN Department of Humanitarian Affairs called the UCA was formed to coordinate the different UN bodies in Angola, such as the World Food Programme, the High Commissioner For Refugees and UNICEF. In March of last year it suggested the possibility of coordinating the NGO efforts which meant signing not so much a contract, but an agreement that the NGOs would be coordinated by the Department of Humanitarian Affairs in Angola.

The MSF organisation did not sign this, and maybe this is the most important point of my talk and I'll explain why we did not. In the situation of a country at war, the main activities needed to get this country back to a reasonable level of peace are first, political solutions which are extremely long-term solutions because they have all the social and economic aspects in them. The political solution will finally lead to a peace that's definitely long-term. This is the field where the UN has its major mandate. The second phase or activity is on a medium-term scale and it has not been employed in Angola. This would be military intervention in terms of suffocating or freezing the war situation that's going on. The short-term activity which for us is the most important, is humanitarian aid. I see that in Angola these things that have a completely different duration have been put on the same scale. Things have been mixed up. Political solutions are being mixed with humanitarian actions. I find that extremely worrying and extremely dangerous, even knowing that a country will only find its peace in political solutions and knowing that humanitarian aid is only a band-aid on a deep wound. We should not allow humanitarian aid to be used as a means of procuring political solutions. (*Applause* ****)

Rae McGrath – Chairman, Mines Advisory Group

(Rae McGrath served eighteen years in the British army during which time he received awards for gallantry but not he claims for 'good conduct'. In 1990, he left his job as UN de-mining programme Director for Afghanistan after six months and ssubsequently set up the Mines Advisory Group which is funded by Norwegians and Swedes.)

Ladies and gentlemen, I suppose I am what Reginald Green would call a layman, and therefore I won't address the question why Angola matters, but why Angolans matter. There aren't, as we heard yesterday 1,000 people per day dying in Angola. Some days there are 320, some days there 1,230, some days maybe none, other days maybe 2,000. They are people. They are not political pawns. Let's just hear briefly about some of those people.

Matias José, age 41, he's a male. On July 30th 1993 he was farming a field near Lewana, Machico Province. Six other farmers were injured by mines in the same area and he lost his right leg. Lily Gomez, age 18. She was walking by the footpath with some other girls searching for food near Malange when she activated a mine. Several other people have been killed and injured in the same area in the past year. She had an above knee amputation of the right leg, severe fragmentation and burning to the left leg. Ampanela Rafael, age 12. On November 8th 1993 she was travelling on a crowded cart pulled by a tractor about 30 km from Milawai. The people were taking home their rice to Camacole when the vehicle hit a mine on an earth road. Ampanela does not know how many people were killed or injured but remembers that almost everyone lying around her seemed to be either dead or to have lost a limb. She was 12. Sevano Able, age 21. Total amputation of the right leg to the groin, left leg injured. On February 4th 1988 he was walking on a footpath near his village when he activated a mine. Francisco Dominguez Roseado, age 33. He just lost his arm. Just lost his arm were his words. And you understand why, for on November 7th 1993 he was loading cassava in a field near Ceswa in Mlange Province. He had just packed his cassava and was bending to pick his load up when he noticed a wire running through the grass. He pulled the wire and there was an explosion. Two men were killed instantly and two others were badly injured in addition to Francisco. They died later because they couldn't swim across the river that they needed to cross to get to the hospital.

Ladies and gentlemen, I'll finish this part of my presentation with Jaimé Milonga who had an amputation of the left foot. On 11th June 1993 James was playing with his sister next to his house in Chikala, Machico province. His father was also with the two children when one of the three stepped on a mine. Jaimé's father and sister were killed. Nine other people were killed in separate incidents in and around the village on the same day. Jaimé was aged 3. So it's not 1,000 people per day. It's not a statistic. These are people we are talking about.

So, I want to talk about mines and this is not some extension of military techniques. This is a real humanitarian issue which has an impact on almost everything that has been spoken about in this seminar so far, and yet so far I think, before my colleague from MSF spoke, I believe that the only time mines were mentioned was in one passing reference to amputees. I'm afraid that shows a **remarkable** lack of knowledge about the problems that face Angola, because rural rehabilitation cannot go ahead without effective mines eradication, because the people who live out in the fields and who live out in the countryside cannot exist unless mines are eradicated. And what you should understand is that if you think the situation is bad **now**, the lessons of Afghanistan, of Cambodia, of Kurdistan, of Iraq, of many other countries will tell you that it's only **after** a peace process that you begin to find out how bad the problem of mines is: when people really start trying to farm their land.

Rae McGrath – "no peace for many years to come"

In Milange, Médecins sans Frontières Holland is running a feeding programme for a population which includes 12,000 under-five-year-olds. The World Food Programme ships 30 tonnes of food per day to the city on average but the estimated requirements are actually three times that amount. And that means that people living in Milange, in the city, have to go out into the countryside to look for food. And to do that, they have to negotiate a three kilometre belt of mines. They are regularly blown up. The hospital regularly accepts as many as five civilian mine casualties per day. On exceptional days, they have as many as 25 casualties. Not only are the people moving out from Milange, to go out into the country side to look for food, because not enough is coming in, but people outside the city, who hear that food is being delivered to the city are negotiating the same mine fields in the opposite direction, in the hope of receiving food aid. And that is the situation in the major towns and cities.

So what are mines? Well, not courtesy of Marks and Spencers, here are an assortment. *(At this point Rae bring a collection of mines out of a carrier bag and tips them slowly onto the main conference table provoking gasps from the audience, especially Angolans who associate them much more vividly with human destruction)* I think it's important that you know what mines are. These are real anti-personnel mines. They come in many shapes and sizes. *(One or two Angolan members of the audience approach the table tentatively to take close-up pictures).* They have in common one thing: that these weapons, when there is a peace process, begin a totally new war. These weapons cannot go back into the armoury just because UNITA, the MPLA, the UN and the international community decide that war is over. Once these things are laid they will remain there either until somebody stands on them and sets them off or until they are destroyed by a properly constituted and organised programme of eradication. And it will take years. So when gentlemen, you have your peace process, when you finish talking, remember that will be the day when the new war starts, for those who can't afford to come to Cambridge for this kind of seminar.

Now, who has laid these mines? Where have they come from? Well, it's not an indigenous problem, because landmines have been laid for three decades not just by Angolans but by Portuguese, Cubans, South African forces, and by a smattering of cowboy soldiers from around the world who have gone there to help one side or another. And the mines have come from South Africa, Russia, United States, France, Portugal, Czechoslovakia, Italy, France, Yugoslavia, United Kingdom, Belgium, China and many other countries. In fact, the only truly indigenous factor about this problem is that the people who stand on them are Angolans. All the people who get blown up by them are poor. And they also have in common the fact that they cannot have access to the media to tell them about what's happening to them.

The next question is what can by done about it? Well, we can throw our arms up in the air and say this is terrible. It's one of these awful tragedies. It's a hangover from war. In actual fact, eradication of landmines is quite a specific and detailed technical task. It can be done but it must be done with planning. It can be done and the planning must be done by people who understand that engineering task; and I would address first the UN by saying that if you are going to build bridges it is not really likely that you will have a good bridge building project by having people to plan it who read books about bridges, but have never actually done anything but walk across them.

So far we have had three major operations to clear land mines. In Afghanistan, it started very well. Unfortunately now more people are being blown up by mines, not in Kabul, but in so called peaceful areas, mostly refugees entitled to the protection of the international community, and they are being blown up on a regular basis, in far greater numbers than at the height of the war in Afghanistan. In Cambodia, the UN operation has wound down to some extent. C-MAC was taken over and funding is not as easy to obtain as everyone promised originally. In Northern Iraq, in Kurdistan, the UN hasn't managed to get around the problems of having to work with Baghdad, and so it's left to my own NGO to clear mines in northern Iraq and Kurdistan. But the problem is that, when you look at what is happening in Mozambique, you can understand that the focus is on clearing the infrastructure. The focus is not based on rural reconstruction and rehabilitation. It is focused on clearing mines from roads, from bridges, from electrical powerlines, from industrial centres, from airfield perimeters and railroads. All very important. But what's the point of doing that, if you can only drive down the roads to fields that are mined?

In Angola today you have a situation that is so serious, just purely because of mines, that we cannot wait for the politicians. First of all there is a need for investment in immediate country-wide community awareness, not to teach people **not** to stand on mines, because no one does it deliberately, but to teach them to live and exist with the threat of mines. Secondly, we must teach people to farm in a mined environment. But before the peace process, which we all hope will come, is formulated, we can't allow this kind of tragedy to continue. And so, UNITA and MPLA must co-operate with organisations like the Mines Advisory Group in allowing us to put civilian safe-lanes into these major mine-fields that are killing so many civilians. **There is absolutely no military reason why marked safe lanes cannot be put in.** It would give military advantage to neither side and if you are serious about representing your countrymen, then this should not even be a question about whether you allow it.

Finally, when the ceasefire is agreed, the UN and NGOs experienced in this kind of work must work together to develop a funding base for a surveyed and identified task force, **not** to open a training school, **not** to hand out commercial contracts and ask someone to do a survey to find out how serious the problem is. I would suggest that if you ran an agricultural programme like that, people would lock you away in an asylum.

Then demobilisation. Trainees must be taken from demobilised soldiers and given paid jobs, and obviously only volunteers, to work in mine clearance. It's something they are particularly suited to and it's worked very well in other countries. And then, there must be ongoing, specialist support and monitoring of regional and central record keeping, to ensure that this process goes ahead. The aim must be to establish an indigenous Angolan capability to deal with the long-term problem of mines in Angola. What that will take is an international and indigenous political will to deal with this problem; and a failure to do it will ensure that you won't have peace, because the poor will continue to be massacred. And although on paper you may have a peaceful country, in practice, for the people who live and are trying to exist in the countryside, there will be no peace for many years to come.
*(Thunderous applause ******)*

Sue Fleming – Manchester University:

(Sue Fleming, a social anthropologist, is an Honorary Research Fellow at the International Development Centre, University of Manchester. She worked extensively in Angola in the early 1980s. More recently she has worked as a consultant to various NGOs involved with development.)

Nurturing Grass-Roots Development in Angola

It is hard to follow such an impassioned plea. I would just like to add that I used to live in the Solomon Islands and there are people there still dying from unexploded bombs and hand-grenades that were planted during the Second World War. This is a terrible problem.

Sue Fleming – "more power to the local level"

What is Grass-Roots Development?

In grass-roots development **people** matter and it is what people say that counts. The term covers different ideas and practices associated with the 'local', the 'community', people within their neighbourhoods and workplace. Grass-roots refer to the people at the 'bottom' as distinct from the decision-makers at the 'top'. Donor agencies give funding for grass-roots development, often called community or social development or 'people's' development. This is usually small-scale in character with some form of local management, and so involves different degrees of 'participation' by the community.

Differences in participation are more than questions of style, they are fundamental to any philosophy of grass-roots development and distinguish types and practices. The World Bank, for example, promotes community initiative and local self-reliance, usually in the context of community resources for the provision of social services (health, education and water), as well as credit and savings. In this context grass-roots development is part of privatisation and reducing the role of the state.

The World Bank and some agencies also talk of a 'bottom-up' approach, of empowering through grass-roots NGOs but with the community as beneficiaries, receivers, not designers and owners of programmes. Here community policy-making is either limited to the management of the communities' own resources, or it is about implementing outside resources efficiently. It is about defining how the cake is eaten, not the type of cake, the size of cake or if cake was wanted at all. Other agencies, especially the more developmental NGOs, see empowerment through grass-roots development as promoting self-determination and enabling democratic processes.

The basic tenets of an effective grass-roots development are:

- consultation, where local people's priorities are the basic development needs. This means consultation processes are open to all. Public forums, for example, may be inadequate especially if women and young men are unable to fully participate;

- respect and value for local knowledge and skills; local people as experts, which means that solutions are decided locally, discussed in the local language;

- local organisation as the basis of local management and control, and the partner for development agencies' work. The development of local organisation is a legitimate development objective.

The Angolan Experience

There is little in Angolan history that has supported grass-roots development. The mass organisations of the party were tightly controlled by a centralised bureaucracy. There was paternalism in the state's attitude and work with the peasantry. Changes in the late 1980s revalued peasant systems of production and local knowledge. There was talk of agricultural development based on an exchange between local knowledge and the extension messages of the state. The Institute for Agrarian Development (IDA) was organised as a semi-autonomous organisation to respond to peasant needs and the National Union of Peasant Associations (UNACA) was formed.

Despite these intentions it was difficult to transform the centralising habits of government and party. There was little in-country experience and no models to follow; the task of retraining rural extension workers and their supervisors and managers was immense. Luanda bureaucracies found it difficult to relinquish control to the provinces, likewise provinces to districts and so on. The capacity of provincial and district levels of government was limited and uneven.

The experience with the setting up UNACA showed the difficulty government and party had letting go of control. On one hand there was a concerted and lengthy effort to involve the grass-roots. The processes of forming UNACA included 954 municipal level and 18 provincial level constitutive conferences, resulting in the national conference in 1990. The whole process was presented as something which involved the democratic participation of peasants. But the Party was the major player, their direction was seen as essential in providing both assistance and incentives, although this was intended to be without paternalism and interference. The statutes were defined from the Party perspective, with UNACA as a mass organisation to defend the interests of the Angolan peasantry within the Party political framework, yet the creation of this organisation was pluralistic, and clearly seen as contributing to the process of democratisation in Angola.

Economic Biases

Perceptions of the economy and economic development have focused on large-scale and export production. Colonial policy, for example, did little to encourage the peasantry. Land concessions, the labour market with its forced labour system and agricultural research, training and inputs favoured the large farm sector. Post-independence agriculture focused on the production of export crops through state farms and production cooperatives. It was only after 1980 that the peasant and small-scale private farmers were given increased support.

In 1988 the first structural adjustment package was introduced beginning with stabilisation measures focusing on budget and balance of payments deficits. The adjustments restricted public sector borrowing, emphasised Angolan and foreign private investment, and included devaluation, liberalisation of prices, imports and access to imports. Fiscal policy meant a cutback in government employment and services. These policies give a bias against small-scale operators in access to markets, foreign exchange, credit, inputs and knowledge.

Non-Government Organisations

A more substantial experience with grass-roots development has come about from the late 1980s onwards, through contacts and links with international NGOs, backed with donor agency support. This has stimulated the formation of local NGOs and encouraged development agencies and communities to rethink and rework the established tradition, moving from a top-down to a locally defined development. Opportunities for this widened considerably with the peace agreement in 1991, but the peace was short-lived, with the onset of the post-election war at the end of 1992, and many projects were forced to relocate or close down.

The following examples of grass-roots development work gives an idea as to the scope and range of experiences in Angola. In contrast to the widely held belief that grass-roots development is impossible in situations of war and emergency, many projects have continued through the renewed fighting. Some, in the peri-urban areas of Luanda and government-held cities and towns, or in safe rural areas have not needed to change their working method or objectives. Others have changed location and emphasis as the communities they were working with became displaced because of war.

Development Workshop has been working in peri-urban Luanda focusing on community-based water, health and sanitation programmes. One, Sambizanga Community Sanitation and Upgrading Project is a pilot project in Ngola Kiluange, a shanty town on the northern edge of Luanda. The project focuses on preventive health care through a network of community workers drawn from local community groups. Technical skills in water and sanitation are balanced with negotiating and liaison skills for the community so they can make demands on government authorities.

ACORD also works in peri-urban Luanda, in Viana II a settlement of displaced people of over 500 households. The project, through participatory research and programming, began with low-cost housing moving on to the provision of water supply. There are currently ten locally managed community water points. Other work includes the building of a health post, school, vegetable plots and tree-planting. There has also been discussion about forming an artisan association. The project has been assisting people to organise their documentation. Displaced from the rural areas in particular are rarely on any register and documentation is a pre-requisite for many official dealings such as opening a bank account and enabling your children to matriculate from school.

ACORD work in Kaluquembe, Huila Province along with ADRA, an Angolan NGO helping to reintegrate displaced people. The programme, drawn up with the community, covers rural credit, agricultural tools and health, establishing at the same time local management structures. This work has been suspended because of the renewed fighting.

UNICEF has worked in Chibia, Huila Province, through the IDA structure at municipality level, reorienting the work of rural extension to respond to peasant needs and requests. They have also worked with a displaced people's camp, Vimilapaso, near Benguela, building on local survival strategies on sporadic food aid. These proposals included negotiations for more land for farming, for irrigation technology, and for individual rather than collective farming of available land.

FOS, a Belgium NGO, has been working with school kitchens in the peri-urban area of Lubango. These are run by parent committees, using emergency food for the first six months then moving on to local food production and contributions from parents. The work in Quipungo, outside of Lubango has had to stop due to the fighting.

Oxfam has been working in Benguela Province, often with joint funding with other agencies. Rather than importing teams to bore the wells, where skills would remain outside the area, Oxfam chose to improve water supply through the local digging and protecting of wells. By using more appropriate low-cost easy maintenance technology backed with training of people from the displaced and/or settled communities, knowledge and skills were built in the community. Oxfam's work with mainly displaced people in Dombe Grand focuses on agriculture production with seeds, credit, technology and access to technical advice and land. Oxfam works with the Institute for Agricultural Development in some of its work, and directly supports the development of Angolan NGOs, funding salaries and running costs.

What can be learnt from these experiences?

Grass-roots development is an approach, a method. It is about the process of change, and applies in any context, cutting across the divisions of emergency, rehabilitation and development aid. These divisions can be particularly artificial in Angola, where war reaches into every corner. Communities outside of the fighting zones experience the direct effect of war as they receive the displaced or, with peace, the demobilised.

What does this mean in practice, especially with the huge emphasis on humanitarian aid? For emergency situations it means using food aid to help people re-establish their life, with food for work being food for their own work. It means recognising that the displaced have their own community and are part of wider social and kin networks, they have their own organisations. Grass-roots development builds this local organisational capacity to reduce vulnerability, through access not only to food and water, health and education but economic activity and basic livelihoods. A grass-roots development approach to emergency and would build on local survival strategies to enable self-sufficiency.

Non-government development agencies working with grass-roots development have been quick to point out the problems of top-down approaches to the displaced. ACORD, in a recent report, criticises the use of transit camps. "First of all it deprives the displaced of some of their basic liberties and generally makes them extremely dependent on the State structures and relief agencies. Secondly, given the precariousness of food distributions and its inherent paternalism, the "hand out" mentality is greatly reinforced and traditional coping mechanisms are destroyed. Thirdly, the "transit camps" generally turn out to be relatively permanent camps, with minimal conditions and practically no attempt to encourage the displaced to find other economic survival activities".

There are wider development implications to grass-roots development. There is a need to look at the way grass-roots development can impact on mainstream, top-down development projects. For example, Oxfam raised the problems surrounding the proposed World Bank project in Lobito which aims to develop community stand pipes through private management, and assumes user capacity to pay. The proposal has been drawn up without consulting the population, and has not brought in existing experiences with peri-urban community-based water supply.

Grass-roots development implies fundamental shifts of power. This means a serious and meaningful decentralisation where decision-making is brought closer to the local level. A decentralisation not just to provinces, but down to the grass-roots. *(Applause **)*

(See page 186 for notes on further reading)

Teresa Santana – Angolan Community in the UK:

(An Angolan student living in London, Teresa Santana is a member of the Angolan Community in the UK organisation. Ms Santana delivered a remarkable speech reading from her notes written overnight , replete with the dramatic pause, a varying voice tone and barely controlled emotion.)

I would like to say thank you for having a chance to stand here and say why Angola matters. At this conference you have been witnessing different points of view of the Angolan conflict. We can summarise them as follows. For some of the participants it is the economic potential and the strategic position of Angola that makes it important. To others it is their own personal and emotional feelings that matter. Others are moved by philanthropic reasons. For others here on behalf of the international organisations like the UN, for them Angola is a test-tube to be used for experiments which may or may not be applied in other areas of potential conflict. Others have expressed the view of naked greed for power. Also, there is an attempt to show the view of so-called civil society based on the self-respect and identity of that civil society. These are the views so far expressed in this forum. On the other hand what has been absent from this conference is a collective will of the Angolan people. We have had centuries of historical opposition and resistance. Moreover, during the last three decades we have always tried to express their views. But even in this forum we have been deliberately undermined, ignored and distorted.

For a simple ordinary person like me, without academic capabilities and expertise so well demonstrated by the interventions in this forum, we know that it is irrelevant in the power decision-making structure in the world today whether or not the Angolan people have or have not something to say about themselves. Yet it is their sovereign right to choose their future. So, a place in this forum is not seriously considered for us to raise our voice. I would not be so naive to expect that every individual should be asked to speak for themselves, especially since leading representatives have been invited to do so on our behalf. I may say, there are not enough.

I would like to remind everyone who is interested in Angola, whoever they may be, that in Angola the independent representation of civil democratic institutions has not yet happened. Those who try to make out that democracy is there should know better and sell their wares in another market, because we have learned the hard way, and had enough. I may not have the clarity and fluency to expose my views in a more elaborate or 'scientific' way - I leave it for them

Teresa Santana – "normal lives?"

to do so. What we want to get across is our message coming from the hearts of millions, of thousands of mothers, children, young and old men and women of Angola; and that is very simple, JUST STOP THE WAR IN ANGOLA. Because the reason that it is still going on has nothing to do with us. Even the artificial finger-pointing against the actual belligerents in Angola's so called 'civil war', as much as it can stir our consciences, will not make any difference to us as a people.

Yesterday, at the end of the workshop I had a quick talk with the Ambassador to Angola from the United Kingdom, Mr Richard Thomas, and it is quite amazing to recall what he said to me, when I asked him some questions on the policies adopted by the British government concerning the diaspora of Angolan citizens all over the world. I said some of them left the country for fear of persecution, and he answered that people in Angola are living normal lives; there is no reason for anybody to leave the country for whatever reason because there is freedom in Angola; and yes he is right where the British government is concerned. Yet I can't abstain from commenting on the words 'normal lives'.

It has been said here by almost all individuals that the Angolan conflict has been the worst in the world, where more than a thousand people die every single day. It has been said here that millions in Angola are affected by extreme poverty and starvation. We are one of the countries in Africa in which agricultural capacity is so promising that normally we starve ourselves to death. It has been said that our infrastructure is completely destroyed and yet we still have the capacity of leading normal lives. We live in a state of fierce war and yet we still have plenty of democracy, in spite of the militarisation of the country, with the obvious restraint of civil liberties and whatever scare there might be that this kind of situation brings to the everyday lives of the ordinary citizen. We are now transformed into beggars in order to survive and yet it is normal to do so as a society. We are living in fear every day, of everything and anything, and when we manage to get out of the country unlike thousands of our young men, to avoid this senseless war, we are classed as a nuisance, labelled as economic migrants. We are one of the richer nations in Africa, but we have been made or labelled economical migrants who are going to eat up the contributions of the British taxpayer.

Of course Mr Ambassador we are leading 'normal Lives' in Angola, so there is no reason to worry about migrants from Angola. We are dying for lack of very simple medicines like painkiller; doctors have not been able to perform their duties, because the hospitals lack the most simple equipment such as syringes and gloves. Others have lost their jobs or are kept in a position of non-official dismissal but barred from performing their duties for expressing political opinions that may not be appreciated by their employer, without any institution to defend their rights. Yes we really do have such 'normal lives'. So 'normal', that it's normal to deny our rights as a nation and as people in every possible way or even impossible way, as zeros.

Getting back to the question why Angola matters, I could outline an endless pile of reasons to please everyone but the only reason that Angola really matters is because there are people there, which gives meaning to Angola to exists. Angola is not a piece of land lying there, plenty of diamonds, petroleum, crops, iron, zinc, copper, etc. etc. for the multi-nationals to harvest from a no-man's land. Those minerals and riches belong only to the Angolan people, as it has been deliberately forgotten here. Angola only exists because its people made it and nobody else has the right to claim what is ours, by birth, sweat, blood, sacrifice and the legitimacy as citizens of our own country and the world. That is what matters.
(*Applause******)

Open Session

Pastor Cumandala (Friends of Angola):

I was really very sad last year when I saw Americans fixing their satellite dishes when we in Angola cannot even afford bread for all of our people and in Luanda there are people who live on rubbish dumps. That really upset me. But this morning I find some hope. I have to admit that this session was the best part of the conference. We are moving forward towards finding a common ground where Angolans can come together in agreement.

I would like to say something about the so-called international arms trade. It may explain why the Angolan conflict is still going on. As we heard here, we don't make the weapons in Angola. I want to call on the Angolan politicians to stop buying weapons, using our money to buy those weapons; because I don't believe there is a Western power forcing our Government to buy these weapons that the MPLA and UNITA are using to kill our people. So this conference must address this. The West must prevent UNITA and the MPLA from buying weapons.

Adao Alexandre (Student, College of Ascension, Birmingham):

In Angola we have a saying about killing a snake from the tail. Here we have Americans and British. What are they doing exporting arms technology, if in reality they want to participate in peacemaking in Angola? Secondly, I wanted to ask if the British are aware of the number of companies in their own country that are exporting arms?

Tegegne Teka (Ph.D Student, Cambridge University):

I was moved by the last speaker on the platform and this has encouraged me to speak. It appears to me that both

Tegegne Teka

the MPLA and UNITA have changed sides. But it seems to me both are like caged birds, driven behind the scenes by internal power configurations. The people factor has never been mentioned. Now the lady has mentioned it succinctly and I thank her very much. This leads me to what I want to say. It happens now and then that the elite in the Third World, the middle-classes, the intelligentsia, fights for power in the name of the people, but the tendency is that gradually they will accommodate the demands of international capital. It will be the same in Angola. This is what I see.

Amir Attaran (Student, Oxford University):

I have a very quick question to ask the NGO members of the panel. Yesterday, we heard a journalist mention that there is a risk in carrying out humanitarian operations – specifically citing the risk of lending legitimacy to UNITA, though this could easily be turned the other way around – lending legitimacy to the MPLA. How do you answer that? Does it make you angry?

Joanna Lewis:

Are there any representatives from NGOs in the audience who would like to come in at this point?

Chris Eldridge (Save the Children Fund):

In answer to that question I would like to say that we would agree with much of what Victoria Brittain said yesterday; but we would disagree with her when she said that working in Huambo gives legitimacy to UNITA. There are a number of reasons for this. Firstly, we had a responsibility for our staff and secondly, to the people and children with whom we are working – two and a half thousand children in some feeding centres. Moreover, the Government that was elected in the elections was a government elected for all the people of Angola, not just some of the people, and therefore we have a responsibility, if we are working with the Government, to work also in other areas.

Thirdly, I would like to say that this links with the question of development. Relief cannot be divorced from this. Development is part of a process and we are there as intermediaries in a development process. That, we think, also requires a context, a context of peace. Peace does not come cheap. To paraphrase a previous prime-minister, there are no free lunches; there are no free peaces. And we feel that there should be far more money put together into the UN system. A parallel could be drawn with Cambodia (two billion US dollars) and with Somalia which shows that just money is not sufficient, for it was used wrongly there. And I would like to reiterate the paramount concern in these situations which is the primacy of independent and neutral humanitarian assistance. This should not be used for political ends and should not be hijacked as it was in Somalia by political and military prerogatives.

Finally, related to that point, I would like to say that peace costs money. There has so far been very little money put into the peace process. To paraphrase another person – peace needs to be given a chance. The UN needs to be given a chance. In the last few months, the UN has significantly improved its work, particular through Manuel de Silva, of the Department of Humanitarian Affairs, and we feel at the moment that there is a substantial chance for peace if there is vastly more money put into the UN system and support for the UN processes, than has so far been the case. *(Subsequent written comments from Save the Children on their work in Angola appear below pages 154-155)*

Tony Hodges (Economist Intelligence Unit):

We all agree, I think, that we need a civil society for rehabilitation and economic development. In many parts of Africa we have seen the development of grass-roots civil organisations, particularly in West Africa: Senegal, Mali, Burkina Fasso; some of them involving hundreds of villages. Are there any signs of such self-organisations developing in Angola, or, have the shocks to the society been so great, that it is virtually impossible under current conditions to envisage that kind of self-organisation?

The second aspect of this is that a free press is a vital element in the development of a strong and vibrant civil society in which people's views and opinions are freely expressed. Again there have been changes in legislation in the media in Angola. To what extent have we seen the real development of a free and urban media? If I can give one example which refers back to what David Birmingham said this morning, in a country like Mali there are no less than eight private radio stations. It seems to me that it is this sort of thing that Angola will desperately need in the future.

To what extent will it be possible after the peace settlement to shift or change the urban/rural balance that has become very heavily shifted towards the urban areas, as a result of the war. Between 15 and 20% of the population lived in urban areas in the early 1970s. At least I would think, 50% of the population are living in the cities now. Will it be possible to resettle these people back in the rural areas and what will it take to do it?

And finally, a question to the representative from Médecins Sans Frontières. She made the very correct point that it is a grave mistake to link humanitarian aid to political jockeying for position and negotiation. But she then tied that in to the UN, to the co-ordination of UN aid, as if the UN itself was trying to tie humanitarian aid in some way to the negotiations in Lusaka. Perhaps she could elaborate?

Joanna Lewis:

Well, we have Fernando Pacheco in the audience, the Director of ADRA, an Angolan NGO who spoke yesterday. Mr Pacheco would you mind saying a little about civil society in Angola from your perspective?

Fernando Pacheco (ADRA):

The bipolarisation of Angola is a potential evil that has to be fought against as a very first step in strengthening civil society. After 1990, I think space was opened up for organisations to operate that were independent and autonomous. Our position is not that we are anti-government, but we are non-governmental. *(On the spot translation provided by Patrick Chabal.)*

Kathryn O'Neill (Christian Aid):

I work for Christian Aid and I would like to add something in respect of what has been said about civil society in Angola. I think that something which has not come through in the discussions so far is this: Christian Aid works at the moment in Angola with local churches which, despite all they have been through during colonialism and under the MPLA, retain structures that reach down even to the village level. And I think, when looking at a solution in terms of reconciliation work and building a real and lasting peace, then the churches could play a key role in the future.

The other thing that I wanted to say is that in relation to international response to such huge needs, one of the things that is overlooked is the capacity of Angolan staff. There are Angolan staff that have been denied any education or training opportunities and that has to be a priority, rather than sending in international staff all the time. It is a philosophy that Christian Aid is beginning to approach and I think this is a key area that has to be strengthened. We can't just assume that the problems can be dealt with automatically by sending in more expatriates. I think it's very encouraging to hear what the Angolans have been saying here over the last two days and on a personal level, I hope that the politicians here actually take note of what has been said. *(Applause***)*

Diana Miller (Retired emigree living in Cambridge):

I wonder is it possible for you (Rae McGrath) to give us the name of firms who have made these landmines, especially those in this country, so that we may hold them responsible and make them pay for clearing up these mines? *(Applause*** and shouts in agreement)*

Antonio Neto (Angolan Democratic Party):

We think in Angola that the NGOs have a deep responsibility to support the push for peace in Angola. There is also a problem that there are Angolan NGOs that are growing in number and they must have as a common goal to contact and liaise with each other in order to find common ground.

My first question is to the lady from Médecins Sans Frontières. From time to time in Angola, you have got places where you can find a lot of medicine. If we send a letter to Médecins Sans Frontières saying that we have got people here that are gravely ill and we need medicine, we are refused. Maybe you have to adapt your work to the situation that exists in Angola. You don't get in touch with specific persons. You always deal only with the government. But what we can see is that these medicines are being sold in the black market.

Antonio Neto – "an ecological tragedy"

Secondly, I would like to say to my sister that we have been in exile for a long time in Europe, in Portugal, working for the support of the Angolan people. We in this country, may I tell you, don't agree with the criticism you have made of the Ambassador of the United Kingdom. We must at least understand that what we have to do for Angola is to organise ourselves when in the UK. If the Angolan people need clothes, medicines or cars, or what ever, political support, then organise yourselves first and be strong enough to give a contribution either to the MPLA and others, or to civil societies. Civil society is not divided into political parties. There is only a people that needs to be helped. It is important that nationalism is nationalism but not extra-nationalism.

Another point I would like to make is that when it comes down to the issue of mine eradication, I would like to say that if the people have been affected by the mines in Angola, then so too have the animals. Gorillas, elephants, lions have been blown up by mines and much wildlife has fled to Zimbabwe, Mozambique and other countries. This is another aspect of the tragedy. It is an ecological tragedy. *(The Chair at this moment could not fail to notice Professor Neto's pink and grey tie depicting large African elephants about to charge.)*

Finally, the Angolan government has an important duty in clearing landmines. It is important to do something and I have a concrete proposal. There should be video programmes made to show on TV about the mine situation in Angola and we should call on the UN that those governments responsible for allowing mines to be sent to Angola should be made to pay a levy so that the Mines Advisory Group could be funded to work with the Angolan government. But this programme must not include any military people, otherwise it will not succeed.

Antonio Fernandes (Angolan Ambassador to the UK):

I would like to say to the conference first, please don't allow the intellectual level to go down. I would like to say to my brother at the back, that it is high time for us Angolans to stop asking what Angola can do for us when we have not done anything for Angola ourselves. To Dr Neto I would like to say, please don't think that we want to put the blame on you for what has happened. We are the ones to blame.

To my sister, I would like to say that I was in UNITA for 28 years. And we are the people who fought against the government, against the Russians, against the Cubans for democracy in Angola. And if the country is not democratic today according to yourselves, we are the people who have to fight for it. This government here cannot give us democracy on a silver platter. We have to fight. We have to organise ourselves as our other colleague said, so that the present government which is the majority, which you think is not yet democratic, can succeed in implanting democracy in Angola; not come here and ask the British to give us democracy. They cannot do it. There are certain changes we can make in

Angola. We can tell the international community to leave us alone to see if we can succeed. We can come here and ask for help to feed our children, our poor people. And we can also go to the UN and ask for help to try to bring the two sides together. But not come here and ask the international community to save us. We, the people are the only ones who can save Angola. *(Applause ***)*

George Chikoti (Angolan Vice Foreign Minister):

It is very difficult being in the position on the one hand of a representative in the government and on the other, a participant in this workshop. I think that one of the most important aspects of this meeting is that we have to thank members of NGOs that work in Angola. I was very much impressed by the statement made on landmining. I was very much impressed with the talk from Médecins Sans Frontières. And I think the situation in Angola is a very critical one and I thank the international community for their participation. It is very very difficult to live in Angola right now. And I just wanted to thank Professor Neto as well who made some important points.

I think that Britain, and through Ambassador Richard Thomas, is one of the countries today that has given more donations to humanitarian aid. That is very important. And I think it is about thirty million. Ambassador Richard Thomas is one of the few ambassadors that has been to rural areas. He has been travelling in the countryside looking at initiatives which are not sponsored by the Government but where he thinks there is a possibility of responding to some of their needs.

But we think that as far as the whole process in Angola is concerned, it is very important to work for the consolidation of democratic institutions. We think that we have to start somewhere anyway, but we cannot abandon the responsibility we have. So we are here, in this open environment, and we will be in Angola trying to find solutions; and how these processes in their very initial stages can move forward to a more stable state. And we will be moving these stages forward with the help of the international community. It is very unfortunate that maybe people in London have difficulties. We are compassionate towards the problems they have and we should look at the whole nature of the problem and involve the international community in the solution. *(Applause**)*

Session 5 panelists face the audience

The Panelists Reply

Catrin Schulte-Hillen:

I would like to respond to three points. First, if working in the different zones was legitimising either the MPLA or UNITA. I think there is a clear answer to this. We work with the civilian population. And we have to work in communication with the controlling party. But that does not make us legitimising agents.

The second question was raised about my comments on the UN. I know at this time the UN is doing a very good job. But I would like to remind you of the situation in March last year, when, after signing the contract in Luanda, there were 65 NGOs which were paralysed. Yet they were capable of working. Having signed an agreement with the UN, they were paralysed, working on a global project in the country which I think was a good idea in principle. But for NGOs that are capable of having contacts about how to move in the field, they should have the operational freedom to go to places where the population is most in need. For example, Huambo. The people had suffered great wounds. We were too late going to that area, too late to help the people that had suffered the huge consequences of a fifty-five day war between UNITA and MPLA, until UNITA won the country and the city. We were not able to go there in time. So it is that situation I am addressing, Just leave the operational freedom to the people who take responsibility for going to places that might be unsafe.

The third comment I want to address is this one. I think there is a slight contradiction in Prof. Neto's position. It is usual to find donated material on the market being sold which is why we always monitor our own. We don't give donations to anyone without monitoring the use of the drugs to prevent them being sold on the market. But apart from that, you will always find drugs on the market, even monitoring them as best you can. I think it is the responsibility of the Angolan professional health staff to try to keep control of the keys to the pharmacies. So I would appeal to the Angolan staff to think about whether they want the medicines to be sold out in the sun in local markets by people not knowing how to apply them....*(The speaker is interrupted)*

Professor Neto:

Open a pharmacy. Then the problem will be solved. *(The Angolan Ambassador repeats the comment which the speaker could not hear clearly)*

Antonio Fernandes:

Open a pharmacy in Angola he means.

Catrin Schulte-Hillen:

I think that is the province of the Ministry of Health. You should open a pharmacy.

Sue Fleming:

I would like to emphasise two points which I think are very important. First the question of how do you channel resources into communities in these contested areas without feeding the war. I think the agencies involved have to think more about how to relate their support to the issue of sanctions. And they also have to reconcile their intervention in areas where Angolan NGOs have been prevented from entering.

There are two questions I would like to answer. The first one was the question of large umbrella NGOs – peasant associations in Angola. I think there's never been a chance in Angola to see what can happen. It was amazing to see that in the brief period of peace, there was an incredible growth of self-organisation and a number of institutional spinoffs. But we have never actually seen where it can go. The second question was about the urban-rural balance. From my experience in Mozambique, I can tell you that people are going back to their rural areas to live. They are definitely building big houses and they make it clear that they are going to settle there and farm. They might have relatives staying in the towns as a survival strategy, but it's very clear there is a move back to rural areas. Lastly, I wanted to support what Christian Aid were just saying about strengthening local capacity and that means strengthening the capacity of Angolan staff.

Rae McGrath:

First of all, the question I can answer simply is that we don't employ military personnel. All the other points circle around the supply of landmines and the culpability of landmine manufacturers. I think that you can't hold a British company guilty of shipping landmines, without holding responsible the Government that allows it licences, who is so careless in their control that they allow these shipments to happen. So, the Government must be culpable in that case. And of course, the British Government has rather a strange approach to landmines. At a recent UN General Assembly session, when the moratorium on trading landmines was introduced, initially the British Government was going to vote against this. But after almost international and complete astonishment at that stance, they then changed their minds, and voted for it, but added a clause to their vote, saying that because Britain had such strong and effective export controls on armaments *(derisory hoots from the audience)* that they did not feel bound by this vote. I refer you to the Scott Enquiry *(chuckles from British participants who recognised the reference to the scandal of government involvement in arms sales to Iraq)* .

As far as manufactures in the UK are concerned, there are three major manufacturers: Hunter Engineering; Thorn EMI; and Royal Ordinance. Royal Ordinance is particularly relevant to the Southern Africa situation. Royal Ordinance, prior to the elections, was pushing very hard to be involved in the clearance of mines. Not as a humanitarian gesture, but as a mines manufacturer, wishing to mop up some of the profits to be made from humanitarian funds, and also, one should remember, giving them a very good research and development programme as they were going along. *(tutting from audience)*. I believe that the granting of humanitarian funds to clear mines to mine manufacturers is obscene *(murmuring of agreement from audience)*. And the fact that a British company is involved in that kind of chicanery is disgusting *(shouts of yes from the audience)*. Companies must be held culpable and so must governments. I would also finally like to say to Angolan NGOs that I would urge you to join the international campaign to ban mines because you obviously have a lot of relevant things to say about the damage that landmines are doing to your country.. I certainly would encourage you to come to the second international conference in May and if you contact me, I will certainly do what I can to assist you in going to that conference. Thank you.

Teresa Santana:

First of all I really have to get guts to sit here and say what I just said. What I have to say to Mr Neto is just that I talk as a mother, as an Angolan, as a civilian. Why, when referring to Mr Ambassador, the British Government, do I have to be thankful and not criticise whatever they may do, because I have the chance to come here as a foreigner, so I must only say thank you and be silenced whatever I feel may be wrong? He said yesterday, and my comments were to those words "normal lives". If you have normal lives, I don't have a need to be here. Nor does any other Angolan. Nor would this conference be taking place. I am not addressing the British Government. I am addressing a very real situation.

It has been said here, by Mr McGrath, that there are too many amputees, too many children without limbs. Well, I might ask you all. These children, these people, could be you; could be anybody that is in Angola at the moment. So why is it wrong for me to come here and to say that people are not living 'normal lives'? I have been called ultra-nationalist. Maybe I am, I don't know. I am here just as a citizen. People have been leaving Angola for decades. It is true. People fought against the colonialists. It is true. That's why I'm here and why you are here. I am telling you that the Angolan people exist. That we have a reason to be. And that we matter. *(Long and loud applause for the panelists' replies *****)*

Joanna Lewis:

It just leaves me to thank you all very much....

(At this point the British Ambassador jumps up from his front-row seat, takes the mobile microphone, sits back down and starts speaking)

Richard Thomas (British Ambassador to Angola):

Sorry but could I please just explain and clarify this. I have taken a bit of a mauling this morning and I haven't enjoyed the experience. But, if it helps Angola, that's perfectly alright....

Joanna Lewis:

Well, only if you could be very quick as we are overdue for lunch.

(But a number of voices call out in protest at this deviation from the workshop's established rules)

One voice:

I don't think this is on.

Another voice:

No, it's not on. Nobody else is allowed to do it. Why should he?

Joanna Lewis:

I'm going to side with the majority view coming from the audience and I'm going to close this session. I would like to thank all the panelists for such an impressive performance this morning and you the audience, for giving them such good questions.

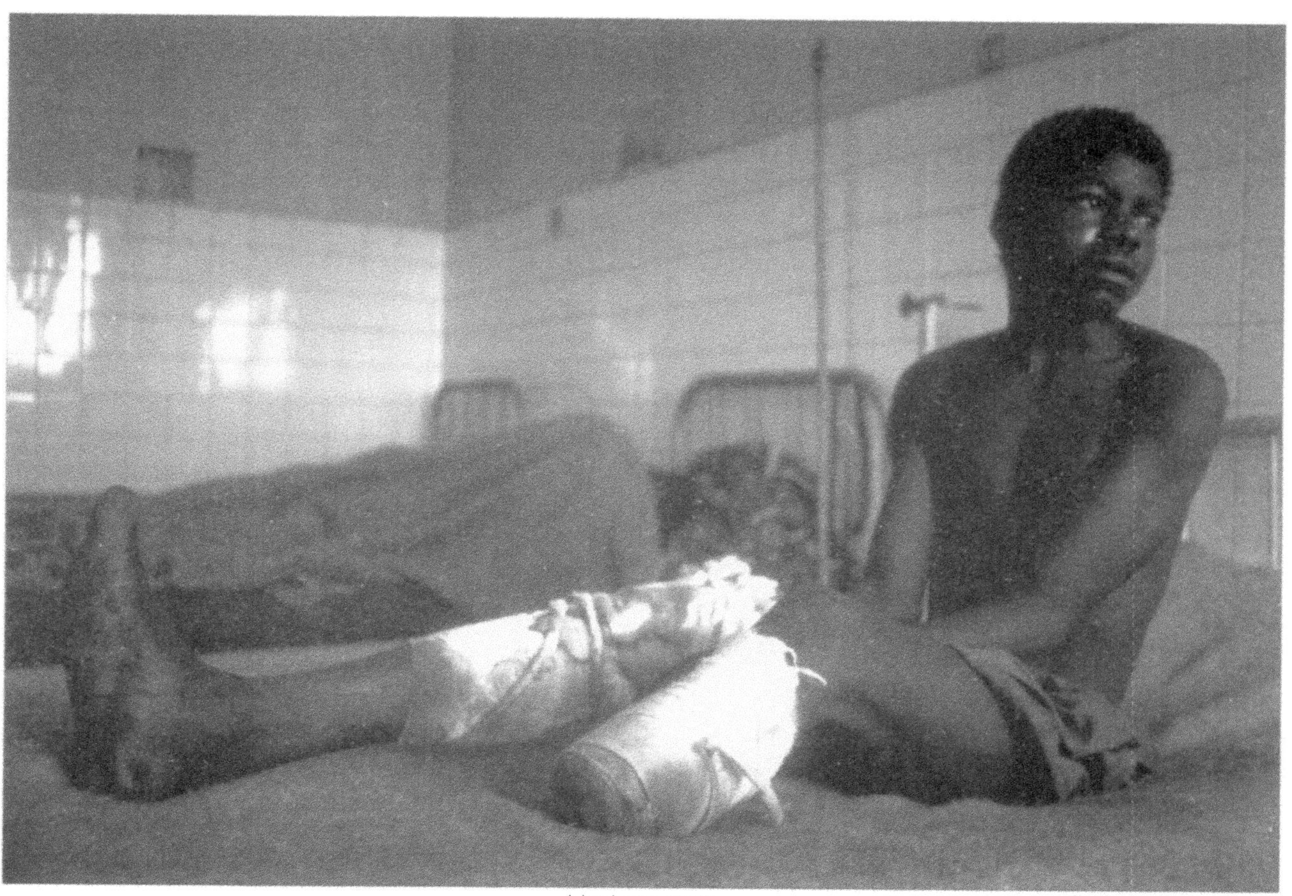

A land-mine victim Photograph by Zed Nelson

Session 6

Africa in the Media

Keith Somerville

Ahmed Rajab

Alex Holmes

Zed Nelson

After lunch, we trooped back to a packed library with the aim of addressing the issue of mass-communication between Africa and the wider world, using Angola as a pertinent illustration of this. We had an impressive line-up. Two different generations of media hands and, within each generation, two different experiences and perspectives. Keith Somerville and Ahmed Rajab have long careers in journalism, one in radio, one in print. One is white, the other black. Next contrast Alex Holmes and Zed Nelson, both at the beginning of their careers. The former makes programmes for a regular TV slot with the responsibility of keeping an audience of over five million watching each week. Meanwhile Zed Nelson is a free-lance photographer, hot-footing it around the world to create images that challenge stereotypes as well as recording what editors at their desks in Britain are looking for to nourish their readership. What this composition produced was two older hands offering penetrating critiques of Western media coverage, one historical, the other more polemical and contemporary, followed by two practical lessons in how Africa is recorded and packaged for a British audience: Alex Holmes talking us through specific programmes he had made on Angola and Somalia; Zed Nelson using photographs taken during his visits to the same two countries.

This neat arrangment however, was more the product of chance than of careful design. The panel had taken its final form only days before the conference started; and anyone contemplating organising a similar venture should bear in mind three things which we learnt the hard way. First, journalists are willing to talk but are often called away on assignments. We lost John Simpson and George Alagiah this way. Secondly, finding women journalists, and African women journalists in particular, is extremely difficult. In a male-dominated area, they are a rare breed indeed; so allow plenty of time for some hard searching. Thirdly, if there is any technical equipment to be used, do not allow academics to get involved with setting it up as this is a recipe for disaster. (Apologies again to Zed Nelson for the delay with the slide projector: those responsible know who they are!)

Introduction from the Chair

Keith Hart:

Welcome to what will in effect be the final session. We have a panel on Africa and the media and we are going to lead directly from this into the issue of what message we might want to send from this meeting to the rest of the world. At this stage I don't have any concrete plans to draft such a message because I don't want to spend the last part of our gathering bickering over words. However, we will face all that when we get to it.

The first item on the agenda is the question of communications. We have had an interesting group of sessions which have shifted in emphasis the political weight that might be given to different factors; and in this final session we again approach the issue of communication, how the professional media seek to bridge the gap between a country like Angola and a country like Britain. We have an interesting panel and we start with Keith Somerville.

Keith Somerville – BBC World Service:

(Keith Somerville was then Executive Producer of Current Affairs of the BBC World Service and soon after Editor of the The World Today and Feature Programmes. Before that he was deputy head of the Middle East and Africa section which published the daily summary of World Broadcasts.)

Africa and Angola in the 90s: Blank Pages for Western Writers?

Angolans danced in the streets of Luanda on 31 May 1991 to celebrate the signing of the peace accord which promised to bring an end to 16 years of brutal civil war and over 30 years of armed conflict. The deal provided for a ceasefire between the governing MPLA's forces and those of the rebel UNITA movement, for an 18-month transition period to multi-party elections and for a UN presence to oversee the processes of military disengagement, demobilisation and electoral preparation.

This long-sought agreement between bitter enemies was seen by Western observers as the latest episode in an unfolding political drama in southern Africa which had started with the quadripartite talks (Angola, Cuba, South Africa and the USA – with the Soviet Union as an active observer) on South African and Cuban disengagement from Angola and the independence of Namibia. Those talks had started in mid-1988 after a military stalemate was reached in southern Angola between Angolan-Cuban and UNITA-South African forces in and around the town of Cuito Cuanavale.

Flowing from those talks appeared to be a stream of internationally-assisted meetings, agreements and political advances which brought independence to Namibia, drew foreign forces out of Angola and encouraged the dialogue and eventual constitutional process in South Africa.

The rapid and positive political developments in Southern Africa coincided with, were influenced by and, in turn, had their influence upon a wave of democratic renewal in Sub-Saharan Africa. Domestic pressure groups suddenly were able to make their voices heard inside and outside Africa, calling for an end to one-man and one-party rule and for the development of participatory and plural politics.

Stepping back again to take an even wider view, commentators at the time saw Africa's politics taking shape against the background of the end of communism and one party rule in eastern Europe and of the end of the Cold War as the Soviet Union moved away from communism and confrontation and towards pluralism, private enterprise and international partnership.

As the African events unfolded, it was a common theme among Western journalists, writers and politicians to relate the democratic upsurge in Africa to what had happened in the USSR and eastern Europe. Just as teenage violence, crime and inexplicably anti-social behaviour is all too simply blamed on television, the cinema and video nasties, so the allegedly anti-social behaviour of African politicians and political systems could most easily be explained by portraying Africa as a blank page on which a variety of

Keith Somerville – "picture-led and soundbite obsessive"

foreign scribes had tried to write their stories, leading to a tangled jumble which had distorted Africa's development.

So developed the western policy of supporting the democratic upsurge in Africa blindly and with little examination of the individual circumstances of states, with no understand of the underlying political, economic and social processes at work in Africa and with an unshakable belief in the ability of Britain, France, the European Union and the United States to exhort and, if necessary, coerce African states into accepting change.

Never at the top of the political agenda for the West – despite periodic flurries of interest due to perceived 'Red threats' to western economic interests such as during the Congo crisis in the early 1960s and the southern Africa conflicts in the mid and late 1970s – Africa now sank to near the bottom of the agenda as the source of the main 'Red threat', the Soviet Union, disappeared completely. But some western politicians retained an interest and believed that they could push forward the democracy bandwagon at minimal cost and with minimal effort.

In the early 1990s, 'good governance' became the slogan for western dabbling in Africa. It was to be achieved by dismantling one-party states, holding internationally-observed multi-party elections and using western aid more efficiently. Countries which resisted – Kenya, Malawi and Zaire, for example – would be lectured, threatened and deprived of economic aid if they failed to follow the accepted formula of a constitutional conference, perhaps a referendum on multi-partyism and then elections monitored by international organisations. Democracy was to be introduced at a pace set, so western governments believed, by them and with all too little regard for the driving forces for change in African states, the need of their populations and their embryonic parties to develop their own approaches at their own speed and the need for domestic political forces to find common ground and consensus rather than have it thrust upon them.

The western attitude, adopted by governments and the press, was a very patronising one. States which moved quickly and in ways which suited western interests were praised and rewarded with meagre increases in aid (e.g. Benin, which elected a former IMF official as President), while the recalcitrant ones were deprived of aid (Kenya and Malawi). Western ministers took a very condescending view of offending states – when I was deported from Kenya in March 1991 to prevent me from interviewing democracy campaigners about the process of change, a British government minister told me that she would give the Kenyan High Commissioner a "slap on the wrist" next time they met.

This whole outlook was one that has proved ineffective, if not downright dangerous in Africa. It was based on the premise that the West knew best and that Africa lacked strong political and social dynamics of its own that would govern the process of change. Africa was the blank page and the West held the pen. The page had become blank when the effects of superpower competition had been erased.

I would not argue that Africa is in any way removed from the effects of the international political, strategic and economic environment in which it exists. Far from it. Africa's economic and military weaknesses have made it porous to foreign intervention – whether economic or military – and have rendered it politically vulnerable to outside interference. But it is not and has never been a blank page; and for all their meddling, the West or the superpowers have not been the determining factor in African politics since independence. They have been a distorting or divisive factor but not the final determinant of the course of events.

The rise in the democratic movements in Africa to a great extent pre-dated the end of communism and the fall of the Berlin Wall. Certainly as members of pro-democracy movements in Tanzania, Zambia and Zimbabwe told me in 1991 at the height of the democracy wave, the successes of the eastern European civil and political movements encouraged their counterparts in Africa, but they did not give birth to them. Similarly, western pressure for change was welcomed by many African civil rights movements but they did not believe that European or American encouragement for them or warnings to autocratic leaders were the answer to their political problems, they were just a part of the answer.

To return now to Angola, the naive belief in the political power of external forces over Africa led to the mistakes made in the international approach to the Angola peace and political process, to the unenlightened approach to Angolan events adopted by much of the international media and to the shock with which the descent back into civil war was greeted. Part of this immense misunderstanding in the West was undoubtedly due to the belief that the end of the USSR and the breaking of its hold on eastern Europe would undoubtedly destroy what credibility was retained by former Soviet allies –usually dubbed proxies or clients of the USSR – in Africa. Mengistu had fallen in Ethiopia (though, as it happens, brought down by a movement with a more rigidly socialist ideology than Mengistu adhered to himself), Benin's pro-Marxist leader, Mathieu Kerekou had been voted out of office and leaders from Benin to Zimbabwe were pulling back from their socialist rhetoric and policies. Therefore, it was only a matter of time before the MPLA in Angola was swept away – as quite obviously it had only been a stooge of Moscow and Havana and there was no indigenous constituency for it.

On the other hand, Jonas Savimbi of UNITA – dubbed by one journalist 'A Key to Africa' (something he has now effectively retracted) and by another 'the Gucci revolutionary'- was waiting in the wings. He still received $50m in US financial backing after the peace deal was signed and he had built, with US and South African assistance, a very slick propaganda machine. America, in particular, backed him to the hilt and would continue doing so until he finally showed them his true colours – though these had been all too apparent to some observers from the beginning.

So, a common view in the western media and in government was that the Cold War was over, the MPLA would eventually crumble and the charismatic Dr Savimbi would romp home. Democracy would triumph in the form of a UNITA victory or, in the worst-case scenario (to adopt a typical US view), a hung election result which would bring a government of national unity to power in which the bitter enemies would suddenly work in harmony. This sort of attitude was all too obvious in the writings of intelligent, knowledgeable people who should really have known better. Chester Crocker, the former US Assistant Secretary of State for African Affairs, who had initiated US financial and military aid to UNITA in the 1980s and helped negotiate the independence of Namibia, wrote in his oddly-titled book, High Noon in Tropical Africa (and we need little imagination to see who was Gary Cooper in that one), that the end of foreign interference in Angola (itself a wildly inaccurate statement) would mean that the "Angolans could now begin to shape their own destiny" and that the end of the Cold War was a great opportunity for democracy in Africa as African dictators "lost their freedom for manoeuvre". Tell that one to the opposition movements in Kenya, Ivory Coast and Malawi!

This optimistic view on the part of leading decision-makers or opinion formers led to the development of policies towards Africa which relied on penny-pinching meddling, cheapskate international monitoring operations and an unwillingness to look below the surface to see what was really going on.

When the Bicesse peace accords brought an end to the civil war in 1991, a UN operation, dubbed UNAVEM, was set in motion in Angola. It was pitifully small, poorly funded, had little support from the UN in New York and too few people and resources to really do more than scratch the surface. Having said that Africa is not a blank page, I'm not now arguing that a massive operation would have solved Angola's problems; however, I do believe that the paucity of funds, manpower and commitment put in by the UN and the international community meant that the UN effort was bound to fail regardless of what the Angolans did. Had a large UN operation been launched – on the scale of Namibia in 1990 or Cambodia in 1992-93 – then those Angolans who wanted to entrench peace and civilian politics might have had more of a chance to defeat those who wanted power at all costs.

The solution was for the Angolans to find, but an accurately targeted, properly funded UN operation could have helped them in the search. As it was, the UN spent around $132m on Angola against $430m for Namibia and a staggering £2bn for Cambodia. UNAVEM in Angola had 350 military observers, 90 police monitors and around 400 civilian electoral monitors to cover a country five times the area of Britain, with 5,820 polling stations and massive logistical problems. In the bitterly fought-over region around Mavinga in the south-east, there were two observers to cover 84 polling stations.

Combined with this meagre international commitment to assist Angola, there was a view among western governments that the election date was so sacrosanct that the very holding of the vote would in itself entrench democracy. So when the UN team and its military observers warned that the demobilisation process, the integration of the new army and the preparation for the elections were all behind schedule, they were ignored. The MPLA and UNITA made mutual accusations against each other of violations of the peace deal, but the UN had no means with which to respond. The minor parties constantly called for action to give them a fair chance against their huge and heavily armed rivals – nothing was done because both the MPLA and UNITA had more to gain from a poorly-monitored election than from one controlled strictly by the UN. Thus the vote went ahead and we've all seen the result.

The resumption of the civil war was treated in the West as some appalling aberration that could not have been foreseen – that is with a few exceptions, notably articles in the Independent in the weeks before the elections reporting the warnings by UN military personnel that the failure to demobilise and disarm UNITA and government forces and the failure to monitor the paramilitary police could end in bloodshed and disaster. There was also an attitude of shocked innocence on the part of the Americans about

Savimbi's behaviour – despite the fact that throughout the election campaign he had made clear that he would not accept any result that went against him.

Since the war restarted, western interest in Angola has been patchy and largely overshadowed by Bosnia and the Middle East. More people have died daily in Angola than in Bosnia but it is hard to get Angola regularly on to the news agenda – even in internationally-oriented media organisations. When it does go on to the agenda it is often because a correspondent has been able to get to the scene of a particularly appalling tragedy and to get out pictures of starving children and horrific hospitals. The international media is becoming so picture-led and sound-bite obsessive that a complicated and remote conflict like Angola is just too hard to follow. It is, of course, complicated by the massive problems of getting journalists into conflict areas, besieged towns and rural areas. It has recently been reported that more journalists are being killed in Angola than in any other conflict – but as none have been British, it warrants little more than a footnote.

Angola is remote, peripheral and hard to cover, so for most of the time it doesn't exist for much of the media. There are western economic interests there, but no lasting strategic or military interests. Occasionally there is a flurry of interest but it doesn't last. And occasionally, there is a reversion to type, when publications think they've spotted the real reason for the war or for a military success by one side or the other – foreign intervention. The government is suddenly doing well because ex-South African soldiers have trained a small, elite commando unit; UNITA has taken an oil port because it has got foreign mercenaries fighting for it. Something happens only because of foreign involvement. Foreign involvement has been a constant factor in Angola's political development since the 16th century, but we need to understand more about the indigenous roots of the conflict and not just the surface gloss put on it by foreign involvement.

If a solution is to be found in Angola, it has to be found by the Angolans, whether through decentralisation, the total military defeat of one side by the other (an unlikely prospect), a sudden assertion of power by the Angolan people such as refusing to fight on or even a painful decision that for many of the population Angola only exists as war zone and that a reversion to the state forms which predated colonial rule and therefore a splitting up of the state is the answer.

The international community can have a role to play in cooperation with the Angolans, but not in spite of them and only if there is the political will to commit the resources necessary to help them achieve what they want and not just what western decision-makers feel is desirable – elections come what may. Multi-party elections are just a mechanism in a whole process of change and political development; they are part of the means to an end, not the end itself. Penny-pinching dabbling in Africa with elections as the desired end does nothing to help Africa sort out its problems and find its own solutions. It is just another symptom of a patronising and ill-informed view of Africa as a porous and easily-influenced, but essentially-peripheral appendage to Europe and America. (*Applause* ****)

Ahmed Rajab – Africa Analysis:

(Ahmed Rajab is Editor of Africa Analysis, a news magazine produced in London. He previously worked for the BBC World Service (Africa Section). He has also worked for UNESCO, Index-on-Censorship Magazine and Africa Events).

To me as an African and a hack, Angola matters because the reporting of it in the West epitomises much of the reporting on the rest of Africa by the Western media.

Ahmed Rajab – "half-baked reporters"

I see that Victoria Britain and Richard Dowden have escaped and I blame you Mr Chairman for not seeing fit to detain them at our pleasure so that we could quiz them and they could tell us about the workings of the mainstream media vis-a-vis Africa - why they constantly under-report Africa.

There is of course a lot that is wrong with the Western media coverage of Africa. It is both under-reported and mis-reported. Perhaps their foreign editors or the editor of the Sun should have been invited to come here to tell us why they are determined to take Africa off the map. What is their excuse for assigning the whole continent of 52 countries to one staff person, if at all? Luckily, the African editors for both the Financial Times and The Independent are known to be people who are personally committed to the continent of Africa, who have caught the African bug, and we know that daily they fight for space in their respective newspapers. The Guardian has no Africa editor. The Financial Times, the Sunday Times and the BBC have staff correspondents only in Nairobi and Johannesburg. Elsewhere almost all the mainstream newspapers and BBC radio and television rely on freelance correspondents even in a vast country such as Nigeria.

It is now almost three years since the UN established its presence in Western Sahara - yet not one major article or TV programme has appeared to explain the issues involved. President Houphouet-Boigny dies in Côte D'Ivoire - a country which he had ruled for more than three decades - and his death does not merit a mention on the BBC TV's Nine O'clock News. Four days later, some British MPs were detained in Somalia but in conditions which were not life-threatening and their adventure makes it on to the prime news slot. It reminds me of the 1960s during the troubles of the Congo (now Zaire) when foreign editors on Fleet Street were said to be clamouring only for news of white nuns who had been raped in Katanga.

Certain countries appear to have fallen completely off the map. Where is Tanzania for example? Who reports on this country - East Africa's largest? Now that Idi Amin is not in Uganda and the country is busy rehabilitating itself, who can tell us about the new Uganda? Must Africa always have bogeymen to warrant decent coverage? Amin, Qadhafi, General Aidid, and in the case of Angola, the 'Idi Amin with a Master's degree' - Jonas Savimbi?

A few weeks after the earthquake in Los Angeles, an earthquake of the same force hit western Uganda. Who reported on it? The Ugandans were crying out for assistance, but where were we to listen to their cries?

At its charitable best Western journalism turns voyeuristic - looking for the exotic. All the islands of the Indian Ocean are 'perfumed' - but what of the sweat of the islanders? What of their daily struggles? Comoros for example hit the headlines for a few days in 1978, when a bunch of white mercenaries invaded the islands and held them hostage until 1991. Not much was reported on the islands in the intervening years despite the fact that the mercenaries were using them for gun-running to Renamo rebels in Mozambique and for busting sanctions against apartheid South Africa. The Comoros bounced back onto the map in 1991 when the mercenaries killed the president they had installed. We had then to look again at the map to see where the Comoros were. The islands were news again only because France and South African whites were involved in ejecting the mercenaries who also happened to be white. Much has been happening there since 1991 but who cares for a country with a tuppence economy? Who talks about Mayotte - Comoro's other island -which is still ruled by France?

A white Kenyan loses his job in a Kenyan government department and it makes the news in the West. But had Dr Richard Leakey been Richard Kariuki or Richard Odhiambo, would he have commanded the same attention? Despite the pros and cons of the case of Leakey, the other side were not given the space to air their views - however spurious they may have been.

On the other side of the continent the Tuaregs, when they are discussed at all, remain the exotic indigo men or blue men. Yet there is a Tuareg rebellion in more than one country in West Africa. And who talks of the issues involved?

Before the situation got worse in Somalia, the NGOs operating there were so desperate to have the plight there covered that they were willing to pay Western journalists to visit. They were ignored. Nobody cared for the nomads with a complex system of clans and sub-clans which nobody else understood. Of course, when CNN got there - luckily they have a correspondent in Nairobi - and especially after US troops began to arrive, the situation changed dramatically. TV screens were saturated with images of a dying nation and of heroic saviours - but those were not the images that the NGOs had been praying for.

The Somali experience in fact shows us two things. First, that the gathering of news is now satellite led; and secondly, that Western NGOs - rather than Western news reporters - are more in tune with what is happening in marginal areas of an already marginalised continent.

Africa is under-reported and yet information - correct and full information - is essential in policy formulation. In certain cases, of course, the situation is reversed in the sense that instead of policy makers relying on the media, it is the media that relies on an already formulated policy in the West. A case in point is Algeria's conundrum.

It amazes me to see how the same supposedly highly-principled journalists who rightly opposed General Pinochet in Chile when he killed a democratically elected President and installed a military junta, were later to encourage and applaud the military takeover in Nigeria after the country's first free elections. If the Algerians - while exercising their democratic right - had committed a mistake by voting in the

Front Islamique du Salut (FIS), surely it is their democratic right to make a mistake - just as it was the democratic right of the British voters to have made the mistake of voting in the Tories. But then there was no bogey of the so-called Islamic fundamentalism in Nigeria as there was - or is - in Algeria on the southern flank of Europe.

What I am saying here is that objectivity, when it comes to much of Western reporting on Africa, becomes a slippery entity. And just as it is said that national economies are far too important to be left to economists, the same I think could be argued to be equally true of Africa - be it Angola, or Kenya, or elsewhere, indeed of Africa in general. The reporting of Africa is just too important to be left to half-baked reporters who visit countries for 48 hours and then return to write informed pieces with the help, of course, of the ubiquitous taxi-diver who is always there to provide appropriate sound-bites. I have yet to see a taxi-driver being interviewed by Jeremy Paxman for example, as an authority on dictatorships, one-party systems or fiscal policy.. Yet it happens time and time again in Africa.

News of Angola and/or Africa in general should not be the preserve of 'specialists' with business interests in Africa. It is necessary for people in the metropole to be aware of the problems of Angola; only if there is enough information available would pressure develop which would force Western governments not to turn a blind eye.

It is important too that journalists in a country such as Angola where there is conflict should report from both sides. At the moment there is too much news emanating from Luanda. We should not allow ourselves to fall prey to government wire-services where sources are dubious. Nor should we allow ourselves to be taken in by UNITA junkets or government-organised tours. We should learn to listen to opposition parties whose voices are seldom heard in the Western media. And it is our responsibility to listen to what the Angolans are saying: that there is a civil society. As the conflict goes on, the people who can speak with independent voices are made mute - because we do not reflect what they have to say. For example, the market woman, the parish priest, the primary school teacher, the agriculturalist - they all have something to say. Voices of the NGOs are seldom heard. And here I am talking of indigenous NGOs, not of expatriate NGOs.

Africans are tired of being shown that they only survive as a result of food aid from Western relief agencies or projects run by expatriate NGOs. No doubt expatriates help; but please, let us endeavour to reinforce the confidence of the African which has been damaged by centuries of slavery, colonialism and misrule. Let us give them back their confidence by noticing and paying attention to them when they do things for themselves. Let us listen to them when they talk. Let us have the humility to acknowledge and record their efforts.

If one considers the democratisation process in Africa to be a desired thing, then we must also consider the same to be true of the democratisation of the flow of information. We must be prepared to break the structures of dependence in African countries and between African countries and the West. In Angola, for example, we should encourage the development of independent media outlets, whether newsletters, newspapers or community FM radio stations, as Tony Hodges suggested earlier. It is a good thing that the Catholic Church in Angola is now in the process of getting back its radio station.

Those are just some of the things that can be done to redress the situation. We can also attempt to put on the ground reporters with some facility in local languages, or better still, to train local reporters who can serve as correspondents, say in London, instead of relying on the same people who do not understand the local cultures, and who do not understand the history, and who do not understand how African societies work.

Mr Chairman, when we repeat the cliche of the world being a global village, we should constantly ask ourselves what in reality does it mean for the neighbourhood that is Africa? How come its voice is not heard? If it is true that the medium is the message, we should also ask, in the case of Africa, 'whose message is it'? *(Applause *****)*

Alex Holmes – World in Action:

(Alex Holmes is a programme-maker for the award - winning World in Action television series at Granada TV, based in Manchester. In the past year he has made documentaries on Somalia and on Angola. He was once a student of Keith Hart's but has not let this hold him back.)

I differ from the last two speakers in so much that the programme I work for, World in Action, is not so much concerned with news. World in Action has a long and strong tradition of covering foreign stories. However, over the last years, the nature of those stories has changed. Gone are the days when World in Action could go off to some part of the world and shoot a story about that place and bring it into people's living rooms, thereby informing them of what was going on. That is now the job of the news media as opposed to current affairs programmes like World in Action. We can't just go there and take a slice of the world and bring it back. We can't compete with what is on the News at Six, the Nine O'clock News, Channel Four News. They are now running news slots that are almost as long as our own programme; therefore we have to find a different approach, and in the way that we go about looking for this different approach, I may be addressing some of the issues raised by our previous speaker –I'm not sure I'll be answering them, but I will be engaging them.

Alex Holmes – "unashamedly populist"

The fact that we can't bring back a story self-contained any more from far-flung parts of the world means that we have to approach foreign stories in a different way. We have to tell our stories in a different way to make them distinctive and we have to ask ourselves much more rigorously what is their relevance for the people who are going to watch them. Because World in Action is an unashamedly popular strand. Its audience is well into the seven or eight millions each week. And if we are to keep that number of people viewing, which we are instructed to do if we are to survive - but also we want to, because we feel you are only telling people things if they are viewing - then we have to find ways of engaging the viewer and making them have access to the stories we are trying to put across. And in the process of telling the story maybe they will come to new understandings and find new ways in which they can associate themselves with what is going on in other parts of the world.

There are probably three ways in which people identify with what they see in our programmes, first of which is the very basic fact of human suffering. If you see men, women and children suffering in extreme circumstances, your heart goes out to them and you will want to know about that place and what has given rise to these events. However, just showing human suffering in itself is not enough. In fact we have found that programmes we have made where suffering is the main element have done disastrously and have produced very little response. People have a shut-off mechanism. Why should they be concerned? So you have to introduce questions of responsibility. What does this suffering have to do with you and furthermore, what can you do about this suffering? How can you exercise that responsibility?

Now these were all issues and questions that came up in relation to the making of a programme which World in Action recently broadcast on the problem of landmines in Angola called Fields of Fire. We had originally looked at making a programme on Angola some 12 months previously. When we looked at the situation it was difficult to find a way into the story, a way that would make people turn on in the first place to watch it. It would have been good and interesting for some people if we had made a programme then about the restarting of the war and the results of the elections, but unfortunately few people would have watched it. The question came up again when as a result of a lull in the fighting some access could be gained to the cities of Cuito and Huambo. But here again this was a situation where we could not compete with the news media. Reports of the suffering brought back by people like John Simpson told that story very well and it was necessary that we find another way in. And fortunately for me, that access was made available after I had been looking at another issue in a wider context: the issue of land mines. There were further developments in this field in that the British government was being forced out into the open with regard to its objection to the banning of these terrible weapons. Therefore the two issues of the situation in Angola and the situation regarding the landmines came together and enabled us to make a programme that we hoped would illustrate what was going on in Angola but also would have the attention of a large number of people.

That was our criteria of going there. The programme itself was structured around following a man who had been sent out there by the Mines Advisory Group, whose Director, Rae McGrath spoke to you earlier today. We followed him through his mission to discover the extent of the problem that landmines posed. As a result, we had a guide through for what many people would be a very strange experience. We had a way of telling that story. And I am glad to say that the response from the viewers was quite tremendous. People in the office could not easily remember when there had been such an outcry produced by a foreign story in recent years. The only way we did that was by finding ways into the story: finding a way that people could feel involved in what was going on; could feel responsible for what was going on. And could perhaps feel there was something they could do about it. Now I know that this is not necessarily reporting based on the most ideal criteria, but we are in the business of making programmes that make people watch and making them feel involved; making them feel responsible and making them feel they can do something about it. Such are the economic constraints that we have to leave to the news media the job of bringing back information.

World in Action has made another programme which I was also involved with in Africa in the last six months, and this was set in Somalia. It is another example of the way in which we can tell a story about a place and explain the circumstances by using a device or a mechanism, and I think it highlights some of the problems that this necessity creates. The story was called Dan Eldon's last assignment and it was an attempt to tell the story of what had happened in Somalia over the last few years culminating in the dramatic and disastrous UN intervention spearheaded by the US, through the pictures of a photographer Dan Eldon, who was tragically killed when a US attack, in which many Somalis were killed, went wrong.

I say it raises many of the difficulties because that was a story of one young man's tragic death and there is no doubt that he was a very fine and courageous photographer. He was only 22. But his coverage of Somalia was outstanding and his work was recognised as such by all this colleagues who had been there for many years. But we were in danger of eclipsing the deaths of the other people. Not only the people who were killed in the attack but the people who had been killed in the weeks, months and years previously to this by focusing on one white British person. But we asked ourselves the question, Do we let this stop us making the programme or do we make a programme and through that programme and through Don's pictures which we made extensive use of, do we bring to a wider audience the suffering of the people in Somalia, and the increased suffering as a result of the UN intervention? And do we allow that mechanism to help us criticise the West's wider involvement? Then the answer we came up with is yes.

This may not be an ideal situation, but it is a way in, and a way in which we can bring the situation of a country like Somalia and like Angola, different as they are, to a very wide audience; and while there are questions as to the amount of information which is published by the media, there is also the very important point of who has access to that information. Extensive surveys in the Financial Times or in-depth analysis on Newsnight are one thing; but if you really want to motivate or change public opinion, then you need to reach a very wide audience and in order to do that you need to find a way of telling the story.

And so that is why we came to use the British position on landmines to tell a story on Angola or the death of a British photographer to tell a story about Somalia; and it is only through using mechanisms like that we can reach the millions of viewers who watch us every week.
(*Applause* ***)

Zed Nelson – Photo-journalist:

(Zed Nelson is a free-lance photographer who has worked in numerous war-zones throughout the world, including Afghanistan where he survived an attack on the car he was driving. He recently had a photo-essay on Angola in The Face magazine.)

I was recently in Angola for two reasons: working for the Independent on Sunday Review Magazine and also for a magazine called The Face which has a very different readership aimed mostly at young people who essentially have no interest in these kinds of issues. So I found myself in an odd position trying to please both of those audiences. Through that came the question of finding the best way to interest people in subjects such as these, which is a problem I often have. I work freelance so I am constantly trying to get editors and picture editors interested in issues I think are important. This is very difficult especially since I have to get the funding up-front. In this case both magazines put money up, but it took me some months to get this to happen.

One thing that happened throughout the trip was that, as usual as a photographer, you tend to concentrate on negative aspects: the sad, depressing things. But increasingly I worry that this perhaps builds up into a rather negative impression of different countries I have visited, so I make a point of trying to balance that out. These pictures are negative. They are very sad. This is a picture of a landmine victim. It is an awful thing to look at. And it is also a picture which I have taken in countries all over the world. I have been in Afghanistan, Somalia and Cambodia: it is the same story, and increasingly I am trying to draw out the parallels of that story. Angola is unique, but what happened to it is so similar to many other countries who were used as pawns in the Cold War. I hope to show this in a book I am working on at the moment.

The other problem is trying to get magazines interested in stories like this. They wait until it is essentially too late. Until there are pictures like this, until that point, no one is interested. I was in Somalia and I had the same problems there. I spent a month there during October 1992 and that became a big news story. But it had been happening for six months; people had been dying: it just hadn't caught the media's attention - it wasn't bad enough yet.

This is a feeding centre in Minongue. These children are showing all the signs of malnutrition, but they are not yet starving. They haven't got stick limbs, so it is difficult to get the pictures published. My Somalia work was very widely published because it was a situation that had become so bad. In a way this generated my interest in Angola because I thought what is interesting is the history of the build-up of the events which allowed this to happen. The famine was a story but it wasn't **the** story. It was just the end-product.

For about two weeks it was front-page news. I was sending pictures back and they were being used every day. I have been in a situation many times before when my pictures haven't been used, are never published. It is just the luck of the draw; whether the media spot-light will end up on that country at that time. As a journalist or a photographer all you can try to do is to raise interest and talk about the issues that matter.

This is back in Angola. Personally I have to ask myself what are the reasons for going there. What am I hoping to achieve? The obvious reason for me is that you need humanitarian aid to help solve an emergency. But often you get two weeks of intense media interest. Money is raised. Everyone has their story and then it is forgotten. No one ever talks about the politics or the history of the situation. There are children now, and I have met many such children in my travels in Angola, who have been born into war and have never experienced anything else. This is obviously very worrying; when people get used to living in a war and they have never known anything different, then you have the potential for the problems to just carry on.

Zed Nelson – "finding a balance"

This is the kind of security people living in Luanda have, if you have the money. As the infrastructure breaks down, there are more and more problems with law and order. But what struck me most was the way people managed to continue their daily lives **despite** all the problems. And that is something that gave me hope about Angola. I found people very optimistic and with a good sense of humour.

I have been to countries where there is no optimism and no humour and I have felt very depressed by these places. There is no feeling of hope. In Angola this is not something that struck me. Everybody is carrying on in some way; everyone has a scheme, a way of surviving.

This is a supermarket. There is very little food in the shops, but food is available. It's all on the street. It's all on the black market. Food is there if you have the money; it's all about economics. Even in Somalia, the pictures you saw of starving children: a hundred feet away, there was a market selling fresh fruit and vegetables and camel meat. And again, it is very difficult to get those kind of images published. Everyone wants a starving child, but to juxtapose that against a bustling market is too complicated. It takes too much space to explain. So all you can do is try to find a compromise.

You see here businessmen. Mafia types. Dealers. Middlemen. Aid bureaucrats. All really parasites on the situation. Angola is a country full of resources, but the Angolan people seem not to be benefiting from these resources. It's the outsiders who gain and a few Angolans, the elite. There are signs of wealth in the cities and government workers driving around in flash cars.

A vast market just outside the capital where everyone is buying and selling. Life goes on and, as I got further into the story, I tried not to just focus on grey, black and white images of starving people, the depressing aspects, but I tried to portray the country as a lively place with all its problems.

These are drugs that have ended up on the black market. Most of the hospitals have incredible shortages of drugs and medicines; but the drugs are there, they are just being diverted into the side-lines of the black market. Everyone is working hard in some way. Angola is not a country full of victims. I have been to places where they have reached the bottom of the line. There is a passive "we need help" feeling. But here everyone is too busy surviving and working, which left me with quite a positive and optimistic feeling. There seemed to be a high level of motivation and of political awareness; a need for change and a hope for the future.

This is a wonderful beach in Luanda with an offshore oilrig which ought to be providing wealth for the country not the war effort or foreign companies.

It is a difficult game you have to play as a photographer or journalist, to make people realise that in these far-off countries which don't really enter their daily lives there are people who actually need help, without giving a purely negative picture or overwhelming people with a situation they can't relate to. If I sound confused about the issues, then it is because I am. As an individual there are all these problems in your mind as to what your responsibilities are; what you are really trying to show and I think that is something you have to address in your own mind and through the media. *(Applause ******)*

Open Session

Keith Hart:

I would like to thank the panellists for bringing us closer to our conclusions in such a constructive way.

In my paper which I never summarised *(ironic cheers)*, I did make a point about death, dying, illness, hunger and killing as the usual image we have of Africa. Yet a population that has grown so much in the last century is much more about life and living. It seems quite hard for that to be conveyed and certainly it is impossible to consider Africa's future without a sense of the burgeoning youth that its population represents, which is both a source of inspiration and a threat, especially to those who are trying to cling to the remnants of power in our middle-age *(a few snorts of laughter and some sheepish faces)*

Antonio Fernandes (Angolan Ambassador):

At the end of Alex Holmes' talk, World in Action, did I understand you to say that for the British public to follow a story you need to take advantage of a journalist being killed, instead of presenting the story itself, the suffering of the people?

Alex Holmes:

People are more likely in the first instance to watch a story about Angola, a place they have probably never heard of and therefore have no reason to care about it, if they can **identify** with something to lead them into that place. In the case of the programme about Somalia, it was one of those situations when we wanted to cover the story for a long time, but it was a situation where we needed to find a mechanism by which we could tell this story, but also that would first of all get people to turn on, and secondly, keep them watching all the way through. Now I am quite prepared to admit that approach has serious problems in that you are in danger of allowing your focus on the death of one white British photographer to eclipse all the other deaths.

The incident which gave rise to Dan Eldon's death killed about 70 people. Now should we not have focused on one of those 70 to tell that story? Well, I'm afraid to say that we have a certain amount of power to inform the way that people think, but we also have to respond to their attitudes in the first place. And if we don't get people to turn on and watch in the first place, then we don't necessarily have the chance to show them a different way of thinking.

If we made a programme about the death of a Somali in a UN operation, it probably wouldn't have got half the viewers it did. Having got them to tune in, saying it was about a young British photographer who died as a result of a UN intervention, we have them there, almost captive for half an hour, which gives us the opportunity to explore other issues and engage other sympathies they might have.

Ahmed Rajab:

I don't fully share that view. Somalia, a country that people had never heard of, yes, probably. But is it not our responsibility to educate the people, so they know the issues, they know where Somalia is, they know what is happening.

Keith Hart:

The tradition of documentary-making in this country is a very conservative one. There are many conventions that the people in the trade believe are immovable; and I think Robert Fisk recently had a go at this, commenting on his own documentary about the Palestinians and the clashes with the people he was making it with.

Keith Somerville:

Taking the issues of why people turn off or don't switch on - and I think unfortunately it is just human nature and it's particularly bad in Britain - people aren't particularly interested in what happens in the rest of the world. But it happens in Africa as well. I was in Botswana last year. I was bombarded with questions by listeners of the programme I worked on. 'We're not interested in Cambodia. We don't want to hear this rubbish, who the Mafia have blown up in Italy. We want southern Africa and nothing else' was the cry of the majority. This happens everywhere unfortunately. It is human nature. We have to try to work with it as well as against it. We do our best. We don't always get it right but we try."

Sir Roger Tomkys (Master, Pembroke College):

This has been absolutely fascinating. I found myself in total agreement with almost everything that Keith Somerville said, with one exception. I very much agree with him that the pressure for change in Africa got portrayed as coming from the West, more or less exclusively from outside. It comes also, as is right, from the inside. I agree with him when he says that very often western policies, government policies are patronising, in style and sometimes in substance. I also very much agree that they often pursued simplistic lines and simplistic principles in rather complicated circumstances locally.

Diana Miller – "racist coverage"

I disagree with him on one point and that is that he speaks of the media and public opinion as often following the same lines as the governments'. In my experience it is much more often the other way around; that is to say that governments were led over recent years very much by pressure of media coverage and of domestic public opinion, in America for example, not founded on a very clear understanding of what was happening on the ground.

To have, following this, the World in Action presentation, I think, was absolutely fascinating, because it shows what drives the need to reach a mass audience. Then, if that need to reach a mass audience then drives government policy, the media bear a very heavy responsibility, a moral responsibility and a factual responsibility. So too do governments.

Diana Miller (Retired emigrée):

About the media coverage in Africa, it seems to me a question of which came first, the chicken or the egg? About Yugoslavia we have had hours and hours every day. About Angola we don't get even a half a minute a month. And I want to ask why is your coverage racist? Because it all boils down to racism when a white journalist, not British, but a white journalist comes into the scene, the media take it up.

Let's all of us charge the media and the BBC with racism and write to the press and phone in to all news services, radio and TV and cable, at least twice a week and ask what is happening in Angola. Why don't you give us any news on Africa? Why is your service racist? There are over a hundred people here – 300 calls to any one news service would force them to do something. Let's do it. *(Laughter and applause ****)*

Ahmed Rajab:

Yes! We need to bombard newsrooms of the mainstream media, so that we all assist in putting Africa on the map.

Bill Kirkman (Formerly Africa reporter for The Times):

I first became involved in press coverage of Africa 30 years ago and I would very much echo the points made by Ahmed Rajab about the under-reporting and misreporting of Africa. I also very strongly echo the points made by Keith Somerville about the western-centred basis of much coverage on Africa, particularly the example of coverage during the Cold War. What I think has been previously lacking and poses a very strong responsibility on journalists, is the need for a good basis of knowledge on which critical judgements can be made on Africa. For example, if one goes back to the Cold War, it would have made it possible to demonstrate the wrongness of much of the coverage, based on a Cold War approach and would have showed a fundamental misunderstanding of the situation in Africa.

So I think there is a real need for knowledge and I think there is also a need, speaking frankly as a journalist, for humanity. One should be knowledgeable, but should not claim to know best about other people's countries. I am sorry Victoria Brittain has gone because I would like to say to her that her partisan approach is thoroughly deplorable. *(Thin chorus of hear hear)*

Rae McGrath (Chairman, Mines Advisory Group):

One very important point is that I think there is a contradiction in saying on the one hand that people are not well enough informed by the media, and then saying that we should avoid the opportunity to inform people in a better way. If the way of doing that is by using some device to get eight million viewers to tune on their TV sets, this is a start, as long as having once got them to turn on, you say the right things and make that part of the education process.

There is a tendency in the NGO world to be very satisfied with the odd article in the Guardian. I don't see how we are going to change understanding of the situation in Africa by constantly preaching to the converted. Personally I would like a centre spread in The Sun – a page 3 spread in The Sun telling people about the tragedy of land mines in countries like Angola in a way that educates them until eventually they will ask for page 3 to be changed from a tits and bum page.

It is our responsibility as journalists to educate. It appears from my own personal experience being interviewed on British TV that when you go for a pre-discussion before the interview the producer will deliberately make a point of asking you to keep it simple, as if for some reason, when it comes to Africa, the British public is not able to comprehend the issues involved. Their intelligence is diminished. What I think is the case is that there appears to be a determined reluctance on the part of media executives not to educate the British audience.
*(Applause **)*

Teresa Santana (Angola Community in the UK):

It seems to me about the World in Action case, that it is really sad that it needs something to get the message across. Why is it? Why do people turn off, just turn of their TV sets just because it is another part of the world? The big problem here is money-making, because you have to pass advertisements regularly. We have to have a different approach to inform people, not just to aim at getting a massive audience. Finally, I would like to ask the photographer if he really understood why the people in Angola, in spite of their problems, still go to the beach and still dance?

Zed Nelson:

Why are they dancing? I suppose it's because their spirit hasn't been broken. But you can answer that much better than me.

Jean-Emmanuel Pondi (Visiting Fellow, Pembroke College):

It is really sad to see so much prejudice surrounds whatever has to do with Africa. Take the 1990 World Cup. The Cameroon team was taken as a joke basically, especially when it was to meet the mighty Argentina. There were really very nasty reports; it was really denigrating, showing one side of Africa, as if we have nothing to do there. People were shocked after the first game and I was surprised that the Washington Post and the New York Times knew where the Cameroon Embassy was. Here we are not talking about death or about war. There is so much prejudice surrounding whatever has to do with Africa and this is really very tragic.

Keith Hart:

Although I have to say when Cameroon were playing England, in the pub I was in, the whole place erupted with joy when Cameroon scored their second goal, as England were playing so badly and winning and it was such a brilliant goal. *(Laughter).*

Adao Alexandre (Student, College of Ascension, Birmingham):

Addressing the photographer, I would like to say that in Luanda, things have changed. Most of the supermarkets are full of goods. And I wondered if you went to areas outside of Luanda?

Zed Nelson:

It was made impossible for me to visit UNITA areas when I was there. I spent hours and hours on aircraft and on borders trying, but we were stopped. The UN made life quite difficult. They said it was because of their negotiations with UNITA. I'm not sure. Perhaps their programmes were non-existent or going badly.

Alex Holmes:

Operating in Angola is extremely difficult. Objections were raised about going anywhere, by both sides - even out of the hotel sometimes! . I have never spent so much time on airstrips in my life.

Keith Hart:

I think the audience is losing its grip. Perhaps you are tired?

(Uneasy chuckling)

Eleanor O'Gorman (PhD Student, Social and Political Sciences, Cambridge):

I have been looking for an opportunity to say something so I'll take my chance now that the microphone is near. We have spoken about international actors in relation to various aspects of Angola. What I want to know is how come the multi-nationals have not been mentioned and the role of international capital and business? It has been done in passing. We have a businessman here from Defence Systems Limited and I would like to know what they do in Angola, how they are involved in the current processes. They seem, from articles I have read, to be privy to information and negotiations and I would like to know how the media deals with issues like that and why seminars like this can't confront these issues?

One of the Friends of Angola makes his point

Ahmed Rajab:

More seriously, Angolan journalists in Luanda have lost their lives pursuing an independent line in Angola, and that probably is not surprising if we consider that the Director General of ANGRO – the state news agency – Mr Carvalho, is still a colonel in the state security system and he is also the Secretary General of the Angolan Journalists Union. But the situation is no better in UNITA-held areas, at least according to my experiences when I visited Jamba sometime back. You'll find that you are more restricted and news is only available from the voice of the cockrell, Radio Volgan. It is difficult to talk to ordinary people living in those areas apart from the afficianados of UNITA.

Keith Hart:

I think we have been confronting quite a lot. We can't confront everything. By the look of the hands up and the time available, I see that I have now provoked a storm!

Unknown Angolan man:

I want to raise two points. There are reports in the Portuguese media of foreign journalists being badly treated in Luanda. Secondly, we are in England and this is the European Union; but this conference is not addressing the issue of Spain selling weapons to Angola, breaking the Bicesse Accord. If Spain had been selling arms to Bosnia then there would be an outcry; but because it is Angola, it is overlooked. This conference hasn't addressed this.

Keith Somerville:

I agree that this is a problem. A journalist working for my programme during the election eventually had to leave the country after continual death threats and actual physical violence against her by members of UNITA at a press conference.

Keith Hart:

I would like to respond to that quickly by saying that this conference started out as a very unambitious workshop with next to no money, trying to bring together a few people close to home. It expanded without the money being increased, and perhaps this has given rise to the idea that it is a universal conference on Angola in which all topics have to be covered. I hope that we don't spend the remainder of the time available to us – about an hour – discussing all the beefs that individuals may have that they think should have been covered and haven't. I rather hoped that we might pull together some of the things that have been raised so that we can come out of here feeling that we have learnt something, rather than that we have left most things undone. *(Ripple of agreement)*

Anna-Maria Huby (Médecins Sans Frontiéres):

Most of the reporting on Africa is done by spokespersons. What do you feel about that imbalance? Why don't you pass the microphone to our people in the field? Most of the time they are never asked to be included in a story. You say you have spokesperson fatigue. Most of the time you just want a quote. Couldn't you improve on this? Is there not some laziness on your part?

Alex Holmes:

I have appreciated all your comments and it is interesting to hear your views on the position I have tried to outline. The one I would really like to respond to as it encapsulates a number of the issues that have been raised is the question from the lady from MSF. From my point of view, I'm looking for someone who can give first-hand testimony on the ground, who can speak on their immediate experience, so the people we constantly try to avoid are spokespeople. They are the bane of our lives. Often we battle with them because they try to intervene to provide the party line whatever. Having said that, talking to people on the ground does have particular difficulties and this goes to the more general point I was trying to make. You are only going to tell people about a certain situation if they are watching. Our programme on Angola was made without subtitles which was quite difficult. We have to avoid creating a blockage for people.

Keith Somerville:

You can't work against your audience, which is why I sympathise with Alex's problems.

Keith Hart:

Does either of the other panellists have anything to say?

(They decline. At this point, the Angolan Vice Foreign Minister, George Chikoti, tried to obtain the microphone to have a final word.)

Well, since we shut off the British Ambassador before lunch at a similar stage, I feel it would be an equal opportunity decision to end the session here. *(Much tittering)* Incidentally, did anyone hear the BBC World Tonight feature on Angola?

Susie Thomas (Cambridge University Press Officer):

Yes I did. And can I just say that I have worked closely with Keith, Joanna, Salah and Paula over the last few weeks, and I have come from being someone who knew little about Angola to someone who feels quite intelligent about the subject. The World Tonight coverage was very good indeed. It was six or seven minutes long which was astonishing. It covered the issue in some considerable depth. It is unfortunate that we are here in Cambridge but we had only had about one inch in the Cambridge Evening News.

Keith Hart:

Well, its a rag anyway. *(General laughter)* Perhaps we might now move on to consider how we might communicate messages from this gathering?

Session 7

Summing Up

As the workshop drew to a close, participants had their chance to make a final pitch in the arena. The media session drifted into discussion about our own communication: was there something to share with a wider audience and, if so, what? Keith Hart remained in the Chair and the media panelists stayed where they were sitting. Some participants chose to sum up, after two days of eclectic debate, why Angola mattered for them or what the problems really were as they now saw them. Some wanted to register what the workshop had given them. Others concentrated their energies on what should come out of the workshop. Discussion was rather slow to begin with, but then there was a scramble to be heard.

Introduction from the Chair

Keith Hart:

This is such a remarkable group of people, so diverse, so engaged, and from so many different points of view in relation to the issue of Angola, that any document which all of you, or some of you, could subscribe to would represent a very impressive cross-section of humanity, if a common view might be communicated.

On the other hand, I did not want the last part of this extremely constructive workshop to be dominated by squabbling over the wording of some abstract and anodyne statement which would leave us more divided than we were when we started. So, I am in several minds. I invite you to say what **you** think is the overwhelming message that ought be to communicated to the outside world from this workshop, if any, and to whom.

I realise these are very complex and fluid issues. This is not a stage-managed conference: we haven't already got the working statement in our pockets to whip out at the right moment and it may be impossible to reach any definite conclusion in the time available. At the very least, I will certainly make sure that anything that comes out of this will be circulated to those of you who attended for your comments, before anything goes further.

José Campino (Political Affairs Officer, United Nations):

I would need permission from the UN to make an official contribution.

Antonio Fernandes (Angolan Ambassador to UK):

I am interested in producing a written statement.

Diana Miller (Local activist):

A copy of any statement should be given to all local libraries in Cambridge.

Peter Brayshaw (Angola Emergency Campaign):

I share your caution and worries whether this diverse group of people could agree on any one form of words to send to the two sides negotiating at the moment in Lusaka. I find it very difficult and we shouldn't do anything that could be seen as an attempt to force the pace or in any way jeopardise these very difficult and serious discussions.

What we should do, having listened to each other, which is a very important thing in its own right for two days now, is to take all of those views away with us, reflect on them and make sure we understand all the range of points of view. Listening is very very important.

Regarding publicising the work of the conference, there are other things going on, meetings in parts of the country all of the time, and I think people should carry on with the networking, and take away from this conference again a feeling of genuine respect for different points of view; but, underlying it all, a feeling of good will towards the Angolan people; the tragedy that has been inflicted upon them; the different analyses of the reasons for that tragedy; and different solutions for it.

Some of us are going to a meeting in Bristol on Thursday. There will be events up and down the country and I think we should carry on trying to work together, bearing in mind also that Angola **does** matter: it matters above all to the Angolan people themselves. So, I really think we should avoid trying to agree on a ten point communique, but, enriched by this experience which I certainly have been very grateful to you and your colleagues for organising, go on in that spirit.

Susie Thomas (Cambridge University Press Officer):

What about asking the medial panelists for their opinion as to how best to publicise the results of this workshop?

Ahmed Rajab (Africa Analysis):

We will give it the mention it deserves in future publications, as we have already done.

Keith Somerville (BBC World Service):

I think some of the distinguished participants from Angola should make themselves readily available to the BBC World Service for interview while they are in the country.

(There seemed to be stalemate and apparent apathy at this point. Could the participants, now tired and with half a mind on their plans for getting out of Cambridge, collectively produce a drive towards some product that would testify to and reflect what had happened in the Old Library of Pembroke College around the issue of why Angola matters? The Chair tried a new tack.)

Keith Hart:

Well, can I ask what have you all got out of it?

George Chikoti (Angolan Vice-Minister for Foreign Affairs):

I think that in the first place I would like to thank Dr. Hart and his colleagues for the initiative you have started. I think it is important that workshops like this can take place in the future and I wonder if we can have one next year at the same date to look at what has happened in Angola in that time.

As a representative of the Angolan Government, I think things that have been said here are very important and I feel totally committed. And I think it is important that different people have spoken and have different ideas to suggest. The Embassy is open to any suggestions they care to make, as far as helping the poor is concerned.

However, I think that an opportunity has been created to tell both of the parties, in UNITA and the Government, that we all agree on one thing: we all want immediate peace. When I look at most of the speeches that were delivered since yesterday, there was something common. People here are against the suffering in Angola and they want that to end.

Maybe it will be possible that a few words, one sentence like "People met in Cambridge; they expressed concern about the suffering in Angola and wish immediate peace in Angola". That can be something, in my view, very simple. It can mainly express the feeling of many people who have spoken here, because, maybe, going away from here, it can be as if nothing has happened. Whereas I think what has taken place here is extremely important for me and for many people in this room. *(Applause ****).*

Alison Tierney (Social Anthropologist, London School of Economics):

I would just like us to remember that conferences are supposed to result in some kind of effective action and not just some conference next year, when we can all talk about it again.

I would like to comment on the relationship between the different sections of the workshop. The NGO section did raise the fact of human suffering. It certainly provided some heartfelt responses from the audience. One member of the audience said it was **the** best section of the workshop: there's no doubt about that. The only problem was that the focus was on European NGOs rather than Angolan NGOs and it's interesting that the one Angolan representative was put in a different session.

However, the NGO session did remind us of the human cost of high-level bickering, both national and international, and I would like to relate this to a comment made by Keith Hart at the beginning of this conference, when he asked in what way is Angola a symptom and symbol of global issues more generally. What is it that we want to communicate as the result of this workshop? And I think we should remember that the word NGO does distinguish those organisations from government organisations. Even though they are linked in many ways, in the way that they often work through government structures, they are nonetheless distinguished from government institutions. They tend to be less bureaucratic and more active and immediate; and they are often frustrated by either national governments or UN official procedures. NGOs are generally recognised as providing effective appropriate action to alleviate human suffering.

Alain Aeschlimann

So the question I want to ask is should we not treat with cynicism the politicians and minor UN personnel who are really concerned with their own interest and their positions of authority? Is it no true that all they say about representing and being concerned about other people is so much hot air? This is a popular negative stereotype of what politicians are; but one supported by much of what we heard yesterday. Is it inevitable that the only effective work on humanitarian aid and poverty alleviation is that carried out by those outside government?
*(Applause ***)*

Sisa Ncwana (London office of the ANC):

I feel that it has been shown by the conduct of this gathering that there is an urgent need to work for a viable and lasting ceasefire; that there is a need to lobby western governments to do their best to influence the negotiations taking place in Lusaka right now so that these negotiations can come up with the only outcome which is the aspiration of the people of Angola. However, that can only happen if those who are seated around the table at Lusaka **do** have the interests of the people and the country at heart. And what is this interest? It is that the people of Angola should live in peace and security and that they should be in a position to get on with the questions of reconstruction and development of their country, which would also lead to a better Southern Africa for us all. The Angolan problems are tied up with the problems of South Africa. They are tied up with the problems of other parts of Southern Africa. Yet at the same time, the destiny of the people of Angola is tied up with the destiny of the people of the whole world. *(Applause ***)*

Alain Aeschliman (International Committee of the Red Cross):

Our organisation has been present in Angola for nearly 15 years since Independence and we have very close links with the country. As a reminder, in 1984 we started a major relief operation. The humanitarian problems there did not start only recently. We were involved in food distribution, seed programmes, medical activities, water and sanitation activities and the rehabilitation of amputees. We fitted more than 150 people a month in Huambo and Cuito with artificial legs. We had expenses of between thirty and forty million US dollars a year.

In March 1992 we decided to dismantle our structure after the last distribution of seeds with the intention of giving to the people a positive input to development. That was planned to start. Unfortunately, with the new outbreak of fighting we had to reconsider our position. We needed our staff to be again active in Angola. We had some difficulties in getting our humanitarian message understood by all concerned. And we insisted and repeated for more than one year that the priority and central point is to create a mutual independent and humanitarian space.

We believe that one of the slogans of this workshop should be 'put humanity first'. *(applause ***)* We think it is important to separate political questions from humanitarian priorities: victims cannot wait. They have to be reached where theie needs are, by organisations working with full transparency and with serious criteria.

Regarding mines, this year there have been several commissions of experts and government experts with the aim of reviewing the 1980 convention on classical arms, especially the Protocol concerning mines. The first priority for the ICRC is to bring more states to ratify this convention. There are only 42 states party to this and three African states. The second priority is to have a formal application of the Protocol concerning mines to internal conflicts. For the time being it concerns only international conflicts. We hope as well it will be possible to introduce national measures of implementation and a system of self-destruction or neutralisation of the mines. We believe that the best way would be to have a ban on mines. This is from a purely humanitarian point of view. But as there are some military necessities, we believe that it is at least very important to improve this Protocol. *(Applause ***)*

Professor Antonio Neto (Angolan Democratic Party):

Angola is working for democracy; but there is no democracy if there is no free press. There is no democracy if there are no political parties working for democracy. So far here, we have been talking about UNITA and MPLA, excluding other political parties. We understand that the marginalisation of the other political parties is well done in Lusaka. Therefore we would like to express the view that the Lusaka peace talks be enlarged to include all other political parties in order to come as soon as possible together for granting peace and freedom in Angola. Secondly, we would like very much that the international community accept responsibility for banning all kinds of weapons in Angola, importing them from Brazil, and chemical warfare which is still going on in Angola today.

We should not exclude NGOs in Angola and we should push the international community to give more support for humanitarian projects; but these humanitarian projects should not exclude the people in the urban areas.

José Campino (Political Affairs Officer, United Nations):

I suggest two or three paragraphs are written for the Lusaka peace talks. Such a letter might emphasise or describe the multiplicity of the people assembled here. We have a common aim to bring peace to Angola. *(Applause **)*

Marco Ramazzotti (Natural Resource Consultant):

I think we are not here to dispense justice. We are here to help the peace process to go on. At the same time, I think it is fairly clear that this workshop did demonstrate that public opinion does condemn in a certain way UNITA, for not accepting the election results. I think that an appeal to both parties for peace and an appeal to respect elections are some of the major points that a statement might contain. *(Murmurs of approval)*

Malik Chaka (UNITA Representative, Washington DC):

The people assembled here owe a debt of gratitude to Dr Keith Hart and his colleagues. I think what is most important is the range of voices they have brought together: people on all different sides of the political divide. But the main thing, as the Vice-Minister has pointed out, is peace and national reconciliation. Mr Samakuva, the UNITA representative to London, for example, said that this was the first time that he had the opportunity to talk to Ambassador Fernandes. It is the first time that I have seen Ambassador Fernandes, the individual that introduced me to Angolan politics, over 20 years ago.

I think the other thing that is important, as well as an agreement in Lusaka, is the implementation of the agreement. It is doubly important and we need to appeal to the UN and to member states to finance the kind of operation that it is going to take for it to be successful. I think it is also important that people here understand that there has been talk of the bipolarisation of Angolan politics. For Angola to move forward, it is going to take the participation of, and the working together of, not only the Government, and the major party of the Government, the MPLA, but also UNITA, other opposition parties, Churches, civil society, if you are to make democracy in Angola (and if we can resolve the problem here, we can fix any problem Africa has), move forward, deepening the democratic process. I believe a message should be sent to Lusaka and I believe that message is that we need to give peace a chance and national reconciliation is necessary. *(Applause **)*

Rajah Jarrah (Southern Africa Coordinator, ACORD):

Bearing in mind that Cambridge is in a privileged position in British society, wouldn't it be a good idea to use this conference as a platform for lobbying the British government to take a lead in rallying support for fund-raising for UNAVEM III, sending a message via the Foreign Office representative to the British Government.

Rajah Jarrah – "lobby the government"

Jean-Emmanuuel Pondi (Visiting Scholar from Cameroon, Pembroke College):

I think we should send some kind of message, so that what we have done here is at least echoed somewhere else, and who knows, it might have an impact.

I think there are a few things we need to look at. And I think we need to look at the way the world is. Throughout this conference there has been the assumption that everyone wants peace. But I'm afraid there are people whose interest it is not to serve peace at all and whose rational behaviour would be precisely to make sure that there is no peace, because a situation of no peace is beneficial to them. There won't be peace; and peace will come only if those people involved have an interest in having peace rather than the reverse. I think it is important to understand that, not to assume that everyone is in our spirit. We should look at the world the way it is and not how we would wish it to be. The merchants of death are omnivorous and I think we have not paid enough attention to the proliferation of arms in Africa, because this has meant that there is now more war in Africa rather than less: an AK47 can be bought for $17 on the streets in Somalia.

The second unspoken assumption here that deserves to be challenged is the idea that democracy will solve things in Africa. I'm afraid people continue to boost systems, trying to put them the way they are here in Africa, hoping they will work. We will be very disappointed. We need some kind of synthesis. We need to ask questions about our culture and how to operate a synthesis between what is good for us. And the reason why democracy might not work is because the main people concerned have not been asked. The majority. Again it is something that has been imposed from outside, from the IMF and so on, and that's why, I'm afraid, it won't work. *(Applause ***)*

Tegegne Teka (Ph.D student, Cambridge):

I would like to answer the question what did I get out of the workshop. I learnt much about the view of the governments involved. However, I have also seen that the two contending parties, the MPLA and UNITA, dominate the forum and I have a feeling that they are problematic to the peace process. But I have learnt from this forum that there are other groups who want to be heard, but who are not recognised in the peace process and who still claim a forum they are not given. As political parties, I think they could become a social force in due course.

I have come to understand that there is a big civil society - the locals, the indigenous, the people - who have been forgotten in this period of peace and reconciliation by the UN and the Angolan Government. The people have not been brought into the peace process. Peace to me is an end to war which paves the way to achieving development.

This assembly here is a mini UN assembly: different institutions, political parties, NGOs, military arms sellers, representatives of MI5, CIA .... *(laughter)* but the important thing is that we all said we should work for peace. The message that the workshop should pass on, without mentioning UNITA and MPLA, is that we support peace. If we mention that UNITA should respect the earlier elections, this would make us partisan, and it would be short of bringing about a government with a broad base. As long as we look for development of the people, we have to look at the local level, at the grassroots: they must participate in the peace process. We must look again at the worth of our people. *(Applause ***)*

Joanna Lewis (African Studies Centre):

I would just like to briefly say three things at this point. First, to respond to Alison Tierney's criticism of the organisation of the rebuilding community panel. When we invited Fernando Pacheco to speak it was with the idea of him sitting on this panel. But we soon realised that putting a representative of civil society on the Angolan panel was also important. We had hoped we could incorporate him more this morning, but this did not work out. Nevertheless, the publicity he received by speaking yesterday was far greater than if he had only spoken today: for example he was interviewed by the BBC.

Secondly, I would be interested in following up Rajah Jarrah's suggestion and including something about mines in any communique with the British government. Thirdly, I would like to thank all our panelists over the last two days for making such an effort to give their time free to be here, despite heavy schedules and, in Victoria Brittain's case, despite ill-health. I have been very impressed by the way they have shown how much Angola matters to them. Thank you. *(Applause ***)*

Reginald Green (Professor, Development Studies, Sussex University):

This raises the problem of worlds as they are, not as we would like them to be. First, peace in Angola is only the first step. If there was one thing the two main contending parties agreed upon during the period prior to the election, it was that no third party should get a hearing. If there is one thing that these two organisations agree upon, not with each other obviously, it is that independent sources of power whether they are local or associated with political organisations, women's organisations, cooperatives or trade unions are dangerous. We have heard plenty of voices here that have raised this in one way or another.

However, my comment would be that one should certainly need to bear in mind, and this is quite central, and anyone here with an ongoing interest in Angola should understand, that the only possible outcome at the Lusaka peace talks is a joint government of the two main parties. This is not unfortunately the quickest way to get space for civil society organisations or any of the other political parties.

On the other hand, we will never get any space for them in war and people won't stay alive. There is no great future for dead people. Whether one is rehabilitating livelihoods or getting space for political parties, one has to get peace first. But in terms of the similar characteristics of the two main actors, there are very considerable problems, whether one wants to call it democracy, whether one wants to call it participatory, or whether one wants to call it capitalist government.

Peace is very much the first stage. But again I would like to point out that the UN may be able to organise the peace process, but to assume the UN is any pertinent judge of how to get freedom for more persons or more participation by civil society, I would only comment that it is an organisation of governments and bureaucrats, and its judgement on anything, beyond trying to get a peace process and an end to war, is so disastrous, that one hardly wants to get to that business.

The immediate message has to be simple. Unless there is peace, there will be nothing else; and if one has an ongoing interest, other than the quiet life for foreign investors and merchants, then peace is very much a first step, because the political situation after peace is going to be very far from what I think the majority of this group, Angolans or otherwise, think is satisfactory.
*(Applause ***)*

Fatima Pimentel (Angola Community in the UK):

My name is Fatima. I am an Angolan and I do voluntary work with the Angolan community, although I speak as an individual and I don't subscribe to any political party.

First of all, I have to give a message to Teresa from the UK Ambassador to Angola. He apologises because he won't be here for this afternoon's session as he had prior commitments. This morning she clobbered him from the panel *(laughter)* and he was not very happy. So he asked me to clarify that, when he said that some of the people who were applying for asylum were leading normal lives in Angola, he meant the few cases he was asked to investigate, mainly of people who came over here on bursaries or with letters of support from organisations and once here, they applied for asylum and, when they investigated them, they were leading normal lives in Angola. He was not disregarding the genuine asylum seekers. He was only referring to those few people. That's the end of the message.

For my part, as I said, speaking as an individual, when doing voluntary work sometimes, I hear stories from both sides. Some people will come and say "Look what UNITA did to me". Sometimes they will say "Look, the Government did this to me"; and sometimes they have the scars to prove it. I find some of it quite difficult to reconcile with a democratic approach.

Nobody wakes up one morning and says "Oh! I'm a democrat". Democracy requires understanding, tolerance and an awful lot of patience; and I'm afraid these are qualities that most human beings are not born with. They have to learn them and develop them. And it takes an awful lot of time to develop tolerance and patience.

I believe that the Angolan people through their suffering are ready for democracy if only the two main parties would stop locking horns. Naturally in a situation of civil war there is a lot of healing to be done and the healing process can only take place once democracy becomes a reality. And this begins with peace. So in my view, the sooner the healing process can start, the better.
*(Universal applause ******)*

Unknown Angolan man:

I am an Angolan. The present conflict is between UNITA and the government, not UNITA and the MPLA. We must not forget the immediate need for mine clearance in the country.

Keith Hart:

Well, thank you all. What I propose is to draft some sort of message, a copy of which will go to Lusaka about our desire for peace, and I think there is sufficient support for the notion that the idea that the peace talks are a duopoly is not widely agreed with; that there seems to be an exclusion of other parties ....

(At this point the Chair is interrupted)

Peter Brayshaw (Angola Emergency Committee):

The National Assembly – that's where this debate should take place. The only reason why the Lusaka peace talks are taking place is because UNITA launched a war when they lost the elections.

(Shouting breaks out from a number of quarters)

Keith Hart:

I think it's interesting that it is an English politician who has precipitated disorder in order to make a partisan point. I was hoping we were going to end with Angolan voices.

Tegegne Teka (Lecturer, Addis Ababa, Ph.D student, Cambridge):

Let us support peace and let us not take sides.
*(Applause ***)*

Marco Ramazzotti (Natural Resource Consultant):

Let us allow Hart and Campino to draft a short message and anyone who wants to see it before can leave a fax number.

(The audience seemed to rally around this.)

Keith Hart:

OK then. Our message should be about the desire for peace and that we do not agree with the current duopoly in place. Can I thank you all once again for participating in this workshop. *(Prolonged applause *******)*

THE CURTAIN FALLS

Beach life with oil platform — Photograph by Zed Nelson

Communiqué to Lusaka and response

DIRECTOR: DR KEITH HART
Tel: (0223) 334396/9
Library: 334398

FREE SCHOOL LANE
CAMBRIDGE
CB2 3RQ

Mr. Blondin Beye,
Special Representative of the U.N.
Secretary-General for Angola,
Hotel Intercontinental,
Room 748,
Lusaka,
Zambia

23rd March 1994

Dear Mr. Beye,

WHY ANGOLA MATTERS

Over a hundred of us, Angolans and their friends, met in Cambridge on 21-22 March 1994 to discuss "Why Angola Matters" to the rest of the world as well as to its own people. Our group included representatives of the Angolan and British governments, UNITA and other parties, the United Nations, non-governmental organisations, academics, businessmen, journalists and students.

Angolans want nothing more than to live in peace now. The presence here of both sides in the war was a powerful symbol of the desire for national reconciliation. This must be reinforced by a strong commitment from the world community to end the human suffering in Angola. Enormous resources are needed to rebuild society there; but there is no more urgent test of humanity's collective will to right the wrongs of the Cold War era.

The future of the Southern and Central African region, especially the transition to democracy in South Africa and Mozambique, depends on international affirmation of respect for the electoral process, for the rule of law over violence. For this and many other reasons Angola **matters** to us all.

The participants in the conference therefore decided to issue an appeal to both the government and UNITA delegations in Lusaka. We urge them to make every possible effort and to show the flexibility and good will needed to reach an agreement which would enable the Angolan people to enjoy the longlasting peace they deserve after so many years of war.

Keith Hart
Director

UNAVEM II
ANGOLA

Missão de Verificação das
Nações Unidas em Angola
II

United Nations Angola
Verification Mission
II

Lusaka, 29 March 1994

Dear Director,

It was with great pleasure that I received your letter by which you informed me of the holding of a conference at the University of Cambridge, on 21 and 22 March, on the theme of Angola. This discussion, which brought together various important personalities - representatives of the Angolan Government and UNITA, university lecturers and students, researchers, historians, pressmen and representatives of international agencies - had the merit of sensitizing international opinion on the tragedy which is playing out in Angola and especially to underscore the need and the urgency of achieving a peaceful solution in this country torn apart by war for close to two decades.

I was deeply moved by your message and, in accordance with your wishes, I shared its contents with the delegations participating in the Angolan peace talks in Lusaka, who appreciated it very much. The mediation, of which the United Nations has put me in charge, is working tirelessly to approximate the positions of both parties and concretize the wish that we all cherish, namely, peace in unity and national reconciliation.

For this very laudable initiative on your part, I reiterate my thanks and brotherly greetings which I would wish you to extend to the participants of the Cambridge conference and I avail myself of this opportunity to present the assurance of my highest consideration.

Maître Alioune Blondin Beye
Special Representative of the
Secretary General of the United Nations

Mr. Keith Hart
Director
Centre for African Studies
University of Cambridge

Later...

Chris Eldridge

Alex Vines

Patrick Smith

Chris Eldridge – Programme Officer for Southern Africa, Save the Children Fund:

Comments on the Claim that by Working in Huambo, NGOs 'Legitimate' UNITA

General

1. Safeguarding children's rights is a paramount concern of SCF and other NGOs. It is the reason for our existence. SCF's founder drafted the Declaration of the Rights of the Child, which was adopted by the League of Nations in 1924. The Declaration comprises the core of the UN Convention of the Rights of the Child, signed in 1989 and since ratified by over 100 member states.

   Particularly important among these rights are the rights to:

   – survival and development (Article 6 of the UN Convention);

   – the highest attainable standard of health, and to appropriate health services (Article 24);

   – free primary education (Article 28)

   – protection and care during armed conflict (Article 38).

   SCF has an implicit mandate to protect these rights. This mandate is recognised by the people for whom we work, by virtue of their participation in the programmes we run. it derives from their governments, who sanction our work; the individuals, donor governments, who sanction our work; the individuals, donor governments and organisations who fund our work; and the UN, which recognises the increasingly important role of NGOs in both relief and development.

   These rights are indivisible and inalienable. Our mandate to protect them applies in peace and in times of conflict and disaster. It extends across geographical, political and military boundaries.

2. From the paramount principle of the Rights of the Child flows another equally important principle: that of the impartiality of humanitarian aid, particularly during conflict. This principle should not be subverted or compromised by military or political operations carried out by or on behalf of the UN, as happened, for instance, in Somalia.

Children, above all, are the innocent victims of war. They are maimed, killed, orphaned, separated from their parents, forcibly conscripted into armed forces, and deprived of their rights to good health, basic education and development. Children on all sides of conflict have the same rights, and to all of them werespond insofar as we are able to do so. This qualification needs to be made, since our ability to work in a independent and impartial manner is increasingly constrained by, among other factors:

– shortages of independent funding (income obtained from private funding, and not from bi- or multi-lateral donors);

– the current number and variety of intra-state conflicts: most of the 50 or so conflicts in the world in early 1994 were intra-state (a greater proportion than ten years earlier, when Cold War rivalry often concealed the economic disparities, demographic imbalances, and religious tensions which, rather than ideological differences, are now increasingly the causes of new conflicts).

The complex and varied nature of these conflicts means that we cannot conceptualise humanitarian work in terms of 'sides'. Conflict, like famine, kills children on all sides of political and military divides (and to a much greater extent now than in previous centuries, as a result of technological advances which allow destruction to be delivered from great distances). Talk of legitimising a particular group reflects a misunderstanding of the role of NGOs, a misunderstanding which reference to children's rights should remove: NGOs concerned with children should be striving, in the areas where they work, to safeguard the legitimate rights of all children, regardless of where they happen, by accident of birth or family location, to be.

A related misunderstanding sometimes arises from the use of the term 'neutrality'. Neutrality is a specific concept in international law, where it means studied non-involvement. It therefore seems inappropriate in a humanitarian crisis. One cannot be inactive or silent – one cannot be neutral –about the suffering and death of children.

Perhaps a more appropriate concept than neutrality is that of impartiality, of being non-partisan, which implies the obligation mentioned above: to strive to safeguard the rights of children.

While SCF aims at all times to be impeccably non-partisan, it is difficult to draw general conclusions from our recent experience in various kinds of conflict about how this aim translates into action, because of the complex and varied nature of these conflicts. What we can do is to take a pragmatic approach and base our work on a considered and individual assessment of each situation. The test we should apply should be: given both resource and security constraints, what approach will be most effective in safeguarding the rights of children caught up in conflict? Depending on these constraints the answer might be: work on both/all 'sides'; work on only one side; do not work. And the nature of the work will vary according to the exigencies of the situation.

The Situation in Huambo:

1. SCF (UK) began working in Huambo in 1990, with family tracing, social work training, emergency assistance and agricultural rehabilitation programmes. We continued until the resumption of the war, in October 1992, forced us to suspend our work. Our work laid upon us a dual obligation to return – an obligation to the people for whom we had been working, and an obligation to our Angolan staff.

2. In September 1992 the MPLA won the Angolan parliamentary elections, which foreign observers and the UN announced were free and fair. Victory in a democratic election gives the winning party or collation a responsibility for all the people of the country, wherever they might be. By working in Huambo – with the agreement of the MPLA government – we are accepting this responsibility on behalf of the government in certain sectors.

   In the absence of government structures in Huambo, we are working directly through our own staff and with our own structures. For example, in the south of the city we are running four centres delivering health and nutrition services: 2,400 children were being fed every day in March 1994.

3. We would therefore distinguish between attempting to strengthen government services, as we are doing in Lobito, by helping the provincial Ministry of Health deliver primary health services, and working in the absence of government structures, as in Huambo, where we are quite definitely not strengthening UNITA health services – we are autonomous (we fly in our own fuel supplies for example), and, moreover, no UNITA health services exist in the areas where we are working.

4. The fact that the MPLA government agrees that an NGO can work in a UNITA controlled area, and that UNITA agrees to accept the presence in Huambo of an NGO actively working elsewhere to strengthen the government means that neither the MPLA nor UNITA can argue that we are working solely for their opponents.

5. Finally, the presence in Huambo of an autonomous and independent organisation perhaps gives people caught up in a conflict over which they have no control the small comfort that they have not been entirely forgotten by the international community.

Alex Vines – Human Rights Watch, Africa:

The Siege of Cuito: A Visit By Human Rights Watch

The human cost since the conflict restarted in October is impossible to determine, but UN estimates put it at over 100,000. In July 1993, the UN reported that as many as 1,000 people were dying daily from starvation, disease, and war wounds. In the besieged government-held city of Malanje alone, 250 child deaths were reported each day in October 1993, though this number had decreased to 26 per day by January 1994.

This is a war notable for human rights abuses. Indiscriminate shelling of starving besieged cities by the União Nacional para a Independência Total de Angola (UNITA) rebels has resulted in massive destruction of property and the loss of untold numbers of civilians. The human cost is staggering. So is the lack of international attention. Angola is being increasingly known as the "forgotten war".

Human Rights Watch's Africa division (recently renamed Human Rights Watch/Africa from Africa Watch) has been publishing reports on human rights abuses in Angola since April 1989. In May and June 1994 Human Rights Watch visited Angola and travelled to both government and rebel held areas in order to collect information on recent human rights abuses. The results of this mission will be published this autumn in War and Weapons: Human Rights Abuses in Angola since the Elections, a book length report.

The plight of the people of Cuito is particularly appalling. The city of Cuito, the provincial capital of the central province of Bie, has been totally devastated following a nine-month siege by UNITA forces in 1993 which began on 5 January. From that date nobody except foreign nationals has been able to leave the city. Those that crossed into UNITA zones are not heard of or seen again by the residents. As in Huambo the majority of people in Cuito had voted for UNITA in the elections.

It is believed that some 15,000 people died in 1993 in Cuito, either from the direct effects of war or indirectly through starvation or related diseases. When fighting started in January it was initially difficult to distinguish who was fighting who because of the fierce street battles around the city centre. UNITA was successfully pushed out of town. But by April 1993, UNITA had been able to break the Government's defences and fight back to within a radius of some 9 kilometres. Subsequent fierce fighting badly destroyed the city and UNITA took control of one area within it. By June the main avenue which led to and through the city had become the front line, marked out by lines of stones, waist or shoulder high walls of sandbags splitting and barricading divided streets, with anti-personnel and booby-trapped explosives in gutted backyards and buildings along the line. The fighting had reduced the city's fine colonial buildings and pastel-painted villas to ruins. Not a single house emerged unscathed. Whole apartment blocks have been gutted; they spill their interiors onto the streets below. Many people had moved into the city centre buildings to take refuge from UNITA's progress mid the artillery shells, mortar bombs and sniper fire. The inside of these buildings had become blackened shells, housing thousands of refugees, mainly women and children, living side by side in squalid conditions, permanently covered in a thick grey smoke from cooking pots

From June, UNITA inched its way forward, fighting block by block. By November, some 40,000 people, including non-combatants, soldiers and civilian militia, were trapped in an area of I0 blocks. Between June 1993 and June 1994 the government held the eastern part of the city, containing most of the city centre and some mud hut "bairro" neighbourhoods. UNITA controlled the western and south-eastern areas, including the central hospital. As UNITA advanced toward the hospital in May, residents brought its medical supplies and equipment into their side of town, but a UNITA shell hit the shop where it was kept. A ruined primary school was then turned into a hospital for the seriously wounded, while first aid posts sprung up across town. The one remaining Angolan doctor left the city through hunger in August 1993, crossing into UNITA zones. Paramedics and nurses continued meanwhile to try and treat victims without anaesthetic and with rudimentary instruments. In July and August, 1993 1000 rounds of heavy artillery shell rained down on Cuito every day. Every building in Cuito is damaged and UNITA had clearly made little attempt to target its shelling. Casualty rates were high. On June 11, 1993 one shell resulted in thirty nine people being killed in central Cuito. Several families were wiped out in this incident. Shrapnel wounds are common. During the period June to October 1993, the local population survived by eating leaves, grass, banana roots and toasted maize. Thousands of children died and the adults lost between 10 and 25 kilos on average. It is currently officially estimated that about 30,000 remain in the town on the Government side. The population on the UNITA side has in contrast been able to take refuge in the outlying villages and soldiers are the only people from the UNITA side to be seen in the town. The previous population of the town was 150,000.

On 21 September, 1993, a unilateral cease-fire was declared by UNITA which led to a fragile suspension of hostilities over the following weeks. A UN mission to Cuito was sent on 12 October to assess the situation and make contact with the local authorities on either side. As a result, the first World Food Programme (WFP) cargo flight of humanitarian assistance was completed on 16 October. However on 17 October, although three WFP relief flights were scheduled, the third flight was not authorized to land by UNITA. This led to three WFP staff members being unable to leave Cuito. UNITA officials declared that they had not intended to detain the UN staff members but were concerned that operational modalities needed to be discussed before further cargo flights could be carried out. The WFP staff stayed in the city for three days until flights resumed on 21 October. On 29 October, the UN evacuated from Cuito to São Tomé 121 non-Angolans (Portuguese and other foreigners), who had been trapped since the commencement of hostilities.

During the siege of the town, the Government has carried out airdrop operations targeting the population in Government held areas (Cuito and Cunje). Since the UN started airlift operations, the Government has continued airdrop activities for civilians in Cunje and the military in Cuito. Incidents involving exchange of fire or disputes occur when parachutes of supplies fall on no man's land or UNITA territory. In November, recurring incidents of this nature resulted in heavy fighting between the Government and UNITA forces in the area between Cunje and Cuito and around the town. All foreign personnel were evacuated on 23 November and humanitarian aid flights suspended. On 24 November, the situation was calmer and the WFP flights resumed In December, the situation remained quiet, apart from an incident on 11 December when a WFP staff member present in Cuito witnessed a Government plane drop four bombs in UNITA areas close to the town.

On 5 February, 1994 intense fighting between both forces broke out and continued throughout the week, killing hundreds of civilians and soldiers. A dispute originated over a tree branch in no man's land which government troops attempted to drag flack to their side for firewood. Shots began in the air, but were aimed later at individuals, deteriorating into a fire-fight. The WFP was obliged to cancel relief flights and international NGO staff were evacuated by road to Huambo. Following negotiations by the UN with Government and UNITA officials the WFP was able to fly again to Cuito on 14 February and the NGOs returned.

The WFP was flying 90 tonnes of food each week to Cuito on average to provide 100,000 people, or 50,000 on each side, with a minimum diet. With probably some 30,000 living on the government side, these weekly shipments provide some cushion for residents when fighting halts the flights and when extra quotas are taken by soldiers. UNITA benefits more. There are no civilians in its sector of the city as they had been forced to evacuate to the surrounding countryside. The food for UNITA is taken to a warehouse located a few miles from an important UNITA logistics base.

After lengthy negotiations UNITA also allowed UN and NGO officials to visit the government held town of Cunje on 16 March by road from Cuito. Cunje had been isolated from external contact for over a year. The mission estimated that around 25-30,000 people were in need of assistance.

What is Human Rights Watch?

Human Rights Watch conducts regular, systematic investigations of human rights abuses in some seventy countries around the world, including Angola. It addresses the human rights practices of governments of all political stripes, of all geopolitical alignments, and of all ethnic and religious persuasions. In internal wars it documents violations by both government and rebel groups. Human Rights Watch defends freedom of thought and expression, due process and equal protection of the law; it documents and denounces murders, disappearances, torture, arbitrary imprisonment, exile, censorship and other abuses of internationally recognized human rights.

Human Rights Watch began in 1978 with the founding of its Helsinki division. Today, it includes five divisions covering Africa, the Americas, Asia, the Middle East, as well as the signatories of the Helsinki accords. It also includes five collaborative projects on arms, children's rights, free expression, prison conditions, and women's rights. It maintains offices in New York, Washington, Los Angeles, London, Brussels, Moscow, Belgrade, Zagreb and Hong Kong. Human Rights Watch is an independent, non-governmental organization (NGO), supported by contributions from private individuals and foundations. It accepts no government funds, directly or indirectly.

Further information about the activities of Human Rights Watch can be obtained from: Human Rights Watch, 33 Islington High St., London N1 9LH.

Previously, the civilian population (mainly women) had been allowed to come to Cuito on foot through well-known paths, but could only carry back two kilos of food.

On 26 May, a day after Human Rights Watch had been in the city, fighting broke out again in Cuito, allegedly because drunk UNITA soldiers threw first rocks and then grenades at a house in which a government military commander was holding a meeting. Hundreds more civilian casualties were reported. Nine days later, on 4 June, international NOD workers were evacuated when a brief cease-fire was arranged. Two ICRC workers decided to stay but were eventually evacuated. Cunje was also attacked by UNITA and heavily shelled. In this fighting the government, against expectations, succeeded in pushing UNITA out of the city, using air support. On 2 June, government aircraft bombed UNITA positions including the Central Hospital. Aerial bombing of outlying UNITA positions continued on 10 and 11 June. A UNITA counter-offensive in August has recaptured some parts of the city and fighting continues.

Surprisingly fraternization between the soldiers of both sides was common during lulls in fighting. Human Rights Watch noted groups of UNITA and government soldiers mingling in the middle of the road along the front-line, effectively no man's land. There were also examples of games in which government soldiers gambled salt or tins of sardines from government parachute drops for UNITA batches of firewood, a rarity in the city. Trade had become so regular that UNITA troops had set up makeshift breweries to produce "cachipembe", a strong maize-base liquor, for sale to the government side. This was exchanged with government soldiers on the front-line in barter deals. A women trader called Alice admitted that:

"The soldiers control all trade. I get my produce from a commander. He takes most of the profit. He gets some things from UNITA: that is how it is."

Olegario Cardoso, one of the most prominent of the businessmen who remain in the city, explained at his business premises, known as Casa Ford:

" For a while the government decrees a ban on trade with UNITA or UNITA issues orders to stop selling to the city, and the business stops. But it soon resumes because we need the firewood and they need salt and cloths. There are cousins and sometimes even brothers fighting each other across that line. This is a crazy war of crazy people. One minute they do business together and the next they kill each other"

Sniper Fire

Sniper fire between June to September 1993 caused many casualties along government held buildings facing the front line. To avoid snipers, people tore holes in walls, connecting all houses in each block, but still had to risk going out to get supplies and water. One particular sniper was very effective - being located on top of the cinema where he got a fine view of the front line. On one occasion a rope was thrown out from Casa Ford to an injured women to fish her in safety before the sniper finished her off. Such testimonies are widespread in Cuito. Alice, a twenty four year old, lives across the road from Casa Ford at the ruined Hotel Cuito. She was an eyewitness to countless UNITA sniper shots.

"Eleven people I know were killed by that UNITA sniper. He had a telescopic sight because it sometimes caught the sun. He shot old, young, women and children. Everybody was a potential target. He wanted to kill. Marcela, my sister was shot in the leg by him. But refused to stop. He shot her three times to ensure she was dead. We did not go out in daylight unless in an emergency and then only by running fast and not in straight lines. Moonlight was also really bad. But we needed fresh water. That UNITA can't be from around here. He would never try and kill his own people in that cold way."

Hunger

Between April and September 1993 food security deteriorated rapidly in Cuito as government airdrops to the city were inaccurate and not substantial enough to feed the residents in the government held sector. A response to the growing scarcity of food and malnutrition was the forming of "batidas". These were large groups of desperate people who would cross the lines into UNITA territory to fetch food from the countryside. Sometimes two hundred strong, these groups braved heavy UNITA gunfire and mine fields to find food. Casualty levels could be as high as one third of the party that set out. Hunger weakened the city's defences. As the batidas became larger and had to venture out further, soldiers abandoned their positions in search of food. Alcinda went on several of these batidas. She describes what happened:

"We were so hungry that we had to get out of the city and find food. We tried to do this silently as we already knew the paths. The danger was that UNITA had laid mines on these. In July [1993] I was with a group which entered into a newly laid UNITA minefield. Ten died and several injured crawled back. Soldiers came with us to help us find food and provide cover gun fire if UNITA saw us. Usually a batida ended up in gunfights as UNITA also kept a look-out for us, especially when we were heavily laden on our return. They could then collect and keep or sell to us what they had taken from our dead."

A nurse at the hospital confirmed that casualties were high during the period of the "batidas". She said: "We knew when a batida had taken place because the next day the injured would arrive. Sometimes they would reach us several days after the event having only crept back at night because of UNITA snipers".

The desperation for food in Cuito was so acute that there was no coercion into joining a batida. However Human Rights Watch obtained testimonies from women who had been forced by government officers to go into no man's land to collect parachute supplies intended for them but which had missed their target. A women related the following:

"A few weeks ago [May 1994] when parachutes came down José, a Ninja, ordered that I and some others go into the bush to pick up some supplies for them. UNITA did not cause my injury but government soldiers, they fired at me and then at the police who fired back. A lot of confusion followed. Two civilians were killed and the others are in the hospital."

Human Rights Watch visited the hospital. A government official told us that all those injured in the hospital from gunshot wounds were casualties caused by UNITA. When interviewing later, without government presence, it was established that they were from this gunfight between police and army over parachute supplies. According to the medical staff at the hospital fighting also starts when government soldiers sneak into UNITA-held territory to retrieve supplies of foodstuffs, cigarettes and ammunition dropped from high altitude parachute drops. Even when they hit their target, they provoke clashes among government soldiers and police. In an attempt to reduce this squabbling parachute drops for the police and army are made on different days. But residents say they have seen little improvement. When UNITA is not shelling, and humanitarian aid is not suspended, exchanges of fire between different government military groups are the single greatest cause of civilian casualties.

Divided Families

There are countless accounts of divided families. Eduardo Sauro suffers badly from leprosy and his colony was taken over in early January by UNITA while he was in town looking for treatment. It is a few miles away behind UNITA lines and he waits for the day he can return home to join his wife and four children.

Vitor is an nine year old boy from Cunje. He was brought to Cuito for medical treatment and could not return when fighting started in January 1993. His mother, who had been with him, was killed in July by UNITA shelling. He does not know whether his father is still alive in the government held town of Cunje, seven miles away.

Both are innocent victims of this war and depend for their survival on the relief work of international agencies when the government and UNITA rebels are willing to allow these to operate.

Burial of the Dead

Because the cemetery remained on UNITA's side, the dead in Cuito are buried in gardens, parks, sidewalks, and front yards. They were also buried in balconies and roofs by scattering whatever was available over them. Some of the mounds are marked with simple wooden crosses, others with bottles or branches of withered leaves.

Why Cuito Matters

Cuito's civilians have experienced terrible violations of their human rights ranging from indiscriminate shelling by UNITA to conscription of children under 15 by government forces defending the city. Such abuses are in violation of international laws, such as Article 3 of the 1949 Geneva Conventions and the UN Convention on the Rights of the Child. These abuses should not be forgotten, they matter. Human Rights Watch will continue in its efforts to make them matter, especially for those responsible for abuses in places such as Cuito.

Patrick Smith – Africa Confidential:

An update on Angola since the conference

The Lusaka protocol signed on 20 November 1994, while meeting with scepticism on all sides, does address the key issues raised in the wake of UNITA'S rejection of the 1992 election results and return to war. While both the United Nations and the Organisation of Africa Unity supported sanctions against UNITA aimed at weakening its offensive capacity, the thrust of the diplomacy has been to bring enough safeguards into a ceasefire then a peace settlement that will guarantee UNITA physical security and a role in government.

Discussions on the content of a new protocol, which is an adjunct and not a replacement for the 1991 Bicesse Accords, started in November 1993. In the year it took to get to the signing of a new protocol in Lusaka three critical themes emerged from the negotiations:

1. That there must be an agreed power sharing arrangement at central government level and at provincial government level, and to a lesser extent in the management of state-owned corporations. Once accepted as a principle in the negotiations much subsequent discussion centered on which portfolios and which governorships/deputy governorships would be offered to UNITA.

2. That there must be an adequate international peacekeeping and monitoring force to oversee military demobilisation and provide security guarantees across the country. There was agreement on a UN force of some 6,000 - 7,000 (about ten times the size of the UN force in 1992). The hope was that this would prevent the development of 'two administrations' where large swathes of the country are shut off to the central government, and secondly to prevent 'false demobilisation' and the caching of weapons.

3. That regional powers, particularly after South Africa's transition to democracy, will have to play a more substantive diplomatic role and provide much of the personnel for the peace-keeping and monitoring team. The apparent success of the peace agreement and elections in Mozambique (particularly the roles of Presidents Robert Mugabe and Nelson Mandela in keeping the process on track) has engendered more optimism about sustaining a settlement in Angola. Indeed, it is South Africa's position as representative of Africa's struggle for democracy and national reconciliation (in addition to its relative economic and military strength) that provides the new impetus for a regional settlement.

However, the circumstances around the signing of the Lusaka protocol were not propitious. UNITA leader Jonas Savimbi did not attend the signing having said he was unhappy with security arrangements for his transportation from Angola to Zambia, and heavy fighting continued in the north and central highlands after the ceasefire was due to come into force on 22 November. The national mood, too, seemed very different from the time of the 1991 Bicesse Accords when there was a strong belief across the country that a turning point in the war had been reached. Clearly, much of that belief derived from UNITA's enthusiastic participation in the Bicesse negotiations, buoyed by its belief (supported by several Western diplomats) that it would win the elections.

But in two years of post-election war (1993-94) UNITA depleted much of its military and political strength. Its involvement in the peace process is seen by some of its senior cadres as an admission of weakness, and by others as a tactical necessity in the course of regrouping having lost many of its key logistical bases in the central highlands and the north. The government's dominant view expressed by Chief of Staff General João de Matos was: "It is necessary to have a military imbalance to reach agreement." By November 1994 it was clear that the imbalance was decisively in the government's favour, but within the government opinions differed about how far the government should go militarily. On one hand there were arguments that the government should press home its advantage by destroying as much of UNITA's military capacity as possible, and on the other that there was a need to deal with UNITA more on a political level in an effort to start the reconciliation process.

Essentially, post-Lusaka diplomacy had to provide a bridge between two military positions:

a) The UNITA view that the 22 November ceasefire provided an opportunity to regroup after a year of defeats and that, under no circumstances, should it surrender its key resource bases such as the diamond fields in Lunda Norte and Lunda Sul. Much of the fiercest fighting after the scheduled start of the ceasefire was in these two provinces.

b) The MPLA government view that UNITA had to be neutralised as far as possible which would include the destruction of their command and control network (already badly damaged by the loss of Huambo City), together with the cutting of their supply routes from Zaire.

Accordingly Alioune Blondin Beye and his UN team saw political and social reconciliation as far less of a problem than creating and sustaining a framework for military and security joint action. In the words of one UN advisor: "Once the military cooperation starts, the impetus for a political compact will soon overtake it." The critical question remaining in the wake of Lusaka is how soon will military cooperation be effective. The arrival of UNITA's military team headed by Brigadier Isias Samakuva in Luanda on 4 December to sit on the new Joint Political-Military Commission was seen as a considerable step forward after a year of negotiations.

Reviewing the progress at Lusaka, it is possible to discern some patterns:

November 1993. After a six week sojourn in Abidjan in the middle of year, MPLA and UNITA delegations arrive in Lusaka and talks begin on two critical issues - firstly, a ceasefire agreement while negotiations proceed and secondly, UNITA's withdrawal from the areas of the country (then about 70 per cent of the land mass) it occupies. The UN special envoy Alioune Blondin Beye, who took over the job from Margaret Anstee in July 1993, makes it clear that he is prepared to chair the discussions/negotiations for as long as it takes to reach agreement. Beye's style was very different from Anstee's: he used his first four months in the post pursuing some vigorous shuttle diplomacy, followed by detailed soundings in October on the agenda for the Lusaka talks. While the agenda for Lusaka was based on the 1991 Bicesse Accords, Beye opened up the discussions as widely as possible amongst the participants and promptly imposed a news blackout on the proceedings.

December 1993. The initial objective is for a ceasefire by 20 December and demobilisation talks proceed on this basis. Agreement was reached on the modalities of UNITA's return to the Forças Armadas Angolanas (the new national army to be formed from both sides in the conflict) from which UNITA had withdrawn immediately after the 1992 elections. The next stage in the discussions centered on the role of the police during which UNITA demanded the disbanding of the 'Emergency Police' or 'Ninjas'. Progress in the discussions was halted after a government air raid on UNITA positions around Cuito on 11 December. UNITA broke off talks claiming the air raid amounted to an assassination attempt against Savimbi who was reportedly giving a speech in the area at the time.

January 1994. After further stand offs over the bombing of Cuito, UNITA and MPLA delegations reconvened in Lusaka. Talks resume about the restructuring of the police force: although UNITA withdrew its demand for the disbanding of the ' Ninjas', argument continues about the size of the police force, in particular the level of UNITA participating in the ranks and in the command structure. By the end of the month the two sides reached a provisional agreement on the restructuring of the police. While these detailed and substantive discussions continued in the Lusaka between MPLA and UNITA their sponsors in Angola are engaged in sharply escalating hostilities. In early January government forces recaptured the northern port of Abriz and began putting pressure on the oil-producing town of Soyo. Government forces also regained control of the four crossings over the Kwanza river which effectively cut UNITA's lorry convoy route from the rich agricultural areas around Uige to its headquarters at Huambo, in the central highlands. This left only two UNITA supply routes in regular use: one up eastern Angola through the diamond-rich Lunda provinces to Zaire and a second down to the Namibian border near Rundu.

February 1994. Discussions at Lusaka turned to modalities for power sharing with UNITA demanding key ministerial posts such as the Interior and Defence Ministry. The government then submitted counter proposals rejecting UNITA's demands and offering lower grade posts. The division of political spoils became the central issue at Lusaka and prompted a series of internal consultations while the delegates referred back to their principals. Hostilities inside Angola intensfied further: most importantly, fighting around Cuito escalated after 5 February, the worst that the Central highlands had seen before the Lusaka talks began. Also in early February, government army cargo 'planes started ferrying asphalt up to the north eastern city of Saurimo to upgrade the air strip there (the purpose being to accommodate MiG and Sukhoi bombers to start an assault on UNITA's hold on the diamond-mining areas). At the same time the government's long march towards Huambo started: four columns, from Lubango, from Benguela, from Lobito and down from the north: by the end of February government forces were reckoned to be about 80 km from Huambo.

March 1994. Following further discussions about sharing of ministerial portfolios in Lusaka, reports emerged from the talks that there could be a signing by the end of the month. The optimism proved premature when it became clear that the government and UNITA would not be able to agree on the critical question of provincial governorships. The government offered: the ministries of Post, Mining, Hotels and Tourism, Public Works and Commerce; the deputy ministries of Defence, Interior, Social Reintegration, Finance, Information and Agriculture; and the provincial governorships of Cuando-Cubango in the south-east, Lunda-Sul in the east, and Uige in the north (all outside UNITA's main support base in the central highlands); deputy governorships of Luanda, Cuanza Sul, Benguela, Huila, and Bengo. In turn, UNITA demanded the governorships of Bie, Huambo and Benguela (giving it political control of the key swathe of territory making up the central highlands), as well as the three the MPLA offered and deputy governorships of Huila, Luanda, Bie, Cuanza Norte, Malanje, and Moxico. The other major unresolved issue, the reports said, was the future role of the UN monitoring mission, UNAVEM and international observers. Linked to this were arrangements for the second round of voting in the presidential elections: Preside José Eduardo dos Santos won only 49.5 per cent of the vote in 1992 and under the constitution there must be a second round. The fierce fighting in Angola continued to undermine the credibility of the talks; neither side appeared to be negotiating in good faith. Commanders of the Government forces who regained the ascendancy in the war in late 1993 were reluctant to take the Lusaka talks seriously lest they lose the military momentum. At the same time UNITA forces saw the Lusaka talks as an opportunity to slow the war down, and make an interim settlement which could leave them in substantial control of the central highlands (the Ovimbundu heartlands) providing for a de facto ethnically-based partition of the country. On 29 March a report (based on a diplomat's interpretation) emerged that the Lusaka talks had collapsed and would be suspended indefinitely. This was just two weeks after Beye said there had been a 'critical breakthrough' on the power sharing arrangements. This followed a meeting between Beye and Savimbi in the latter's headquarters in Huambo on 12-13 March.

April 1994. Both government and UNITA broke Beye's news blackout on Lusaka and came out with public criticisms of each other's negotiating tactics. Foreign Minister Venancio de Moura called for the UN to impose sanctions and deadlines against UNITA. There were signs of dissension on strategy within UNITA: official spokesman for UNITA Jorge Valentim, who having previously advocated partition of the country as a constitutional solution, backed down and said his organisation wanted devolution of power to the provinces but did not support any division of the country. But Valentim also questioned the viability of the Bicesse Accords as a basis for the Luska negotiations throwing into question the previous five months of negotiations.

May 1994. UNITA's public posture became markedly more conciliatory . It no longer rejected government proposals outright but said they should be the basis for debate which needed some amendment. UNITA defined its starting point in the critical negotiations over power sharing as wanting 'substantial participation at all levels of power, particularly in the ministries of sovereignty and the productive sector'. It wanted a stake in the management of security and the economy, as well as the right to appoint officials in the state-owned oil and diamond companies. Early in the month, there were reports that Washington was putting pressure on the MPLA to compromise in the face of UNITA's military weakness: in particular, MPLA government sources said they were being urged to concede the Huambo governorhip to UNITA. However, the other two members of the observers' troika at Lusaka - Portugal and Russia - appeared to have little sympathy with the United States' position. There were further discussions at Lusaka on the role of the UN, which was considered the least contentious item on the agenda. US sources revealed - perhaps to counter earlier reports about pressure on Luanda - that Clinton had written two personal letters to Dos Santos in April and May, endorsing the government's proposals for power sharing.

June 1994. The agenda at Lusaka moves onto security arrangements for UNITA in Luanda. However the negotiations were further sidelined by the intensification of fighting around Cuito and the disruption of relief flights. Special envoy Paul Hare returns to Washington, frustrated after seven months at the talks but leaving the message that Clinton had supported the government's power sharing offer. UNITA agreed to the government's proposals with one exception: it wanted the governorship of Huambo (after which US official suggested some form of compromise such as a non-partisan administrator taking the Huambo governorship). The new African National Congress-led government in South Africa indicated it was prepared to help mediate in Angola, following Beye's visit to Cape Town at which he referred to Nelson Mandela as a key figure in the regional peace effort. Government military efforts closed in on Soyo, the northern air base of Negage and capital of the diamond-mining areas, Cafunfu. UNITA increased the pressure on Cuito and Malanje, and threatened aid flights to these government-held centres. Intelligence reports indicated that UNITA's logistics were increasingly under strain as a result of the government offensive: despite Savimbi's claims that UNITA had stockpiled enough guns for a decade of war, there were reports of debilitating shortages of spare parts and fuel in UNITA-held territory.

July 1994. A new document on power-sharing is produced by Beye's office and indications were given that UNITA might be prepared to accept the deputy-governorship of

Huambo, rather than the full-governorship. This emboldened Beye to announce that 95 per cent of the agenda at Lusaka had been completed. South Africa continued its intervention with Mandela hosting a meeting with Zaïre's Mobutu Sese Seko in Pretoria, and UNITA representatives visited South Africa for talks about a Mandela-Savimbi meeting. US ambassador to Luanda Edmund de Jarnette publicly urged UNITA to accept the Lusaka package.

August 1994. Lusaka talks moved back to issue of security for UNITA leaders in Luanda, which was negotiated as an annexe to the overall 'reconciliation' or power sharing package. The logistics, structure and composition of the UN Mission and the Joint Political-Military Commission (which will monitor the peace and power-sharing agreement) were discussed. UNITA and the José Tiburcio Zinga Leomba's Cabindan secessionist movement FLEC-Renovada undertook some joint operations in the Belize area of the enclave.

September 1994. The government sharply increased the pressure on Huambo as its four columns moved closer to the outlying areas of the city and its air force stepped up bombing raids. Independent military analysts reckon that government successes had by the beginning of the month reduced the territory controlled by UNITA to some 35 per cent of the country from almost double that a year previously. UNITA temporarily pulled out of the Lusaka talks in protest at the bombing raids on Huambo. There were continuing rumours that Savimbi had either been severely injured or killed in a government bombing raid which knocked out UNITA's communication system; further rumours had him recuperating in hospital in São Tomé or Morocco. However, when it rejoined the talks before the end of the month UNITA representatives publicly agreed to accept that the government would nominate the governor of Huambo. Analysts interpreted this concession as an indication of UNITA's weakness and a tactical move designed to forestall the government's planned recapture of Huambo (it had taken UNITA a 55-day bloody siege to capture the provincial capital in 1993). The government pushed the UN to impose tougher sanctions on UNITA but the Security Council stayed action for a further fortnight to allow the Lusaka talks to conclude.

October 1994. Optimism about the Lusaka talks increased following agreement on power-sharing and in spite of the intensity of fighting around Huambo and in the north. A timetable for the new UN operation emerged from the Lusaka talks: Within 10 days of the signing of a ceasefire agreement, 100 UN troops would be sent to Angola; within 30 days, 350 troops, 126 police observers, and 14 medical personnel would be deployed; within 60-90 days, some 6,000 troops would be despatched to Angola to supervise and monitor implementation of the ceasefire and demobilisation agreement. The one unmentionable factor remained an agreement on the future role of Jonas Savimbi: indeed, his prolonged silence provoked further rumours about his state of health and state of mind. However, this did not prevent government and UNITA delegations initialling the negotiated protocol in Lusaka on 31 October, just one hour before the Security Council deadline.

November 1994. Government forces captured the oil town of Soyo, then Huambo in the week ending 12 November. In spite of UNITA's pledge to fight to the finish, there were signs in Huambo of it having made a tactical withdrawal taking its armoury and supplies and sabotaging the installations it left behind. Following the fall of these two centres there were several reports of UNITA groups caching weapons. Much of the UNITA high command were reported to have retreated from Huambo to Andulo, Bie Province (north-west of Huambo) which was a key air base to receive UNITA supplies from Zaïre. Fighting in the north and in the Central Highlands raged up until and after the formal signing of the protocol in Lusaka on 20 November. Troops deployed in the UN missions were to come overwhelmingly from countries in the region with Botswana, Namibia, South Africa, Zambia and Zimbabwe all offering to send contingents.

December 1994. A UNITA delegation led by Brigadier Isaias Samakuva arrived in Luanda on 4 December for talks on implementing the Lusaka agreement and assembling a Joint Political-Military Commission. The government's chief delegate was Faustin Muteka.

January 1995. The Joint Political-Military Commission meets on 6 January ahead of a meeting between the MPLA government's Chief of Staff Gen. João de Matos and UNITA's Chief of Staff Arlindo Chena 'Ben-Ben' in Chipipa on 10 January. De Matos and Ben Ben agreed to 'ensure immediate cessation of hostilities' and to disengage troops 'currently close to each other in sensitive areas'.

17 January Angolan journalist Ricardo de Mello, director of Imparcialfax Publications, was shot dead in Luanda. Imparcialfax had carried out a series of investigations into corruption in the government and the military.

February 1995. Second meeting of de Matos and Ben Ben in Waco Kungo on 2-3 February to 'consolidate the ceasefire' and to 'convey a message of peace to the national and international communities'. Both military chiefs were to visit their troops in the field to explain to them the provisions of the Lusaka accords and agree to a programme of limited disengagement in Huambo and Uige provinces. The meeting was designed to maintain the momentum ahead of the UN Security Council debate about Angola. 8 February, the UN Security Council agrees on the deployment of 7,000 blue helmet peacekeepers and drew up a timetable for what is to become Unavem III:

1. Planning and support staff to go in immediately;

2. Logistical units to build accommodation and set up communications networks will be sent in April 1995;

3. The first infantry battalions (6,450 troops drawn from Brazil, India, Pakistan, Romania, Uruguay, and Zimbabwe) to be deployed by mid-May;

4. The operation is to come under Security Council scrutiny in August 1995 when another vote will be taken;

5. The Security Council will then review the operation and debate the renewal of the Unavem III mandate at six-monthly intervals.

The 7-12 February UNITA Congress in Bailundo sent contradictory signals: UNITA leader Jonas Savimbi told Congress delegates that the Lusaka accord was a 'piece of paper with no worth' and was 'full of lies' - he later told foreign journalists that he supported the peace process but was having trouble convincing his generals to support it. The Congress communiqué supported all attempts to bring peace to Angola but contained no specific endorsement of the Lusaka accord. The communiqué added that Savimbi was prepared to meet President Dos Santos if that would help the peace process.

Scavenging next to a busy market in Luanda Photograph by Zed Nelson

Conference Papers

Keith Hart

Reginald Green

Keith Hart – Director, African Studies Centre:

Angola and the World Order: the Political Economy of Integration and Division

Angola and Human Interest

When Annie Hall, in the film of the same name, suggests to Woody Allen that they go out to a restaurant for a meal, he replies that he does not feel like eating because of all the starving people out there in the Third World. The audience laughs ... nervously. It is, of course, absurd for a New Yorker's appetite to be affected by such thoughts. Why now and not yesterday or all the time? But we also know that, in order to get through the day, we habitually switch off feelings which connect us to the suffering of human beings everywhere. We know that what happens to other people matters; and we laugh. Laugh or cry – what's the difference?

One day in January 1993, Marco Ramazzotti came into my Cambridge office for the first time. I had been Director of the African Studies Centre for just a year. "They are killing my friends in Angola", he said. "What are you going to do about it?" The question was absurd. I was used to getting requests to read essays or to sign permits for the university library. What was this? One thing was certain: this man's passionate concern brought the recently renewed war in Angola right into my life. For a moment, all the distance, the barriers of ignorance and indifference were cancelled out; and I had to make a human response.

That was the origin of this conference. I called it a 'workshop' in order to reduce the sense of failure if it did not come off, which seemed for so long to be likely. Marco became my partner in launching the idea of a meeting to publicise Angola's plight here. But then he had to go away and the prospect of major funding dwindled. People said that it was pointless to single out Angola with all the other horrors of our world to think about. I was keenly aware of how slender was my own real connection with the place. But the Master of this college, Sir Roger Tomkys, provided support and encouragement when it was needed, as did my friend, Achol Deng who speaks after me. Then Joanne Lewis threw herself into galvanising preparations for the workshop; and I always knew that I had the experience of my closest colleagues, Paul Munro and Salah Bander, to fall back on.

So here we are. The premise is still unlikely; but it is why we are here. Faced with the fact of an ugly and remote civil war, we are charged with answering a single question: why should the rest of the world think that what is going on in Angola matters to them? In what way are we affected? Even more implausibly, how can a meeting in Cambridge University affect what happens in Angola? Perhaps the answer to both sides of the question is "not very much". But I am still here because I refuse to take that answer for granted. Somehow we have to try to build bridges across the ditches we have dug to maintain our separateness from each other. We have to undermine the walls of indifference that define the contours of our late 20th century world.

Each of the speakers in this workshop has a particular reason for addressing 'Why Angola matters' positively. The first group, beginning with this attempt to place Angola within a perspective of global political economy, are concerned with a world order made vulnerable by the end of the Cold War, examining international law, African diplomacy and American policy. Then some prominent Angolans, including the two main parties to the conflict, will explain why the rest of the world should get involved in a country whose problems are largely the result of outside involvement in the first place. In the last session of the first day, speakers representing the government, the anti-apartheid movement and economic journalism will explore British interest in the Angola question.

The second day stresses Angola's importance for the transition to democracy in South Africa, placing it within a highly integrated set of regional political and economic relations. Angola is also a daunting test case for the international community's ability to help in the reconstruction and rehabilitation of societies devastated by war and economic catastrophe. Finally, some of this country's leading journalists from television, radio and the newspapers will ask how Angola reflects the way Africa is reported in the media. This is turn will allow the conference to consider how our conversation can be transformed into the means of persuading others that Angola, among all the world issues clamouring for their attention, really does matter.

My own effort hinges on the attempt to link Angola and Africa more generally to the sense of malaise afflicting most people I know. There is not a single popular government in the world today. The global economy's downward spiral, despite the signs of 'recovery' discerned by compromised southsayers, seems irreversible. I want to convince the citizens of declining rich countries like ours that their economic insecurity has something to do with the fact that most human beings have no money to spend at all. And I want to link that to the main political choice we all face at this time – to fall back on a narrow and divisive protectionism or to seek more integrated solutions to world problems through outward-looking policies which advance our economic interests as much as our common humanity.

Angola is a symbol of this outlook. Of course it does not directly affect the man on the Clapham omnibus to any significant degree. A glimpse of a mutilated, starving child on TV may elicit a pang, but not for long ('viewers are warned that they may find some pictures disturbing'). Angola is just an extreme example of the poverty and violence which have become routine for the majority of Africans. Somehow people have to be made to realise that endemic western unemployment is tied to the fate of those fly-blown children; that governments who care more about arms deals than effective aid are the problem, not the solution.

On the fiftieth anniversary of Bretton Woods, the jubilee year of the birth of the international undertaker, the IMF, I would like to summon the intellectual mastery and poetic prose of Maynard Keynes in support of such ideas. But this poor sketch will have to do. Keynes knew that his recipes for national demand reflation had to be international in scope; and he was thwarted in 1944. In the middle of the most terrible depression since the 1930s, with war looming everywhere, our task is to translate his vision into terms which reflect the integrated world economy of the 1990s and address the political structures inhibiting true recovery on a global scale. We might begin by recalling that jubilee once meant the cancellation of debts, both financial and real.

Our task at this time is to find a new, more inclusive concept and practice of community, one which builds coalitions of shared interest across the divisions of a world split by race, nation and religion, not to mention the inequalities of wealth and power, gender and generation. We aim to look ahead to a better future, but we cannot ignore history. Many Africans at home and abroad would point to their having suffered 500 years of racism at the hands of 'western civilisation', first slavery, then colonialism, now apartheid and continuing discrimination in Europe and America. There is talk of victimisation, collective guilt and reparations; and the rhetoric of white versus black echoes the Panafricanism of the anti-colonial struggle earlier this century.

Angolans have had good reason to feel hard done by. They provided slaves for centuries; their experience of colonialism was not kind, except perhaps for a small coastal elite. Their war of colonial liberation against the Portuguese was prolonged and intensified by the involvement of the superpowers and South Africa. Despite the end of the Cold War and apartheid, international forces still sustain the viciousness of the war. Belated recognition of their government by the sole remaining superpower has not banished the threat of the country's dismemberment or of its being engulfed in yet another regional war. If Africans all over the world have yet to find the political forms which guarantee their right to democracy and development, Angola is a powerful symbol of that collective frustration; and the malign role of 'whites' in all this is palpable.

Nevertheless, if the wounds of racial inequality are to be healed, whites and blacks will have to learn to live together. This is why the transition to democracy in South Africa, taking place at this moment, is so crucial. Cooperation at this stage will be made easier if the vision of history we share is less relentlessly one-sided. For whites and blacks have been jointly responsible for the iniquities of history; not equally responsible perhaps, but it is not the first time that we have been in this mess together. Certainly collaboration on a massive scale was necessary to slavery, colonialism and apartheid. Neither party in the Angolan war can blame the brutality entirely on outsiders. Moreover, the struggle for emancipation from racial inequality has always linked Africans with their friends elsewhere – the abolitionists, the colonial mavericks, the anti-apartheid movement. And finally, the mixture of peoples in Africa makes it essential to find concepts of community and alliance more enlightened than those destroying Yugoslavia today.

In a real sense then, what is happening now in Angola and South Africa matters to the rest of us because it is a test of where the world is going in the aftermath of the Cold War. Like Palestine and Northern Ireland, the issue could go either way, with consequences magnified by the continental and diasporic scale of Africa's involvement with the West. We have heard the voices of chauvinism loud and clear since the fall of the Berlin Wall. Intellectuals, politicians and journalists everywhere stare transfixed by the spectre of a nationalism which they themselves have lived by for the best part of a century. The countervailing movement for international solidarity and inclusive coalition politics has barely been able to make itself heard. Where one side promises a return to atavistic certainties, the other's rallying cry is muted and unsure.

The idea that humanity has a common interest in making progress towards the integration of world society, rather than accept the inevitability of division and conflict, is too abstract to lure most people out of their insularity and indifference. The direct experience of war might do the trick, as it has before this century; but some might think such a solution too drastic. As modern politicians know, the most compelling arguments are economic, an appeal to material self-interest. I, for one, do not see why the highest ideals should not also be consistent with general economic improvement. If the abolition of slavery was linked to the rise of wage labour, that does not make the humanist ideals involved less compelling. It means merely that what was right had economic history on its side. So too today, we must search for general material interests which reinforce a policy of integration over one of separation and division. It is apparently not enough to say that peace is better than war, democracy than dictatorship, if the world's economic powers have a direct stake in the wrong arrangements.

Africa and the Global Political Economy

My analysis assumes something undemonstrable, namely that the conflict of our time is between nationalism and regionalism with a global dimension. I believe that humanity is in transition from national organisation to something both more inclusive and more local at the same time, perhaps regional federations linked to a more explicit concern for global unity. In the case of Subsaharan Africa, emergent regions include South Africa and its neighbours, Nigeria and ECOWAS; these two countries contain the industrial growth poles of the continent, but they are themselves much divided. Kenya is the link between the Horn and its former partners in East Africa; Angola has the wealth to be the driving force of Central Africa, yet it is also very much part of the Southern African region. Out of the fact of regional integration wider associations may develop, including African unity and beyond.

Our century of wars could be on the brink of universal democracy or of something far worse. Political institutions are unlikely to remain the same, even though the world's rulers cling tenaciously to existing forms of government. Yet most discussion assumes the indefinite continuation of an order whose origins lie in two world wars not long ago. We have become used to thinking of society as a nation-state; and for some time now this identification has been breaking down. What happens if we start thinking of society as all the human beings in the world? To some extent, we already do – the United Nations expresses a fragile political unity and publishes statistics on global trends; satellite pictures of planet Earth reinforce such a vision. It takes an effort; but we can do it.

What do we know about the human predicament today? Our numbers have increased five or six times in the last two hundred years, while energy production has expanded at double the rate. The city has overtaken the village as our main type of habitat. The world's population consists of an older minority which is rich and white, linked to the vast majority which is young, poor and darker. This is the culmination of a demographic explosion which began in Europe in the 19th century and has continued in the Third World since 1945. The children of Africa are the replacement generation for a western population which now has difficulty reproducing itself. The inequalities marking that division are almost unimaginable and not many people want to contemplate them.

Africa stands today as a symbol of one extreme in this polarised world. Its population was half of Greater Europe's in 1950, is roughly equal today (around half a billion people) and is expected to be double Europe's early next century. This population is very young and increasingly lives in large cities thrown up by Africa's own urban revolution; many emigrate, if they can, to Europe and America. The continent cannot feed itself, despite having abundant land and a higher proportion of farmers than anywhere else. The export crops and minerals which drew colonists to Africa in the first place now sustain a dwindling share of world trade and, outside South Africa and Nigeria, there is little new industry to replace them.

Africa's main business is government, closely linked to armaments and war. The dream of development has been abandoned – most Africans are worse off today than at independence three decades ago. Funds are haemorrhaging into the black hole of the foreign debt. The harsh monetarism of the IMF and World Bank (an ideology of recolonisation known quaintly as 'structural adjustment') reduces corrupt regimes to the status of passive collaborators in a new phase of asset-stripping ('privatisation'). The prevailing mood of the African middle classes is one of despair; who knows what the masses think and feel?

The emergent states of Southern Africa have a tangential relationship to this continental picture. Angola and Mozambique have been fighting a war while the rest of Africa deteriorated with rather less excuse. Namibia has just won its precarious independence; and the South Africans take refuge in the idea of their own exceptionalism during the run-up to historic elections. There can be little doubt that the political outcome in this region will have profound consequences for Africa's trajectory more generally. The buoyancy of a successful transition to majority rule in a region which has epitomised racial domination for so long could fuel the struggle for democracy and development everywhere

Nor is the picture in the rest of Africa as unrelenting as we may sometimes imagine. The prevailing impression is one of death and dying – disease, hunger and killing. Without wishing to impugn the integrity of journalists and charity workers, there is an institutional interest in stressing this side of Africa. Perhaps the population threat plays a part in shaping the audience's unconscious preferences too. Yet the extraordinary rise of Africa's people during this century speaks of life more than death, of burgeoning youth rather than premature mortality. And the cities, largely built and serviced by Africans, are remarkable for their commercial vitality. Demographic dynamism also translates into a cultural explosion (music, films, literature) which is making a global impact. International diasporas maintain networks whose social potential has not yet been fully felt. And, as Nelson Mandela well knows, it is the young who take to the streets in revolutions.

Given this thrilling (and no doubt alarming) outburst of popular energy, now focused on South Africa's hectic emancipation from apartheid, how can we explain Africa's failure so far to meet even minimally its people's aspirations for independence? The answer surely lies in the institutions of the post-war world which shaped their states and economies. The anti-colonial struggle spawned Panafricanist sentiments; but independence brought the uniform strait-jacket of the nation-state. There was then, as the lady used to say, no alternative. The context of the Cold War led the western powers to treat all African attempts at self-determination as potentially communist-inspired. When the money ran out and popular consent seemed unattainable, coercion in one form or another became the accepted basis of government. Rulers had to please their international creditors, not their own people.

The accelerated shift of population to the cities was sustained by the state's concentration of power and expenditure at the centre. A flourishing informal economy grew up there to meet the needs of these urban masses. The next step should have been a boost to commercial agriculture, as Africa's farmers supplied the cities with food. The benevolent spiral of rural-urban exchange is well rehearsed in the text books of early development pioneered by the Scottish political economists. Instead Africa was flooded by cheap food imports from Europe and America (and to a lesser extent Asia). The terms of trade for export-crops deteriorated owing to competition with other Third World regions and manufactured substitutes. Farmers and herders retreated into a defensive self-sufficiency and famine stalked the land.

Why did this happen? It most definitely was not owing to lack of enterprise on the part of African farmers whose resilience as producers is well-known to historians and anthropologists. The main cause lies with the structure of world trade. After the second world war, the victorious powers committed themselves to an arms race and to food self-sufficiency, pouring the benefits of industrial growth into defence and agriculture. The result was that offloading the products of both onto dependent Third World states became a higher priority than securing their economic growth. In any case, when industrial countries subsidised farmers out of taxes and poor countries taxed theirs to the hilt, the latter were priced out of the market. Any attempt to protect food agriculture was, of course, vigorously resisted. It is hard to overstate the significance of this handicap to Africa's development.

The sight of a handful of French farmers threatening to wreck inadequate GATT reforms is an evocative symbol of the global inequalities which reproduce Africa's under development. Obviously the supine local ruling classes are deeply implicated in this unsatisfactory situation; they long ago gave up representing the real interests of their own people. But true progress will only come about when a powerful constituency within the industrial world recognises that our own halting economic performance is the result of the same institutions which have reduced Africa to misery. How to link food mountains and the nuclear terror to the plight of Africa's deprived masses? That is the question.

The intellectual means already exist in Keynes's recipe for ending the Great Depression. However credit can be created, a good part of it must become effective demand where it is most needed. A benevolent spiral will be generated by transfers aimed at bringing producers and consumers back into the exchange economy. On a world scale, Africa is just an extreme example of the human majority which has effectively dropped out of the money economy. The collapse of Stalinism has merely added to that mass, while encroaching depression in the West threatens to finish the job. How can these areas be best brought back into a world market from whose expansion the advanced economies will be inevitable beneficiaries? Must the rest of the world just sit back and wait for the Asian tigers to work a miracle? The parochialism of national politics precludes addressing these questions; but, unless we do, the future is dark indeed.

It is ludicrous that public effort in the West at this time should still be directed at maintaining a medieval complex of food and armaments, the security state of the bully throughout the ages. African countries need the chance to develop local exchange of food, simple manufactures (e.g. clothing) and construction materials, just as the industrial west needs to invest in communications, hi-tech manufactures and infrastructure provision for the world market. Africa has a global comparative advantage in certain cultural products, low-tech manufactures and raw materials. The market for high value-added goods produced in the West will grow only if the bulk of the world's poor get a chance to exchange on terms which suit their local endowments. This means drastically dismantling the structures organising world trade in food and textiles, for example. It would mean endorsing and even financing protective measures aimed at building up internal trade between agriculture and the city (such as price support systems funded by the rich countries).

If these measures seem preposterously large and impracticable in scope, then so too is the long-term decline of the global economy as a whole. Yet this is the context within which South Africa and its unlucky twin, Angola, are struggling to enter the world of independent nations. They cannot be expected to be successful, if that world remains fundamentally unchanged. And it is in all our interest, human and economic, that some such change should take place soon.

Everywhere the political choice is relatively simple. Some fall back on national isolationism and the division of 'us versus them' that this implies; they include most of the world's ruling interests who would like to believe that the 20th century state is history's last word. Others seek more local control within a framework of regional and global integration, often at the expense of nation-states which are 'too small for the big things and too big for the small things'. Most of Europe's political parties are split down the middle on this issue. In Southern Africa the division is between those who affirm racial, national or ethnic separatism and others who are engaged in building non-racial and supra-national coalitions. At base it is a question of Africa's unity or its continuing fragmentation for the benefit of foreign powers allied to local elites.

Our late 20th century world is economically exhausted and morally bankrupt. Africa is not a place 'over there' with its own special problems. It is part of the institutional decadence that is dragging civilisation everywhere down into barbarism and despair. It is also a vital source of the common humanity that can save us, if we overcome an indifference to others which for too long has been symbolised by the wrong colour of skin. Perhaps the suffering of distant strangers reminds us of our own privileges and comforts; but it ought to remind us of the inhumanity of a system which draws the line at a national border or even at our own front door. We **are** affected by living with such inequality, in many more ways than we are yet aware of.

To speak specifically of the British, at this miserable stage of our national decline, if we retreat further into moral isolation from a world that we made the way it is, we deserve to languish for even longer in the dustbin of our post-imperial history. Each of us can, however, begin dismantling the barriers of indifference at any point, on any issue.

And that is why Angola matters.

Reginald Herbold Green – IDS, Sussex:

Angola Through a Cracked Glass Dimly: Peace, Reconstruction, Rehabilitation, Regionalism

Out of Africa there is always something new.
– Pliny –

Introduction

Angola is potentially one of the two $ 7,500-10,000 million economies among the southern African eleven. While very much smaller than South Africa's $ 70,000 million, it is potentially a substantial economy and one with sufficient initial export base to allow rapid growth.

However, the key word is potentially – actual GDP is probably under $ 5,000 million as a result of a third of a century of wars. Except for the petroleum sector and, up to a point, Luanda, the country is a wasteland of shattered towns, wrecked infrastructure and devastated countryside. Over half of the people exist in absolute poverty with malnutrition and infant mortality rates among the highest in the world. External trade is basically oil and (dominantly illicit) diamond export for war supplies, some basic consumer goods and relief food for Luanda and some provincial towns plus amenity/luxury goods (both legal and condoned illicit) for the elites of the two combatants.

In the absence of peace and physical reconstruction Angola's economy and – more particularly – economic relations with southern Africa will not grow much except to the extent South Africa can displace Portuguese and Brazilian suppliers. Without rehabilitation of livelihoods (problematic even with peace) there are serious question marks about both socio-political stability and the sustainability of enclavised Petroleum/Luanda growth.

Independent Angola's primary regional priorities have been political plus energy (hydro and petroleum). At present it is in no position to pay much attention to economic regionalism (or indeed any medium term economic strategy) and finds regional political solidarity less relevant to the present elected government UNITA conflagration than it was to the MPLA Government/RSA-UNITA alliance conflict of 1980-1991.

Potential – yes; Prospect – yes; Problematic – very; Present Priority of Regionalism – marginal. Like the supposed main locomotive to haul southern Africa forward (South Africa) the Angolan auxiliary engine is in reverse gear and is unlikely to be even in medium forward gear until two years after a lasting peace emerges.

Time Past – Road to Present

Angola has a number of special features which are integral to its present and prospects. To see it as a typical SSA economy, a typical second line oil exporter or (perhaps a *fortiori*) a twin of Mozambique is to obscure not merely details but basic structural realities.

Angolan politics and regionalism are heavily influenced by four pre or early colonial era kingdoms – the Congo in the North; the quasi-autonomous military settler/Creole one in the highlands behind Luanda; a nationalist cum pragmatic neo-colonial one directly south of it and a perhaps less unified Ovimbundu Plateau state. Each combined indigenous African and Portuguese administrative, military and religious features and each developed a Creole elite (meaning Europeanised African not necessarily with European blood relatives).

In the late 1800s and early 1900s, after more direct Portuguese rule covered much of the territory, this elite (or rather these elites, as one centred on the north, one on Luanda and one on the Plateau and its ports) was prominent in government (up to an acting Governor General), commerce (including substantial firms trading direct with Europe) and the military (including senior commissioned officers). While paralleled in French and British West Africa possessions, this 'false dawn' of an African professional and business class was most pronounced in Angola.[1]

At that point in time colonial powers did view Africans who spoke, dressed, ate, worshipped and studied European as at least potential candidates for middle level (and promotion to higher level) government posts and, by and large, as useful complements to, upcountry agents of and intermediaries for coast based European merchant houses. This was especially true of Portugal for two reasons: greater intermarriage or quasi-marriage of Portuguese (and Portuguese Asians) and Africans and the highly hierarchical neo-feudal class/caste structure of Portugal, whose ruling elite saw itself as so much 'above' an ordinary Portuguese person that a Portuguese cultured African (except for a handful of top posts) was – in Africa – not seen as very different.

The 'false dawn' was rapidly blotted out after 1900 – in the case of Portugal (and perhaps more generally?) by greater democracy. The Portuguese Republic – unlike the Kingdom –set priority on jobs for the boys (at least middle class ones) and opportunities for thrusting petty bourgeois/aspirant bourgeois traders. These were hard to find in the decaying backwater on Europe's south-west fringe so the evident quick fix was in the Empire and the key tool much more systematic racism against Europeanised Africans.[2]

However the old elite – while pushed down (and thus a source of nationalist leadership) – was not reduced to the level of ordinary Angolans. By and large it held on to Portuguese living styles, education, clerical posts (public and private) and military non-commissioned officer (or lieutenant) status, some intermediary and outpost commerce for Portuguese merchants and, in the northern elite case, coffee planting using Plateau migrant labour very much on the Portuguese settler (and labour practices – or malpractices) model.

A 'new' Creole elite also emerged – basically from Portuguese-African marriages or quasi-marriages. This did not merge with the old elite (except perhaps on the Plateau) and was more radical in rhetoric, tended to hold somewhat more technical and church posts but was (as was to become crucial) under-represented in the military. Initially the MPLA was largely – though not exclusively – led by 'new' elite members. After the Alves coup attempt and the resurgent South Africa/UNITA alliance for aggression, the enhanced military weight in Angolan politics swept the old elite back into power in Luanda with the new in a secondary, technical role. That is a unique African political history – no other 1870/1910 Creole elite has regained power or now leads a government.

Mercantile Backwater to Petro Boom Land

Portugal's 'new state' valued its colonies economically and feared it would lose them to foreign control if foreign investors had a free hand.[3] However, poor Portugal (practising an austere fiscal policy and impeding foreign investment at home) had no funds (state or private) to provide both infrastructure and enterprises to use it. Therefore, until the 1950s a low level mercantilism prevailed – outlets for Portuguese high priced manufactures and suppliers of escudo raw materials plus net foreign currency providers via coffee in the Angolan case (and labour plus transit traffic in the Mozambican).

In the 1950s the political economy of Portugal's main African colonies became much more dynamic. Settlers, Portuguese capital (state for infrastructure, private for commerce and an initial industrial tier as well as high rise urban buildings) and Portuguese civil servants and professionals came in what – compared with the past – amounted to tidal wave proportions. 1955-1972 were boom years in both Angola and Mozambique, as readily seen from looking at central city building ages. This burst of growth did little to open opportunities for Africans partly because the human investment in Africans base was very small, even by colonial African standards (albeit perhaps not so very much worse than in Metropolitan Portugal's own poorest provinces), and because the goal of economic opportunities in the Empire was even more energetically carried out by settlers (several hundred thousand in Angola) than in the 1920s.

From the mid-1960s (with the Liberation War in progress but not really threatening Portugal militarily in the field – as indeed it never did) Angola became an oil boom economy, largely because in that sector at least foreign capital had been made welcome. While adding to Luanda's skyline and factories, this colonial deathbed development did not substantially alter the other production, infrastructure or human services/investment sectors before independence, not least because the oil was offshore of an isolated enclave. It did mean that the new Angolan state would – assuming it kept the sector safe – have very substantial revenues, probably rising rapidly as more oil was developed.

Scrambles to War

Angola therefore approached independence with an uneven but generally weak rural infrastructure and very low levels of education and health services but also with two strong segmented (regionally) elite sets and with prospects of very substantial and, as yet, unused government revenues.

This proved a recipe for conflict. The regional divergences and the elites linked to them would probably have ensured that even in the absence of any ideological differences because the key prizes were the central governments cash flow and job roster.[4]

Angola's fractions in any case were subject to a series of outsider interests. The ideological concerns of the USA (whose businessmen came to trust the MPLA as prudent bourgeoisie partners even as its government came to see them as emanations of a hostile, offshore, demonic 'great power', i.e. Cuba), the Portuguese desire to hold on to economic opportunities, the French wish to acquire oil provinces and the South African policy of creating cordon sanitaires plus, perhaps, securing sanctions proof oil as well as the USSR's desire to secure a solvent African socialist junior partner (and defeat the USA and RSA as well as China – then UNITA's prime backer) and Cuba's to promote world revolution visibly and viably[5] all led to interventions first politically and diplomatically and then in the RSA and USA cases, followed promptly by Cuba and the USSR, militarily.

The first war of liberation ended in 1976 with the MPLA government controlling virtually all areas of much economic interest but UNITA very much a guerrilla force in being with a regional support base. That continued to 1980 with Luanda blossoming for the elite (but not in peri-urban areas);

real advances in health and education; some recovery of non-oil output (probably less than in Mozambique); a bureaucratic explosion limited only by the limits to even half plausibly qualified candidates and the general complacency of an export boom regime assuming its revenue growth will continue indefinitely.

The second liberation war (or war of Plateau resistance from a UNITA rank and file supporter optic) exploded when South Africa launched a forward strategy of total onslaught (on both coasts) to protect its own borders (and Namibia's) well beyond them and to lock in its landlocked independent state markets.[6] It is that war which reduced Angola to a functioning petroleum enclave, a more or less functioning capital zone core, an archipelago of just surviving provincial towns and rural pockets amid a sea of devastation.[7] By the 1990/1 termination of the second war most of the infrastructure and human services were non-functional, non-oil production was less than half what it would have been dead without war and over a million people who in the absence of war would have been alive were dead (out of ten million).

The second war ended partly because of external environment changes and partly – it appears – because both MPLA and UNITA believed they could win an election. With de Klerk's initial new pragmatism aimed at an internal settlement added to P. W. Botha's prior decision to cut losses and leave Namibia, the Angolan involvement was a net looser for South Africa, especially as it impaired the chances of building up trade links. For the USA the withdrawal of Cuban forces (plus the continued US business interest in Angola) also meant that UNITA was an embarrassment as a combatant, albeit useful if it won its way into a coalition government. For the USSR ending the cost of supporting the Angolan government while seeing it win an election (and perhaps have funds to pay back bills) was highly attractive.

And so to the 'false peace' which ended when UNITA discovered it could not win an election.

Angola's southern African regional links date to the two liberation wars. It was associated with the OAU and more particularly Zambia and Tanzania during the first war. During the second it saw the Front Line States as important to its international diplomatic position and SADCC (as a *de facto* economic wing of the FLS) as useful in the same way and as a means to working through the regional potential markets for its petroleum and hydroelectric sectors. Economically colonial and independent Mozambique have had limited regional links – transit rail traffic, some trade with South Africa, minute trade with Mozambique.

Peace: When? How?

Angola can neither rebuild, rehabilitate nor be relevant regionally in economic terms until it is at peace. UNITA has enough of a support base and of military cadres plus (at least for the foreseeable future) military hardware and munitions to make large parts of Angola ungovernable and to threaten security virtually anywhere.

Logically, the parameters for a peace settlement do exist:

a. both parties are exhausted and debilitated;

b. neither believes it can win militarily;

c. the fiscal prize of oil revenues remains (because so much has gone to pay for the war substantial peace reallocations will be possible);

d. the government (with pluralities in 17 of 18 provinces) is confident enough to offer UNITA one or more governorships, about 20% of ministerships (and 30% of vice ministerships) and presumably comparable proportions of other plum positions;

e. subject to bargaining on numbers, such a deal would seem attractive to most of UNITA's leadership;

f. and a coalition that did bring peace and stable payoffs, at least internally to itself.

But to-date logic has not prevailed for three reasons:

a. the government's distrust of UNITA was vastly increased by the return to war – it really had demobilised most of its infantry and much of its heavy equipment which UNITA – as became only too clear – had not;

b. UNITA's distrust of the government was increased by the violent reaction of the (ex army) armed police and MPLA militants against UNITA leaders and supporters in government-held towns after UNITA went back to war;

c. Jonas Savimbi, the unchallenged master of UNITA, has devoted 33 years to one goal – becoming master of Angola (his one consistent policy) – and is thus not pensionable nor accommodatable in a comfortable, prestigious, powerless post.[8]

Thus it is neither predictable nor projectable when peace will be achieved nor – given the third factor – whether it will be stable. An early, stable peace would be based on a merger of elites cutting in UNITA's and presumably a parallel political distribution of prestige projects plus basic services reconstruction/expansion. It would not open the way to political competition – quite the reverse. Third parties would find their paths – at best – steep and the fields they sought to till infested with – at least – rocks. That would not necessarily prejudice (albeit it would influence) initial reconstruction, rehabilitation and renewed growth nor much affect regional policy. Given the very great (even by African standards) inequality evident in Angola (between carteiros in Luanda, among provinces, between the oil enclave and the rest of Cabinda), it might well pose longer term socio-political stability risks and, by its skewing of domestic demand, be less than a good thing for industry.

Reconstruction – Task and Means

Angola at peace will face a massive nationwide physical and operational reconstruction mountain. To ask what is destroyed, damaged, out of operation or functioning fitfully leads to such a long catalogue it is almost easier to ask what is, or could quickly be put, in good working order:

a. the petroleum sector (including the relevant enterprise and government institutions) is basically in good shape and in a position with peace to expand. Third War damage is limited and rapidly repairable;

b. the cimento (core European-made city) of Luanda is itself in need of moderate restoration albeit its external infrastructure (water, power) need more rehabilitation – a situation relevant to the 500,000 odd not-so-poor to affluent Luandans and to the restoration of large scale business activity though not so relevant to the other 1,500,000–2,000,000 Luandans;

c. most of the basic dam structures (not the transmission systems) are structurally sound;

d. the Luanda and – where and when accessible – top of the market urban centre trade and commercial network is functional and has proven remarkably resilient (given an abiding state 'blind eye' based on mutual interests of the elite and the traders).[9]

For the rest there is a mix of utter devastation (most provincial towns, most water systems, many health and education units, most bridges), near irreparable (short of total reconstruction) non-maintenance (most of the rest of infrastructure and non-Luanda large and medium scale directly productive enterprises) and extended forced neglect for up to three decades (most medium and small scale rural production including the family small farming sector – sector familial). The same holds true of most non-Luanda public services and of sub-provincial town commercial and related market access networks as well – *a fortiori* – as of internal rural labour migration patterns.

Costs of Putting Right – Time Needed

A rough physical reconstruction cost estimate can be of the order of $ 25,00 to $ 40,000 million, albeit the underlying physical destruction estimates may be on the high side and perhaps $ 5,000 million relates to full restoration of the Copper Belt-Lobito rail link which is fairly certainly uneconomic and – less certainly – unlikely to happen. Given limits on design and construction capacity (even with imported personnel) this is a 10-year exercise even assuming lack of financial constraints, a rather unrealistic assumption as total available state revenue and non-oil enterprise and household investible surplus at the start is unlikely to exceed $ 1,500 million a year (assuming a Polish model debt rescheduling and payment of rouble debt at the current rouble/dollar exchange rate).[10]

The more binding time constraint may, however, be institutional. Angolan large and medium sized enterprises are badly run down as functioning units and as to personnel as well as in respect of physical plant. Given the past welcome to joint ventures – and the positive response from Brazil and Portugal businesses in the 1976-80 interwar near peace – this may remedy itself fairly rapidly – especially if genuinely flexible and entrepreneurial (the exception not the rule) South African business joins the party (and party it will be for the early and successful).

The present parallel economy can convert to less Byzantine (and more production linked) approaches fairly quickly so far as the enterprise portion goes. So far as the linked public sector goods supply/public sector incentives side goes, the problems are much greater especially because standard Structural Adjustment approaches to ending a very much integrated system of public low priced goods access (legal through illegal but fully condoned to grossly illegal) [11] for resale/exchange on the 'parallel' market as a means of providing incentives to key personnel do not in practice amount to a costed buyout so much as a draconic and unpredictable slashing which may well reduce actual inequality, because formal wages and preferential access were apparently not highly correlated, but is sure to reduce incentives among previously sheltered professional outside the petroleum sector.[12]

That transitional problem (potential disaster) is compounded by the need to reconstruct bureaucratic procedure which is now vaguely effective at producing a large number of low wage/salary jobs and at nothing else. Portugal's very complex paper administrative control system – which seems to have worked rather approximately and *ad hoc* to ensure that results were attained – has been transformed by the former GDR into an edifice only highly trained Baltic (including Nordic or former DBR) bureaucrats can understand, much less operate.[13] Reforming it will not be made easier or quicker by destroying senior personnel incentives.

Resources and Possible Results

Angola has two major asset flows on its side in tackling the reconstruction mountain range:

a. about $ 1,000 million in present oil revenues divertible from war import bills;

b. perhaps 10,000–15,000 artisanl and professional military employees (out of a national total of perhaps 16,00 to 25,000 divided Military 10,000–15,000, Hydrocarbons 2,000–3,000, Other Government 3,000–5,000, Other 1,000–2,000) who can largely be redeployed to civil state and enterprise use.[14]

This is in a sense the upside of a 1983–1993 resource allocation policy that gave first priority to petroleum (the key foreign exchange/fiscal source); second to the military (the means to survive); third to elite – including key personnel[45] – incentives; fourth to survival relief and education/health; fifth (effectively negligible) to anything else. With peace, the second priority could be cut at least 75% to the benefit of the fourth and fifth while rationalising the third in the new context.

Given the import capacity-fiscal-human resources and the potential for both to grow rapidly (the petroleum and – less certainly – technical/tertiary education sectors can expand rapidly with peace) the priority half of physical reconstruction could largely be done in five years. With supporting enterprise evolution that could boost GDP from –say – $ 4,000 million to $ 8,000 to $ 10,000 million in the sixth year of peace.

Livelihood Rehabilitation: Food, Society, Stability

However, reconstruction and GDP recovery to near the levels the petroleum sector opening up would have brought without war, is not as unproblematic as it may sound. If attained by centralised, elite welfare prioritised, private productive/commercial sector (including joint ventures) fuelled methods it may do little for livelihood rehabilitation, regional and urban/rural disparities or food production/food access (entitlement) security. The combination of a modified New Economic Policy (à la Lenin/Bukharin) and neo-liberalism in an elitist/oligopsony-oligopoly context (à la the Fund and Bank) is singularly ill-suited to prioritising livelihood rehabilitation or absolute poverty reduction because the components in each half which facilitate (up to a point) those processes are cross cancelled by constraints imposed by the other half. The heritage of elitism, urban bias, war-enforced rural neglect and war-resource allocation prioritisation is also an obstacle to rehabilitation. The fact that rehabilitation is not central to initial GDP recovery (as it is in Mozambique) means an export/urban/elite enclave approach could be adopted and for some years implemented with apparent success.

The nature of the problem can be seen from a rough breakdown of Angola's 10 million [16] people:

a. Internal and external refugees — 1.5–2.0 million

b. Pauperised in place (in war ravaged rural areas/towns) — 2.0–2.5 million

c. Other absolutely poor people — 1.5 million

Sub-total – Absolutely poor — 5.0–6.0 million

d. Military household members — 1.5 million

e. Bureaucracy household members — 1.5 million

Sub-total – At adjustment risk — 3.0 million

f. Others above absolute poverty line — 1.0–2.0 million

Turnpike prioritised reconstruction with market access provided where it pays is unlikely to draw in more than 10% of groups a-b-c to an extent allowing them to escape absolute poverty. The petroleum sector is not itself a large employer or local purchaser – its overall economic impact is dominated by what use is made of the rents and domesticated profits from it. Absence of war will not restore small farming household ability to produce enough to be above the absolute poverty line for the descendants of half who were there in 1970, much less the half who had never made it to that level.[17] Nor in the absence of rural sources of supply and markets is it easy to see how it will bring more than a few urban absolutely poor households up to the poor or not so poor levels (say $ 900 and $ 1,200 annual **household** incomes).[18]

Demobilisation – at least nominally vital for reallocating resources – means up to 70% of the military household members are at risk assuming 10% have skills needed for reconstruction and 20% stay in the armed forces. Demobilisation without resources to establish rural or urban livelihoods means absolute poverty and the risk of freelance banditry. Indeed, a better option might be Ghana's of the 1980s. Separate functional and 'reserve' units and provide the latter with quarters, food, low pay and *de facto* opportunities to daylight while not providing new weapons, vehicles, ammunition or fuel to limit both discontent and the ability to threaten the state.

The civil bureaucracy at 250,000 is not so much absolutely too large (in terms of, say, World Bank Long Term Perspective Study goals for 2000) as the wrong people in the wrong posts with most unsatisfactory public service and remuneration (absolute and comparative from crushingly low to absurdly high – the former for most employees) structures. To clear space for needed artisans and professionals (from demobilisation and new graduates plus returnees) means sacking perhaps 20% minimum and retraining 30% to 50% with most of those sacked 'redeployed' (the Bank's term) into absolute poverty [19] and no net gain in employment.

This is **not** a necessary outcome. Rural, small works labour intensive reconstruction, seedcom (literally and more broadly) assistance to small family farming households (logically especially returnees-demobilised- pauperised in place, but since that is 90% of rural households operationally probably best universally); credit to small rural trader/transporters to restore, market access could break the back of the rural absolute poverty crisis in a decade and – by increasing rural effective demand –substantially reduce the urban. An effective urban analogue is harder to articulate, though not necessarily impossible.

However, such an approach requires a decentralised, articulated, small 'project' oriented approach Angola has never had and – until successful – is none too interesting to the moneyed private sector. Only its health and education components have historic precedents (1975-80) and both fully applied Marxian and World Bank scriptural validation. Because it is not central to GDP recovery in Angola (indeed might well slow it marginally over the first five years though probably not thereafter) it is not saleable as necessary (as it locally is in Mozambique).

There are two negative GDP consequences of a non-rehabilitation focused reconstruction.

a. mass market demand will grow slowly deterring large, medium and small ('informal') industry and commerce;

b. food output will rise slowly leaving physical deficits (and larger needs invalidated by entitlements).

But on a petro-focused growth strategy to allow maximum investment (in physical assets and skills) – whether on a Marxian: Invest, invest, it's Moses and Our Prophets or a neo-liberal: Invest, Invest it's Hayek and Our Profits basis – these points are answerable. Petroleum exports will cover food import needs validated by effective demand and still leave a surplus for investment as well as being larger in GDP terms than the short term potential for 'a' plus 'b'.

The 'pure' economic case against the narrow turnpike approach is not overwhelming. 'Export more oil and import more maize'; build GDP and investible surplus rapidly and then turn to rural income and decent wage/productivity employment expansion'; 'finance human investment cumulatively out of achieved production gains' **are** neo-liberal slogans but have a rather wider credibility and modelling logic base.[20] Angola's small farming and urban wage earning (recorded or 'informal') household sectors are **not** the key to its GDP growth to 2,000 (as they are in Mozambique or Tanzania but not Botswana or Namibia).

The 'moral economy' case that no national can be great and prosperous if a majority of its people are poor and miserable traceable back through Adam Smith to the medieval Schoolmen (e.g. St. Thomas Aquinas and St. Antoninus) and that it is the state's business to create a context in which the majority can become educated and climb out of absolute poverty **is** relevant. Unfortunately it is rather out of fashion (or at least operational programming priority) with safety nets having a higher current profile (even in some applied – as opposed to long term conceptual – World Bank work). How to empower an absolutely poor majority of households to produce their way out of absolute poverty **is** hard to conceptualise in an articulated, contextual way, harder to programme and near impossible to 'prove' in hard numbers *ex ante*.

However, the political (or socio) economic side of the moral economy argument is more clearly binding in Angola with the nature of UNITA's initial marginalised small farmer/exploited migrant worker base and of Nito Alves 'lumpen proletariat'/would be 'lumpen petty bourgeois' base its heralds. A petroleum enclave looking after its own fenced off from adjoining rural poverty; cimento/canisa divides (especially in Luanda) dwarfing colonial era ones in depth and visibility; revived northern Angolan planters exploiting Plateau labour again; exploitative/oligopsonist-oligopolist rural traders; well paid senior officials and poverty line primary teachers and nurses; massive dams and power lines in/through subsistence agricultural areas; goods in shop windows for all to see – but only 10% to afford to buy – do not add up (especially in Angola) to a guidebook to lasting leadership/base trust nor socio-political stability. With four centuries of resistance to successive rulers to draw on, the implication (and one hopes the macro economic) costs of that scenario, however vague as to form and time, are clear.

But what form reconstruction will take and with how much rehabilitation is intensely problematic. There is no strong case for deep pessimism, but still less for bubbling optimism.

Angola's Economy and Southern/South Africa Regionalism

The Southern/South Africa Region is regularly seen as a locomotive principle case with South Africa as the main and –sometimes – Angola as the auxiliary locomotive. There are only three problems with that approach:

a. both locomotives have been in reverse for several years;

b. each will face major – even if dissimilar – domestic economic and social restructuring challenges with much higher priority than economic regional issues over the next several years;

c. neither, at the moment, sees the region as central to its trade strategy at either state or major enterprise levels.

Angola's present export pattern of oil, or even one with revived diamond and coffee components, is not one to which regional markets matter much. It may be a low cost crude supplier for South Africa and perhaps competitive for Tanzania and – if it expands refinery capacity – for products more broadly. However, the margins – for either party – are slim as Angola will be in no position to increase regional sales by providing soft medium term credit.

In respect to hydroelectricity Angola does seek to become an exporter and could be one within a regional grid whose main export units would be on the Angolan Plateau and the Kurene (Namibia), at Cahora Basa (Mozambique), Kariba (Zambia) and Stieglers Gorge (Tanzania) and probably a Botswana coal fired plant [21] with South Africa and Zimbabwe (plus Kenya in eastern Africa) the main importers. Indeed its leadership in the SADC energy sector turns in part precisely on that interest. In the medium term it is sensible economically but in the short the capital cost of building any new dams (or perhaps even rebuilding power houses and building transmission lines) pose problems because of limited cash flow potential and priority reconstruction areas. The same applies to major refinery capacity increases which could benefit from regional markets and probably reduce costs for product imports but would be very capital intensive.

In the natural gas field coordination is desirable. Tanzania, Mozambique, Namibia and Angola all have commercial reserves and South Africa a field which is commercial on a sunk cost basis. Initial uses seem likely to be in South Africa (including imports from Namibia and Mozambique) and Tanzania for power generation. However, one ammonia urea plant – but not initially two – would be viable globally if it had a regional base (in which it would be the low cost source) as, perhaps, would be a single methanol plant. Angola, with larger reserves and less need to exploit them rapidly might be inclined to wait and opt for global lpg export specialisation near or after 2000.

Other short term Angolan exports to the region are likely to be virtually non-existent. Revival of transit traffic operations is unlikely – the Lobito Bay line when existing was viable but, with both Dar es Salaam and Beira options open to Zambia and Zaire,[22] will not be economic to rebuild beyond the point justified by Angolan traffic.

Angola may find the region more relevant as a source – if South Africa and Zimbabwe can compete with Brazil, Korea, Japan and Portugal in manufactured goods and large scale construction contracting. How much regional preference it is in practice willing to provide (nominally it does provide significant preferences to Zimbabwe and other regional states except South Africa and Botswana and on manufactures Zimbabwe have shallow credit pockets compared with Korea and Japan and probably even Brazil and Portugal which enjoy certain advantages as respectively the centre of the Lusophone world and the traditional metropolis – both speaking Portuguese.

Because Angola for at least several years is likely to be a grain and meat importer – it is a logical purchaser of Zimbabwean and South African maize [23] and of Namibian beef and, perhaps, lamb/mutton. In the case of sugar South Africa and Zimbabwe are the logical suppliers as is Zimbabwe in the case of tea (at least until Mozambique has a blending plant). Other potential primary or semi processed imports include small volumes of copper, copper wire, lead, zinc, aluminium sheet and aluminium circles while steel products offer a larger market but a very highly competitive one for the products which South Africa and Zimbabwe export. This rough sketch suggests moderate to substantial regional sourcing but little short term regional marketing plus a more important medium term interest in Regional hydroelectricity – natural gas – petroleum and products production and trade.

That is an advance on the historic pattern (especially since its lead component transit traffic has ceased to exist and is unlikely to be resuscitated).[24] It could provide the basis for a buoyant import trend as SADC/PTA manufacturing sectors become more competitive with plausible exchange rates (which Angola does not yet have) and physical upgrading/re-habilitation as well as more regional market oriented. The export side – beyond electric energy and petroleum products –is harder to project. Initially Angola's manufacturing sector is – assuming success in restoring GDP growth – likely to be able to sell all or almost all its output at home. How rapidly larger, more export-oriented industrial units might arise and in what is not at all clear. If Angola does opt to develop a petrochemical sector the prospects would change but, however useful the regional market, the decision would be based primarily on global supply-demand-access considerations.

In the short run (peace plus five years) it is most unlikely that regional economic policy, beyond the established energy sector mode, will have high or even medium priority. Angola is more likely to respond to rather than take a lead in regional integration and trade promotion initiatives. At present priority is still lower because without peace economic regionalism (beyond normal seaborne trade with South Africa and – via Walvis Bay – Zimbabwe) is impracticable and the political solidarity value of economic (or for that matter political) regionalism is much lower in the current phase of the government-UNITA war than earlier when UNITA was a dependent ally of South Africa (as well as a USA supported instrumentality) and the Angolan war was perceived in the North as a subsidiary but important Cold War hot front. Again Angola is neither withdrawing nor unwilling to respond positively to initiatives but has neither the senior personnel time nor the resources to follow a pro-active approach.

In short Angola's history and economic potential mean that for peace plus five years economic policy and resource allocation will be primarily domestically focused –especially if livelihood rehabilitation is given high priority for socio-political reasons. But it also means that Angola will be a substantial market open to competitive regional manufacturing and construction firms as well as a moderate food and a small metal importer – and that it will have hard currency to pay. The last point is crucial as, with the possible exception of crude oil to South Africa, Angola's regional exports are likely to be low to trivial.

For endnotes see page 185-186 below.

Notes

Notes

Achol Deng

Peace-Keeping and Peace-Building in Africa

1. This position in classical international law has found modern expression in Article 2(7) of the Charter of the United Nations which reads "Nothing contained in the present Charter shall authorise the United Nations to intervene in matters which are essentially within the domestic jurisdiction of any state or shall require the Members to submit matters to settlement under the present Charter, but the principle shall not prejudice the application of enforcement measures under Chapter VII".

2. Rosalyn Higgins, 'Internal War and International Law', in Cyril Black and Richard Falk (eds.) *The Future of the International Legal Order*, Volume III, Conflict Management, Princeton University Press, Princeton, New Jersey 1971, page 81. See also: G. Fenwick, 'Can Civil Wars be brought under the control of International Law?' *American Journal of International Law*, 32 (1938); Hans Wehberg 'La guerre civile et le droit international' *Recueil des Cours de l'Academie de droit international de la Haye*, LXIII Paris, 1938; Roger Pinto 'Les Regles de Droit International concernant Guerre Civil' *Recueil des Cours*. CXIV Paris, 1965; Richard Falk '*The International Law of Civil War*', American Society of International Law, John Hopkins, London, 1971.

3. See *The Geneva Conventions of August 12, 1949*. International Committee of the Red Cross (ICRC), Geneva; *International Red Cross Handbook* ICRC and *The League of Red Cross Societies*, 12th edition, Geneva, July 1983; *The Geneva Conventions of 12 August 1949*, Commentary published under the general editorship of Jean S. Pictet, 4 volumes, Geneva, 1952–1960; Fritz Kalshoven, *Constraints on the Waging of War*, ICRC, Geneva, 1987.

4. See generally, Gunnar Ferman, *Bibliography on International Peace-keeping*, Martinus Mishoff, Doidrecht and London, 1992. An excellent and up-to-date work is William J. Durch (ed.) *The Evolution of UN Peace-keeping*, The Henry L. Stimson Centre, Macmillan 1993. Durch identifies 14 UN Peace-keeping operations in the Cold War period (1945-1985) and 13 such operations during the New Era (1985-1992). Indeed many more such operations have since been put in place and there is uneasiness about the financial and administrative implications of this proliferation.

5. UN Document S/2411, June 17, 1992 also reproduced in 31 *International Legal Materials* 953 (1992).

6. *Abid* p.960.

7. Chapter VII of the UN Charter generally deals with action with respect to threats of the peace, breach of the peace and acts of aggression. Article 39 reads: "The Security Council shall determine the existence of any threat to the peace, breech of the peace, or act of aggression and shall make recommendations, or decide which measures shall be taken in accordance with Articles 41 and 42, to maintain and restore international security". Article 41 deals with economic sanctions whereas Article 42 deals with armed interventions.

8. See Chester Crocker 'Peace-making in Southern Africa: The Namibian Angola Settlement of 1988' in David D Nursohn (ed.) *The Diplomatic Record 1989-1990*, Boulder Co. Westview Press, 1991; F. William Zirtman, *Ripe for Resolution: Conflict and Intervention in Africa*, New York, Oxford University Press 1989; Robert Jaster, *The 1988 Peace Accords and the Future of South-western Africa*, Adelphi Paper 253, London, International Institute for Strategic Studies, Autumn 1990; Virginia Page Fortna 'United Nations Angola Verification Mission I' in W. Durch *The Evolution of UN Peace-keeping*, Macmillan 1993, p.377-387.

9. Prior to the signing of the accords Angola and Cuba sent formal letters to the UN Secretary-General requesting the assistance of the Security Council. See United Nations Documents S/20336 December 22, 1988; S/20345 December 22, 1988; S/20336 and S/20337, both of December 17, 1988.

10. See International Institute for Strategic Studies *Strategic Surveys 1990-1991*, p.235; Virginia Page Fortna in United Nations Angola Verification Mission II in William J. Durch, *The Evolution of UN Peace-keeping*, Macmillan 1993, p.388-405.

11. UN Document S/22609, May 17, 1991.

12. UN Document S/23191, October 31, 1991.

13. According to *Jane's Defence Weekly*, August 1991, p.219, no sooner were the Accordas de Paz signed than some 300,000 mines were cleared by a joint team of MPLA and UNITA troops.

Jean-Emmanuel Pondi

Angola in African Global Diplomacy

1 These figures were finally released by the Portuguese government. See Elisabeth Morris, Portugal's Year in Africa in *Africa Contemporary Record (ACR) 1974-75*. London. Rex Collings, 1975. p. 73.

2 Two thirds of the 350 resolutions that were drafted by the OAU between 1963 and 1973 dealt with political issues. Of these, more than half were concerned with the situation in the African territories still under colonial rule and apartheid. See Laurent Zang, L'action économique de l'OUA in M. Kamto, J. -E. Pondi & L. Zang *L'OUA: Rétrospective et perspectives Africaines*. Paris, Economica, 1990.

3 Harold Nicolson, *Diplomacy*. London. Oxford University Press, 1959. pp. 4-5.

4 For a good analysis of this first OAU meeting, see Colin Legum, *Pan-Africanism: A Short Political Guide*. London, Pall Mall Press Ltd., 1965. pp. 187-195.

5 See William J. Foltz & Jennifer Widner, The OAU and Southern African liberation in Yassin el-Ayouty & I. William Zartman (eds.) *The OAU After Twenty Years*. New York, Praeger, 1995, p. 250.

6 See Stephen Wright & Janice N. Brownfoot (eds.) *Africa in World Politics*. London, Macmillan, 1987.

7 The ALC was given statutory responsibility by the OAU for negotiation with the liberation movements and OAU member states on such questions as their contributions to the special funds of the ALC, transit facilities for the guerrilla forces, agreement on sites for their training camps, in addition to international fund raising and diplomatic support. See *The ACR 1974-75*. op. cit., p. 23.

8 In reality, many African countries of the French speaking area had signed defence agreements with France in 1961-1962, thereby breaching a major tenet of non-alignment.

9 See OAU Draft Resolution on the Activities of the African Group at the UN, CM/Ctte A/Draft. Res. 10. Rev. 1 of 1975, in *ACR 1974-75*. p. 13.

10 See Alan James, *Sovereign Statehood: the basis of International Society*. London, Allen and Unwin, 1986. p. 20.

11 See the special file published by *Jeune Afrique* No. 1724 of 26 January 1994: FCFA La Déchirure. pp. 36-52.

12 See Daniel Volman, 'Africa and the New World Order' *Journal of Modern African Studies (JMAS)*, Vol. 31. No. 1, 1993. pp. 1-30.

13 For a very detailed analysis of its workings, see Djierina Wembou, Lenouveau mécanisme de l'oua sur les conflicts *Afrique 2000.* Mars 1994. pp. 5-20.

14 See Suzanne Cronje, 'The return of colonialism', *The Africa Review 1993-1994,* London, The Economic Business Report, 1994. p. 2.

15 *The Kampala Documents: Towards a Conference on Security, Stability, Development and Cooperation.* Kampala, Uganda, 1991. p. 8.

16 'The Merchants' descent on Africa', *Africa Analysis.* No. 190, 4 February 1994. p. 6.

George Wright

United States Foreign Policy and Angola: The Prospects

1 Among many see: Patrick Smith, 'Angola: Free and Fair Elections!', *Review of African Political Economy*, 55 (November 1992). pp. 101-107.

2 Mark Hertsgaard, 'Minutes of the Meeting: The Secret Life of Henry Kissinger'. *The Nation*, October 29, 1990. p. 398.

3 David Martin, 'Angola Still Awaits U.S. Recognition', *Southern Africa News Features,* (Southern African Research and Documentation Centre, Harare). February 1993. p. 1.

4 Shawn McCormack, 'Change and the Military in Angola: The Impact of the World Order on the Process of Conflict Reduction and Democratization in Angola'. Presented at the African Studies Centre Seminar, The University of York, May 13, 1993.

5 Roy Laishley, 'U.S. Sets Out its Africa Policy', *Africa Recovery.* June 1993. p. 3.

6 Among many see: Fred Halliday, *The Making of the Second Cold War.* London: Version Press, 1983.

7 See: 'Angola: Recommended Policy Framework', *Washington Notes on Africa.* Fall 1993.

8 'U.S. Threatens Savimbi Over Oil, Press Release. UN Angola Mission', (Source: Agence France-Presse International News), January 25, 1993.

9 *Ibid.*

10 Martin, *op. cit.* February 1993. P. 2.

11 See Alex Vines, *One Hand Tied: Angola and the UN,* Catholic Institute for International Relations Briefing Paper, June 1993.

12 Victoria Brittain, *Angola's Transition: The Background to the Return of the War.* London: Anti-Apartheid Movement, January 1993), p. 1.

13 For example, see: Karl Maier, 'UK Toils for Peace as Angolan Rebels Create a Capital'. *The Independent* (Britain), February 19, 1994.

14 See: *Landmines in Angola: An Africa Watch Report.* New York: Africa Watch. January 1993.

Reginald Green

Angola through a cracked glass dimly

1 In Mozambique it was less prominent because the old military/administrative Creole establishment of the Zambesi Valley was smashed in the Prazeiro Wars and the separate Lourenco Marques civil one was much smaller.

2 The vast majority of Africans had been exploited, suppressed or ignored throughout. The change was for the 1% to 2% Creole community.

3 In the 1900-1940 period Mozambique was arguably a British economic colony under the Portuguese flag.

4 Compared to these no sub-national economy orientation was very attractive. Cabinda – where all of the oil then was, and most still is – was so small geographically and in population as to be virtually a bystander in the political manoeuvring – then and now.

5 Angola paid Cuba's military costs – and probably most Cuban civil professional personnel salaries – from oil revenues. USSR arms purchases, initially in cash, were substantially on loan account from the early 1980's.

6 Whether South Africa had serious designs on a sanctions poor oil supply from Angola is unclear. Its actions show interest in using UNITA to reduce Angola to chaos rather than to install it in Luanda. The offer many in southern Africa feared – **Angola** to deny SWAPO bases and sell 10 million tonnes of oil a year at world price plus 10% for 20 years with **South Africa** halting all supporting to UNITA and providing reconstruction technical assistance and, at a price, construction services – never came.

7 This is **not** to say UNITA governed or even held most of the rest of the country. Part was fought over, some controlled on day vs. night shift basis, some reduced to *terra incognita* in a grim parody of pre-colonial existence. UNITA's actual governance perhaps covered 15% to 25% of people and somewhat more terrain (like RENAMO, UNITA tended to occupy large tracts of virtually empty and relatively useless countryside when it could, but neither government chose to do so).

8 In this he is very unlike Renamo's Alfonso Dhlakama who appears both resigned to total electoral defeat and to be concerned primarily (now and after) with payoff in life style for himself.

9 It is ironic that historical support patterns have clad an ultra state bourgeois/private entrepreneur oriented regime rather comparable in nature to those in Abidjan and Douala in Marxist-Leninist rhetoric and –occasionally – practice. In fact, the chosen policy, as illustrated in the petroleum sector has been at the most Leninist New Economic Policy, and parallel markets have been seen as part of a necessary, complex mechanism of preserving incentives for the bureaucratic, military and business elite.

10 The collapse of the rouble means that Angola's $ 3,000 plus million of rouble debt at 1980s exchange rates is not worth at most $ 3 million at current rates.

11 For example, various categories of employees had legal access to beer at low prices and beer factory workers to allowances of free and low price purchase quotas – all exchangeable at a profit on the 'parallel' market. But in addition at least 15% and perhaps 30% of beer was quite simply stolen by various groups in various ways.

12 In petroleum the private and public enterprises will find a way to see their employees and key associated state employees protected. Similar efforts will be made elsewhere ironically, it could well be naked, condoned but ill-coordinated or monitored bribery instead of a more open, if Byzantine, official entitlement system. On the

face of it that converts quasi controllable quasi rents into uncontrollable 'pure' rents not into open market related incentive payments.

13 Inexperienced Angolans – even if well educated – cannot, and anecdotal evidence from multiple sources suggests Russians could not either, while Cubans blithely ignored it when convenient (perhaps in a more Portuguese – or at least Iberian – style than anybody else!). A parallel GDR advised 'rationalisation' in Mozambique was (as it never has been in Angola) systematically and officially short-circuited, bypassed, treated to a Nelsonic blind eye. Lack of formal reform means that there is no functioning bureaucratic system at all (in the sense of patterns for routine operations) which has its own high costs, but quite different ones from Luandan procrusteanist straitjackets of unworkable rules.

14 Angola **won** its high tech war with South Africa and won it with a superior self-operated airforce and competent artillery, armour and logistical services plus maintenance, not massive use of infantry (in fact Angola's armed forces' weakest link).

15 The system was far from perfect, e.g. port workers were not an 'official price access' group because (unlike beer workers) their literal product was a service not an allocable good. As the results included a combination of low productivity and massive uncontrollable (if the ports were to operate at all) pilferage, this was clearly an error in the prioritisation system's own terms.

16 10 million is very approximate. It is probably an overestimate. Official data assume a 2.6% annual growth from a 1980 Census base, i.e. **no war**. With war related excess deaths of the order of a million they are precisely wrong. Mozambique projects seem to be up to two million people too high suggesting one and a quarter 'shortfall' on official projections for Angola.

17 Descendants since of 30-35 year old 1970 heads of household a majority are dead today given Angola's low average life expectancy and war toll. Of Angola's 1994 population at least 75% are under 33 and therefore have never lived in a country fully free of war.

18 Based on parallel exchange rate. The numbers are from Maputo based on the official (now basically realistic) exchange rate as of early 1994.

19 Even if the wage lost (often aptly styled salario minimale) is well under the household absolute poverty line it is a key (25% to 50%) component in a set of multi-sectoral, multi person contributions to the household budget whose loss is likely to be catastrophic.

20 Indeed Feldman and Mahalanobis models and Soviet ('socialist') national accounts systems operate on them just as much as does Ricardo's implicit model.

21 Lesotho's Highlands Water Projects' main export will be water, not electricity which is largely for domestic use.

22 Currently used South African routes are economic lunacy and not justified by capacity constraints at or to Beira and Dar.

23 Angola is unlikely to attract much food aid after peace so both the region's commercial exporters should be able to compete.

24 At least until recently, Angola did give priority to rebuilding the whole Lobito Bay – Copperbelt line but in a war context in which this was manifestly impossible. Whether the enthusiasm will survive a hard post-war look at resource flows and overall reconstruction priorities is another matter, not least because no substantial soft credit specifically for that purpose (as opposed to more general infrastructure construction finance) seems likely to be obtainable.

Sue Fleming

Nurturing Grass-roots Development in Angola

(Many thanks to ACORD, Eduardo Mondlane Foundation, FOS, ICCO, ODA, One World Action, Oxfam, SCF, and VOICE for information and discussions about this paper.)

ACORD (1993). *Participatory development in rural and peri-urban communities in Huila Province* – Angola. June 1993.

Fleming, S. (1991). Between the household: researching community organisation and networks. *IDS Bulletin* 22(1). January 1991.

Fleming, S. (1991). 'Peasants and peasant associations in Angola: a look at policy and practice'. Paper prepared for the 1991 ASA Conference on Socialism: ideals, ideologies and practice, University of Cambridge.

Forbes-Martin, S. (1991). *Refugee women.* Zed Books. London.

One World Action (1994). *Angola: building for the future.* London.

Oxfam (1991). *Working guidelines for gender and emergencies.* GADU/Emergencies Unit, November 1991.

Wyer, J. (1994). *Study of humanitarian aid and poverty in Angola.* ODA

Notes to Further Reading

For the general background, see David Birmingham *Frontline Nationalism - Angola and Mozambique* (James Currey, 1992); Basil Davidson *In the Eye of the Storm* (London 1972); Keith Somerville *Angola - Politics, Economics and Society* (London, 1986). On the economy, *Angola 1994-95: Country Profile* (Economist Intelligence Unit 1994); and *Angola to 2000: prospects for economic recovery* (Economist Intelligence Unit, 1993)

Angola's internal problems are many: see *Angola in Strife,* Situation Report No.6, (U.S. Agency for International Development, April 7, 1994). For the most up-to-date account of human rights abuses in Angola, see *Angola: Arms Trade and Violations of the Laws of War Since the 1992 Elections* (Human Rights Watch Arms Project and Human Rights Watch/Africa, 1994); also *Angola: Assault on the Right to Life* (Amnesty International, August 20, 1993). The critical issue of landmines is the focus of *Landmines in Angola* (Mines Advisory Group).

On Angola's significance for the region and the world, see Chester Crocker *High Noon in Southern Africa* (London 1992); Victoria Brittain *Hidden Lives, Hidden Deaths* (London,1988); Michael Wolfers and Jane Bergerol *Angola in the Front Line* (London, 1983). On the effects of destabilisation, see *Apartheid Terrorism: The Destabilisation Report* (Commonwealth Secretariat, 1989); *Children of the Frontline - The impact of apartheid, destabilisation and warfare on children in Southern and South Africa* (UNICEF, 1989). On foreign intervention, see the relevant chapters in Stephen Chan and Vivienne Jabri (eds.) *Mediation in Southern Africa* (London, 1993) and David Smock (ed.), *Making War and Waging Peace: Foreign Intervention in Africa* (Washington, DC: US Institute of Peace Press, 1993).

On the United Nations in Angola, see Alex Vines, *One Hand Tied: Angola and the UN.* (Catholic Institute for International Relations Briefing Paper, June 1993); Margaret Anstee, 'Angola: The Forgotten Tragedy, A Test Case for UN Peacekeeping, *Foreign Affairs,* XI, 6 (1993); *The Lost Agenda: Human Rights and U.N. Field Operations,* (New York, Human Rights Watch, 1993). United Nations Humanitarian Assistance Coordination Unit, *Briefing on Progress of Humanitarian Assistance in Angola, 1993-4.* On the 1992 UN-supervised elections see Patrick Smith, 'Angola: Free and Fair Elections!', *Review of African Political Economy,* 55 (1992) 101-07.

UNITA has attracted a polemical literature all of its own, most recently William Minter's *Apartheid's Contras* (London, 1994); see also his earlier *Operation Timber: Papers from the Savimbi Dossier* (New Jersey, 1988) and *Account from Angola: UNITA as described by ex-participants and foreign visitors* (London, 1990). Elaine Windrich *The Cold War Guerilla: Jonas Savimbi, the U.S. Media and The Angolan War* (New York, 1992) and Fred Bridgeland *Jonas Savimbi: A Key to Africa* (Edinburgh, 1986) offer contrasting accounts. For a UNITA version, see Fatima Roque *Angola: Em Nome da Esperanca,* (Lisbon, 1993).

For further reading on Angola's history, see *The Angolan Revolution Volume I ,1950-1962; Volume II, 1962-1976* (London 1969; 1978); Gervase Clarence-Smith *Slaves, Peasants and Capitalists in Southern Angola, 1840-1926* (London, 1979); Gerald Bender *Angola Under the Portuguese: the Myth and the Reality* (London, 1978); Joseph Miller *Way of Death: Merchant Capitalism and the Angolan Slave Trade, 1730-1830* (London, 1988); and Adrian C. Edwards *The Ovimbundu Under Two Sovereignties* (Oxford 1962). For a general view of African political history and culture, see Jean-François Bayart, *The State in Africa: The Politics of the Belly* (London, 1993).

Obituary

Davidson Nicol (1924-1994)

In an age when national and racial divisions threaten to tear human society apart, we need the example of men and women whose loyalty to their particular origins extends ultimately to a kind of universal citizenship. Davidson Nicol was a true patriot. He loved where he came from; and a life of extraordinary movement and achievement enabled that sense of his origins to embrace finally the world as a whole. His first loyalty was to the country of his birth, Sierra Leone; then to his Cambridge college, Christ's, and to the University of which he was such a distinguished member. He served on West African regional bodies; and upheld many African causes, retaining a special interest in Southern Africa. He was acutely aware of his race as a black African and this led him to assert his kinship with the New World diaspora. According to Chief Emeka Anyaoku, he was also a fervent "Commonwealth man". At the United Nations he combined global diplomacy with international education; and later was President of the United Nations Association. Throughout his adult life he gave himself to the young of the world as a mentor.

The last article Davidson wrote was published in **West Africa** a few weeks before his death on September 20th. Entitled "The Oxbridge connection", it begins as a celebration of some prominent Africans who had attended Britain's ancient universities, an indirect reminder of the author's own success in bridging that particular gap. But the tone then shifts as he exposes the implicit racism in recruitment to Oxford's Rhodes scholarships; reminds his readers of the fund's origins in African mineral wealth; and suggests that more awards now need to be made to Southern Africans in the aftermath of Mandela's revolution. The combination of Panafricanism and a belief in Oxbridge's civilising mission is quite striking.

Davidson Sylvester Hector Willoughby Nicol, CMG, MA, MD, PhD (Cantab) was born in Sierra Leone in 1924 and died shortly after his seventieth birthday in Cambridge. He was an honorary fellow of Christ's College and an associate lecturer in international relations. He was the lone African on the African Studies Centre's committee of management, a situation he had grown used to as the University's first African medical student and its first college fellow (as well as the first to get a first...). He was always a pioneer; but he looked forward to the day when Africans would assume their rightful place as senior members of a university which they now attend in their hundreds as students.

Davidson was a brilliant student, matriculating in Freetown at the age of fourteen. At Cambridge he pursued natural sciences and medicine, carrying out research into insulin. He returned to Sierra Leone, via London and Nigeria, to become the youngest Principal of Fourah Bay College in 1960 and then the first Vice-Chancellor of the University of Sierra Leone. At this time he wrote prize-winning fiction and poetry, under the nom de plume of Abioseh Nicol (notably **The truly married woman** 1964), as well as **Africa: a subjective view** (1965), a visionary work which repays reading today. He became Chairman of the West African Examinations Council in this period and was active in many national, regional and international associations. He left the University of Sierra Leone in 1968 to serve his country in a sequence of diplomatic posts.

Davidson soon moved to the United Nations, where he was Chairman of the UN Decolonization Committee in the early 1970s. But he found his true niche as Director of the United Nations Institute of Training and Research (UNITAR) with the rank of Under Secretary-General for a full decade from 1972. In this period he headed important missions to Angola and Ethiopia and wrote **Paths to peace: the UN Security Council and its Presidency** (1981). He left when UNITAR's mandate had begun to overlap with that of the United Nations University, an institution he had helped to found. Back in Cambridge, he inspired young visitors to his home with his vision of a world in which one could be cosmopolitan and true to ones origins at the same time. We miss him sorely.

Keith Hart

I was rather taken aback by the dramatic effect which the news of Dr Davidson Nicol's death had upon me. However, when sadness eventually yielded to reflection, I understood the reason for this overwhelming sense of loss. For Davidson Nicol had played a crucial role in setting me on the road to where I was when I heard the news. Like so many others, I benefited from his commitment to helping young scholars, especially students of African affairs in whatever way he could. What made him such a potent figure for me was his combination of an impressive intellect that spanned so many disciplines and an unshakable sense of humanity which allowed him to set aside the barriers of race, class and gender.

I first knew Davidson Nicol as a lecturer on international organisations. Despite being non-compulsory, his classes were always extremely well-attended. Nicol's deportment and presentation invariably emited the authority of an elder statesman on secondment. He was far too well-dressed to be a Cambridge don for a start. He wore starched white shirts, tasteful silk ties tied close to the neck, dark classically tailored suits, with a scarf and long camel-haired coat in winter. Tall and upright, his strong features and intense gaze were regularly embellished with a quick smile. For he was also a wit and he heaped upon us a wealth of anecdotes and ironic observations drawn from his many lives. He was one of the best advertisments for the United Nations I have ever seen. First African medical student to win a place at Cambridge, a path-breaking physician, one-time President of the UN Security Council, allegedly once considered such a threat to Sierra Leone's leaders that he was not welcome in his own country, his celebrity carried with it an air of mystery and enigma.

Those students who chose to write on Nicol's subject were always rewarded with an invitation to his home near Girton for Sunday lunch or week-day dinner during his all-too-short stays in Cambridge. He would try to bring people together whom he knew could help each other or who were likely to be marginalised by the North American heartiness of the international relations programme. From helping you off with your coat, keeping your glass filled, encouraging you to take more from the table, bringing you into the conversation, introducing you to some retired ambasssador or making you tea instead of coffee to helping you back on with your coat, reminding you that you had come with gloves and ringing for your cab, there seemed no limit to his social grace and skill. He would do all this for everyone without appearing obtrusive, an old fuss-pot or even breathless. The relaxed social setting he provided gave young people a chance to learn how to remain themselves while negotiating the currents of an intimidating institution.

Beyond even this talent for the social was the way Davidson Nicol behaved towards the individual. If you met him in the street, he would usually suggest a quick visit to Auntie's Tea Shop; and over jam and scones he would want to know how things were going, how was your day, your boyfriend, your grandfather, your thesis. He always made you feel that your story was of great importance to him. I particularly remember one conversation we had in his huge study, sitting in front of the fire in two enormous leather chairs surrounded by his collection of books, ornaments, African art and more books. We talked about the problem of feeling alienated from ones past, of the distance we had travelled between where we came from and where we were now. He understood what it might be like to be an outsider to Cambridge, from the Celtic fringe, a woman, first-generation university student. And he showed how all things could be reconciled.

Davidson Nicol had probably learnt the hard way the pitfalls of reducing individuals to something less than full humanity. He had the ability to rise above prejudice quietly but with style. When someone angrily told me that I should not make plans to study Africa because I was not black, he was furious. "African Studies and Africa needs people like you", he said. "Don't abandon us now." So I didn't. And when I heard that he had (unusually for him) come back to Cambridge for the summer this year, I immediately rang him to let him know I had managed to get my PhD and a research post. Luckily I thanked him then for his part in my life. In August, I thought I saw him across the street, but he looked so different. I u-turned in the road and cycled towards him. I was right, but how gaunt he looked. "Let's go and have lunch in Brown's", he suggested, "my treat". But unlike the old days I had to be elsewhere — something to do with a publication (this one!) — already late, I had to dash. And so we hurriedly embraced, pledged to arrange dinner soon and went our separate ways, never to meet again.

Less than a month later Davidson Nicol was dead. What might we have talked about that day? What wisdom would he have imparted? A friend and ally has bowed out. A few weeks ago I was in Mozambique as a United Nations observer. An academic from Sierra Leone was put in the same district team as mine. I mentioned Davidson Nicol and immediately this manenunciated a chronological list of his achievements any biographer would be proud of. I moved quickly to endorse his praise. "Yes, we shall miss him greatly in Cambridge", I responded. He looked at me sternly and said "Africa will miss him more".

Joanna Lewis

AFRICAN STUDIES AT CAMBRIDGE UNIVERSITY

Cambridge's links with Africa have been strong for at least 200 years, long before the foundation of the African Studies Centre. The University and town were prime movers in the campaign to abolish slavery which began in the 1780s. Apart from Clarkson and Wilberforce, the leaders of the anti-slavery movement included three Cambridge masters of colleges, the University's MP and Prime Minister, William Pitt, the town's mayor, a radical journalist and several prominent preachers. Cambridge was home to Anglican evangelicalism in the nineteenth century and a centre of African mission activity, as well as home to African leaders such as Alexander Crummell, the American civil rights activist and writer, and Joseph Casely-Hayford, the father of Gold Coast nationalism. Since then Cambridge has spawned female explorers, innovative administrators and pioneering scientists who have continued the University's tradition of active engagement with Africa.

The African Studies Centre was founded by Audrey Richards in 1965, largely in response to the great interest shown by members of the University in the newly independent countries of Africa. Three decades later, Africa is still a cause of universal hope and despair, with South Africa and Rwanda revealing the extremes of human possibility, as nowhere else in the world can. In that period over 700 PhDs have been awarded on African subjects across the whole range of disciplines; and no region outside Britain is more strongly represented here. At any one time over a hundred masters and doctoral theses on Africa are being researched in Cambridge; and some 300 residents are registered with the Centre as having active African interests.

The African Studies Centre exists to support research and teaching on Africa within the University. These functions are generally carried out by the various departments and faculties. A major aim is to make research-based knowledge available to meet the needs and interests of African people, while bringing the achievements of African civilisation to this country. In the wake of the communications revolution, the Centre is committed to exploring new ways of bridging the gap between the academy and the rest of society. It also supplies a wide range of services to the community: a library which opens the way to Cambridge's rich African collections; other research facilities; public lectures and seminars; workshops and conferences; a meeting place for Africans and others interested in Africa. Cambridge University is unique in the range and historical depth of its intellectual engagement with Africa; and this involvement is central to its identity as an institution of world rank.

Milton Keynes UK
Ingram Content Group UK Ltd.
UKHW052108070124
435561UK00002B/7